D1260299

Archie Bunker's America

Archie Bunker's America

TV in an Era of Change, 1968-1978

Josh Ozersky
With a Foreword by Mark Crispin Miller

Southern Illinois University Press
Carbondale and Edwardsville

Library of Congress Cataloging-in-Publication Data

Ozersky, Josh.
    Archie Bunker's America : TV in an era of change, 1968–1978 /
  Josh Ozersky ; foreword by Mark Crispin Miller.
        p. cm.
Includes bibliographical references and index.
1. Television broadcasting—United States—History. 2. Television
broadcasting—Social aspects—United States. I. Title.
PN1992.3.U5 O97 2003
791.45'0973'09045—dc21
ISBN 0-8093-2507-1 (alk. paper)   2002012083

Printed on recycled paper. ♻

The paper used in this publication meets the minimum requirements of American National Standard for Information Sciences—Permanence of Paper for Printed
Library Materials, ANSI Z39.48-1992. ∞

To my father

Contents

Illustrations

Plates

Figures

Tables

Foreword

We often hear that the utopian disorder of the 1960s and the early 1970s was brought to us by network television. According to this notion, TV pulled the United States out of Vietnam, because it "brought the war into our living rooms," its frequent bloody revelations and the reporters' overt skepticism subverting the officials' ever-rosy claims. Likewise, we have often heard that TV led the fight for civil rights, by opening the eyes of a complacent North to the intolerable spectacle of troopers beating, gassing, and trampling marchers in the streets of Birmingham and Selma. And we have also heard that Richard Nixon was destroyed by television, his shifty gaze and sweaty upper lip and the doggedness of newsmen like Dan Rather finally ruining him soon after Watergate.

Although this sort of argument has long come mainly from the Right, whose tribunes heatedly deplore TV's alleged progressive influence, there is as well a venerable liberal view of the networks' seeming countercultural effect—a view that _lauds_ TV for its subversive thrust back then. Thus have the likes of Spiro Agnew and Reed Irvine actually agreed, on this one point, with, say, Walter Cronkite and Jerry Rubin (which pair would also have agreed on little else). And yet, despite that odd consensus, commercial TV in itself was surely not the force for change—Aquarian, barbarian—that its champions and detractors seem to think.

The instances above are either groundless or exaggerated. As William Hammond, the U.S. Army's own historian, demonstrated long ago, the nation's disapproval of the war in Vietnam had more to do by far with the increasing loss of U.S. lives than with the TV coverage—which in any case was overwhelmingly supportive of the war, notwithstanding the persistent myth, still prevalent inside the Pentagon, that America was beaten from within, mainly by unpatriotic journalists. TV largely shied away from any too-disturbing looks at "our side" in that conflict—especially after CBS caught endless flak for airing Morley Safer's ugly story on the burning of Cam Ne in 1965. (That report was especially controversial for its image of a U.S. Marine casually torching a thatched roof with his Zippo lighter.) Thereafter, the media's few troubling pictures of the war came not from television but from the print press, photojournalism at that time still thriving:

Eddie Adams's harrowing glimpse, from 1969, of Capt. Nguyen Ngoc Loan's summary execution of a Viet Cong prisoner, and Huyn Cong "Nick" Ut's unforgettable shot, from 1972, of nine-year-old Kim Phuc, her clothes burnt off by napalm, running, screaming, toward the camera. (John Filo's photograph of Mary Ann Vecchio, keening by the corpse of Jeffrey Miller at Kent State, is another searing war-related shot that didn't come from television.) And while TV did shock the nation with its images of peaceful marchers under fierce attack by Southern cops, the salutary impact of such scenes was surely counterbalanced by the news footage of black rioters throughout the 1960s. While many tolerant viewers were roused to righteous indignation by the former, many others were confirmed in their racism by the latter. Finally, Nixon's fall owed nothing to the telejournalists, however impolite to him they sometimes were. Watergate destroyed him only through the efforts of the *Washington Post* (and its anonymous informers in the government).

This is surely not to say that TV played no role in the upheavals of that era. That the world as all had known it seemed increasingly to shake apart, its murals crumbling and its statues tottering, its epic fictions startlingly replaced by stories far more disappointing, was a change deriving in large part from television's rising cultural hegemony. In every newscast whose gray footage deviated starkly from official claims, as in the occasional hard-hitting documentary exposé, such as "The Selling of the Pentagon," and also in those talk shows—hosted by Les Crain, Dick Cavett, and Mike Douglas, among others—that actually encouraged controversial exchange, the networks shook the status quo a bit, by honoring the medium's quasi-subversive thrust. As Joshua Meyrowitz has argued, television has long tended, as if naturally, toward something like subversion, its cool and pointillistic picture of the world effecting a new emphasis on, and inducing a new fascination with, the (seeming) *truth behind* the fine facade. This accentuation of the background story was to some extent reflective of the tonal contrast between television and the older nonprint media—the high and glossy "silver screen"; radio, with its quaint stentorian effects; and the loud strain of vaudeville. Television slowly drove the superannuation of those prior media by introducing into countless homes its faster, cooler, more ironic style—a style apparently *immediate* and therefore tending automatically to undercut the older and more blatant sorts of media performance. Colorless and intimate, this novel medium appeared to be no medium at all and so was perfectly positioned to delight its younger viewers by enabling them to *see through* what now came across as screamingly pretelevisual.

Thus, the rise of television helped to form the spirit of the 1960s, charging that insurgent epoch with "irreverence"—as that quality would soon become commodified and banalized. The medium's low-key, ironic view contributed to a seductive change in style. It was apparent, for example, in the disappearance of the glamorous aloofness of the Kennedy White House and in the bacchanalian arrival of the Beatles (to note two epoch-making happenings of late 1963—the year "the Sixties" actually began). It showed also in TV's gradual generic changes: the rise of parody (*The Avengers* and *Get Smart!*), and the slow extinction of the Western. The new vogue of Pop Art, the cult of "camp," the labored wackiness of fashion, a la Mary Quant—all such novelties reflected television's disenchanting light. And yet, the most important cultural change induced by television had to do not merely with the look of things but with the very *concept* of "the look of things"—a concept that suddenly was under stress to an extraordinary degree.

The cultural ascent of that iconoclastic medium was eerily appropriate to the period's fateful climate of supreme disclosure. Just as television was encouraging a new mass appetite for mundane truths ("The Loud Family" first aired in 1973) and background information ("The Selling of the Pentagon" was aired in 1971), the print media were rocking the Establishment with staggering revelations of what really had been going on behind the masks of U.S. power. The *New York Times'* publication of the Pentagon Papers (1971) shattered the state's forever-Pollyannaish view of how the war in Vietnam was going, while the *Washington Post* (from 1972) destroyed the Nixon team's imperial spin by bringing out the sordid facts of Watergate. And, in mid-decade, the Pike and Church Committee hearings in the U.S. Congress and the publication of such books as Phillip Agee's *CIA Diary* and Joseph B. Smith's *Portrait of a Cold Warrior* finally (and yet only temporarily) publicized the truth about the CIA, thereby undoing years of expert propaganda by the agency itself. All such troubling coverage—duly dramatized by TV's newscasts—drove a new awareness of the gross discrepancies between America's ideals and the actual practice of her postwar managers.

That consciousness found rare expression in the boldest films produced by Hollywood in the early to mid-1970s—*Godfather II, Chinatown, Nashville, Serpico, The Stepford Wives,* and many other movies that reflected powerfully on the disorienting gap between reality and propaganda. The time for such enlightening product lasted through the decade, until the industry became addicted to blockbusters in the mode of *Star Wars, Rocky, Superman,* and *Close Encounters of the Third Kind.* Until that dispiriting surrender to the gods of market research—that is, in the interim between the breakdown of the classic studio system and the triumph of those mammoth parent firms that now own all the culture industries—the American film industry was startlingly adventurous, hospitable to troubling narratives and to artists who held wayward views (as long as they made money).

In *its* entertainment sector meanwhile, TV, by and large, dealt far more timidly with the peculiar stresses of the era (although, by contrast with what's on today, TV's accomplishment back then appears heroic). With a tighter corporate structure than the movie business of the 1970s, and always in a panic to appease its advertisers, TV could not afford to go too far in its reflection on the tumults of the day. While it did sometimes stray onto unusual terrain, therefore, TV largely tended not to deal much with the more important contradictions in the ongoing story of America. Instead, it found much safer ways to please the new mass appetite for (something like) iconoclasm—by pumping up the volume, confecting items like *The Monkees* and *The Mod Squad*, making fun of old white guys and retro styles, and otherwise intently marketing "irreverence."

TV's domestication of the social and political upheavals of the 1960s is the theme of this important book. Josh Ozersky's study is important both for the new light it sheds on an extraordinary moment in the history of TV and for its illumination also of the moment when, arguably, the current phase of U.S. cultural history began. For TV's postapocalyptic move to depoliticize the spirit of "the Sixties" marked the onset of the culture of TV that floods our consciousness today. It is a culture of routine and trivial iconoclastic gestures that pose no danger whatsoever to the status quo—bathroom jokes, nonstop profanity, outlandish body piercings, comic spectacles of broad "dysfunction," nauseating personal ordeals on programs such as *Fear Factor,* nauseating personal displays on programs such as Ricky Lake's or Jerry Springer's, in-your-face performance art, biographies that dwell on unattractive private habits, and all other salably "subversive" stuff that plays well on TV and off. Meanwhile, the political and economic powers of the United States, which were necessarily and reasonably questioned once upon a time, are left untouched, of course, by such crude bits and items, which subvert nothing but the canons of good taste. The cultural tendency toward this entirely apolitical outrageousness begins after the 1960s, on TV. We are fortunate that Josh Ozersky's book is here to help us understand how that occurred.

—Mark Crispin Miller

Preface: TV, Culture, and Cultural History

Few Americans can say that they live outside of the sphere of television: a few Amish, evangelical Christians committed to the home-school model, a patchwork of wealthy or austere individuals with better things to do. For the rest of us, TV is one of the central energies in our society. As a result, TV has from its inception been looked at critically. How does it affect us? What does it do to children? How has it changed society? I don't begin to try to answer these questions in this book. Like a growing number of other cultural historians, I am more interested in how America changed television. For purely economic reasons, as its audience changes, so TV has to change; and the way it changes, I think, tells us about our recent history.

Now, there are two objections that one can immediately make at this point. The first is to say, as my father used to, who cares? TV is crap and not worth studying, except possibly as pathology. This is a valid point of view in many ways, and I should make it clear up front that writing at length about TV as cultural history doesn't involve egalitarian defenses of "the most popular art." Most TV *is* pretty bad and deserves the scorn it gets. But cultural historians are, I think, obliged to be more interested in mediocre art than in original art, because that art by definition owes less to individual talent and more to what happens to be in the air. This book tries to get at what was in the air as the networks attempted, year after year, to accommodate the cultural shifts of the 1960s and 1970s; and the reflexes of an Aaron Spelling or a Jack Webb are more relevant in telling this story than, say, the genius of an Ernie Kovacs or a Jonathan Winters.

The second objection, made more often by academic students of mass media, is that the networks, as corporate entities, brought their own values to the table and that programming reflects this in a very tendentious and unrepresentative way. What is on TV reflects the values of capitalism, or at the very least, pragmatic strategies meant to give commercials a suitable environment in which to sell. This is undoubtedly true, but so what? Television occupies a special place in postwar America, and it changed as America did. The problem is that the relationship between America and television is symbiotic and complex. "The culture industry," as Theodor Adorno called it, has no control over what the public will like and depends on auguries and incantations in trying to make a hit. The audience, for their part, can only speak back by choosing what is often best in a bad lot, and then seldom with unanimity. The two sides are forever courting each other, forever destined for dissatisfaction and misapprehension. Television as a fact of life has informed American life and culture; but television as a day-to-day industry runs after American life and culture like an autograph hound behind a star's limousine. The networks' very cluelessness and desperation in the years between 1968 and 1978 give us a flash of illumination on that murky time, as they, like historians of a future time, tried to understand a changed world.

TV as History

This responsiveness might not have been present in an earlier period; in its salad days of the 1960s, TV networks were content to program innocuous entertainments for a general audience and to vary them only as necessary. But with the discovery by large advertising agencies of the demographic breakdown of buying power, TV in the mid-to-late 1960s found itself forced to seriously study the makeup of its audience for the first time. Conveniently for the historian, that breakdown came along generational lines, which also happened to be, arguably, the most significant division in politics and culture. As a result, TV echoed the larger history of the times.

It is not enough, however, to trace the way in which TV tried to exploit/represent America's search for itself in those years. The questions behind that search— How can we reconcile the cultural changes of the 1960s with the culture of the so-called silent majority? How can we deal with a political life that even the president called a nightmare? What is to become of our families and folkways?—are asked indirectly and only get answered as one show fails and another succeeds. The public mind can only communicate with the networks through the coarsest of membranes—Nielsen ratings and consumer buying power.

To really see the dynamic at work, the historian has to go to the meeting place of network and audience: the TV screen itself. Corporate correspondence or memoirs have only limited relevance, because the networks merely buy shows from producers, themselves executives who neither write, act, nor direct. There isn't much connection between the CBS programming head in New York, his head full of Nielsen figures and quarterly revenues, and the midseason fill-in that becomes an institution, providing the grade schools with new catchphrases and ending up donating its props to the Smithsonian. And yet, that unpredictable confluence of network, producer, actors, writers, and audience produces defining moments of American cultural history. No medium pursues such moments more obsessively or more methodically; no medium has the range and power to create such moments so often. Watching them closely within a historical context, and their myriad stillborn siblings as well, brings us into close quarters with our own cultural history.

This book describes how, over the course of ten years, network programmers lost and found their bearings in changing times. In 1968, as chapter 1 describes, this audience was already breaking apart, but the networks refused to address the fact until advertisers made it very clear that they were interested in younger audiences, particularly the large demographic wave of consumers entering the market courtesy of the postwar "baby boom." Chapter 2 looks at the networks' first disastrous attempts at "relevant" programming, and how CBS hit on a winning formula with *All in the Family* in 1971. Chapter 3 provides an in-depth look at the cultural content of the new programming—how comedy based on conflict was the winning formula for producer Norman Lear's shows, while the MTM studio's brand of consensus-based workplace comedies proved a more lasting success. In chapter 4, we find that network television in the early 1970s mainstreamed the innovations of the 1960s into the nightly status quo, as programming increasingly drew on the entropic forces informing American life—changed gender roles, "law and order," and (significantly) the disappearance of sustaining show-business formal conventions. Chapter 5 describes the reaction to the negativity and unruliness of the new programs: by mid-decade, audiences were exhausted, and after Nixon and Watergate, they were ready for a televisual return to normalcy. The

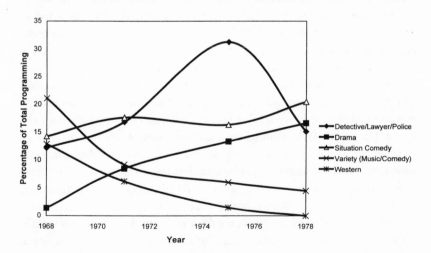

Trends in Programming as a Function of Time. "By twisting this way and that in response to the divergent forces that were emerging, television's mass appeal facade was rent asunder." Ed Papazian, *Medium Rare: The Evolution, Workings, and Impact of Commercial Television* (New York: Media Dynamics, 1991), 169.

pointedly named *Happy Days* and other comedies turned to innocuous themes, albeit leavened with a post-1960s social sensibility, as the social innovations of that era came to seem less deviant or even remarkable. In chapter 6, we see television complete its transformation into a mass medium for a postconsensus nation: by 1978, prime-time programming had adjusted to a fragmented audience for whom television, having survived the challenge of the 1960s, was itself the greatest common denominator. Finally, the epilogue looks briefly at the decades that followed.

"Cultural History" and a Note on Sources

I have referred several times to this work as *cultural history,* a vague term that in practice often means everything and nothing. Readers therefore have a right to know just what I mean by the phrase. Perhaps it would be better to say what I don't mean. Over the last twenty years, a theoretically oriented "cultural studies" has become the dominant perspective among students of American media. The concerns of that perspective—the function of power, cultural identity, capitalist or majoritarian hegemony, the writings of Michel Foucault, Antonio Gramsci, Walter Benjamin, Raymond Williams, and other European theorists—are almost completely absent from this study. What can I say? I am truculently old-school in my approach to history. My heroes are two-fisted, explicitly subjective, narrative storytellers such as Lord Macaulay and George Bancroft. That's my approach to writing history, albeit with a nod to scholarly practice. The preoccupations of much of contemporary media studies, with their sociological sheen and power-to-the-people posturing, never had much appeal. As a result of my primitivism, though, this study draws on no critical vocabulary not available to the general reader, and, in fact, it was for that reader that it was written. Literate citizens, and not professional academics, are the intended audience.

This is not to say that I have not drawn extensively on the existing academic literature. I am lucky enough to be writing at a time when there is a small but very accomplished body of television historians: scholars such as Jane Feuer, Lynn Spigal, Ella Taylor, Aniko Bodroghkozy, and other writers, all of whom have engaged in the project of understanding what TV tells us about the society that produced it. These writers have paid special attention to the ways in which television has functioned within the larger institutional and societal contexts of their times, and also how it has often created a space where those contexts were in some way challenged. Where I have departed from their practice to some extent is in my willingness to write about television from the point of view of a citizen/viewer, as opposed to a scholar/critic; to speak the language of traditional criticism and analyze works of art largely in their own terms—that is, why a joke is funny or why a thriller "works." The refusal to do this is, I think, a big mistake and one reason that some of the most penetrating criticism is relegated to nonacademic sources. While dismissed as merely "journalistic" by academics, the practice of critics such as James Wolcott or Leslie Savan have generally provided the best record of the inner life of commercial TV. The sanctimonious jargon of the history guild, in particular, is destructive in this regard—disguising, as the austere standards of science, what is really a transparent bit of proprietary bullying.

Other secondary sources I have used include books on television by professional media analysts such as Ed Papazian and a number of superb popular histories and reference works, the best of which is the comprehensive, beautifully written, and insightful *Watching TV,* by Harry Castleman and Walter Podzarik. Finally, I have drawn extensively on a relatively small but exceedingly valuable literature by and about some of the key figures in television in that era. Books like Aaron Spelling's or Grant Tinker's autobiographies are no doubt prey to spotty memories, self-serving interpretations, and simple mistakes; likewise, books about television by reporters such as Les Brown or Sally Bedell probably do not attain the lofty standards of verifiability of a work by Henry Steele Commager. Nonetheless, they provide the best picture we have of what happened behind the scenes at ABC, CBS, and NBC in the years considered. A pragmatic wariness about taking these quotes at face value is no doubt warranted but no more so than is true of a campaign biography or a military memoir.

The primary literature is problematic. While the personal papers of writers and producers may be found at a handful of archives, corporate correspondence after 1950 is exceedingly hard to come by. I have depended, in its place, on three major resources to supplant this hole in the record: the papers of key figures collected in archives such as those at the University of California, Los Angeles, and the Academy of Television Arts and Sciences; interviews and correspondence with important surviving figures from the period under question; and the day-to-day business news of the industry, as covered by trade journals such as *Variety*. Beyond these, there is, however, one enormous resource of primary material, and it is what forms the backbone of any study of television history. Television programs themselves are and should be considered primary sources, as essential and central to a history of television as any president's personal papers are to a political biography. In discussing specific episodes of television series, I have cited shelf numbers from what is probably the most definitive single collection of television programs, that of the Library of Congress's Motion Picture, Broadcasting, and Recorded Sound Division. Many of these programs can also be found in the Museum of Television and Radio in either Los Angeles or New York City, on commercially available video release, or even on television itself, where many of the shows are constantly rerun by such networks as USA, Nickelodeon, TV Land, The Family Channel, and many others. It is the programs themselves, watched with an informed and critical eye, that must remain the primary resource. Although the networks' character as economic institutions provides an important backdrop and motive to this story, the essential focus is on *programming*—as both verb and noun.

The other truly important primary source in discussing television is the ratings of the A. C. Nielsen Company, the most important gauge the television business used, and still uses, to measure the popularity of programs. While other ratings systems exist (Arbitron, Simmons, Q ratings), it was the Nielsens that remained the one undisputed and irreplaceable standard throughout these years, and it is therefore the Nielsens that I have used throughout.

Television, like other American cultural institutions, changes with the times or risks anachronism and irrelevance. But rarely in the history of any American institution did a ten-year period see so many changes, abrupt about-faces, rudderless buffeting, and fluid adoption to changing times. The reader may infer something from this of the external upheaval to which television was responding; but that larger America—indeed, larger world—affected television only in the crude ways in which television's primitive senses perceived it. This study does not attempt to describe those changes except in the broadest terms, the terms in which television, a "pitiful, helpless giant" if ever there was one, could grasp them. But if, even through so muffled a signal, television still found it necessary to reinvent itself again and again, some measure of the spinning chaos around it can be taken.

In writing this study, I was helped by a number of individuals who deserve special gratitude and acknowledgment. Thanks to Jerry Dominus, Ed Papazian, and Mike Dann for permission to quote from my interviews with them. Bill Vesterman and Whitney Bolton of Rutgers University got me started down this path in college, and Bill in particular has been a friend and patron such as nature rarely bestows. J. Philip Gleason at the University of Notre Dame provided a model of the scholar's patience, humility, and intellectual grace—inimitable for me on all three counts but ennobling nonetheless. Wilson Miscamble and Jackie Wyatt, also at Notre Dame, showed infinite patience in dealing with my shambling disorder; Jim Carroll provided me with friendship and support when I needed it most. Mark Crispin Miller's ideas have had a fundamental influence on my work. Neil Postman was my first, best model for taking television seriously, and Leslie K. Dwyer deserves a nod of thanks for suggesting I go to graduate school in the first place. Finally, much love and gratitude to Cynthia Ozersky, who was there through the entire process. And nothing I have done could or would have happened without the guidance and example of my late father, David Ozersky.

Archie Bunker's America

1
"Green Acres Is the Place to Be": America and TV, 1968

Few things are more striking, in retrospect, than the sheer oblivious-ness of prime-time television in 1968 to the turmoil surrounding it in the real world. Cataclysm followed cataclysm on the news. January brought the Tet of-fensive, an astonishing rebuttal to official reassurances about the Vietnam War. So discouraging was this news that, in an unprecedented act, news anchor Walter Cronkite himself was prompted to break with all tradition and suggest, onscreen and *ex cathedra,* that the war might be unwinnable. "We are mired in stalemate," Cronkite pronounced, ". . . the only rational way out [is] . . . to negotiate not as victors, but as an honorable people who lived up to their pledge to defend de-mocracy and did the best they could." (President Johnson, watching on one of his three TVs, immediately turned to his press secretary to say that he had now lost Mr. Average Citizen.)[1] April brought the death of Martin Luther King Jr., and summer, the death of Robert Kennedy; each event was the occasion of im-mense television coverage, as well as violent social and political aftershocks. Sum-mer also brought the infamous Chicago Democratic Convention, where such deathless images were generated as Dan Rather being wrestled to the ground and Mayor Daley's police brutalizing protesters. These were defining moments in TV's history (they would later become universal signifiers of "the sixties" for lazy pro-ducers); moreover, they were far from isolated spectacles in 1968. The occupa-tion of universities, most notably Columbia, by student radicals; President John-son's announcement that he would not run again; and most of all, the endless procession of depressing or inflammatory images from the war flooded millions of American living rooms with discord, violence, and ominous instability.

In prime time, however, the shows listed in table 1.1 were rated in the A. C. Nielsen Company's top ten as of April 1968.[2] (*The Saturday Movie of the Week,* which would occupy eighth place, is omitted). The proverbial viewer from outer space, receiving these broadcasts a billion years hence in his recliner in the Crab

Nebula, would infer from them only the most ephemeral of social problems. They consisted of three pastoral comedies, two Westerns, a liver-spotted handful of aging-star vehicles, and a pair of ludicrous sitcoms—one about two cute children in the care of an English valet, and the other about a housewife with magic powers.

Table 1.1
Top Ten Shows, 1968

Program/Network	Rating
1. *The Andy Griffith Show,* CBS	31.8
2. *The Lucy Show,* CBS	27.0
—3. *Gunsmoke,* CBS	25.6
4. *Family Affair,* CBS	25.5
—5. *Bonanza,* NBC	25.5
6. *The Red Skelton Show,* CBS	25.5
7. *The Dean Martin Show,* CBS	24.8
8. *The Jackie Gleason Show,* CBS	23.9
9. *Bewitched,* CBS	23.5
10. *The Beverly Hillbillies,* CBS	23.3

Only in historical retrospect, however, do the Nielsen top ten look so irrelevant. For the networks, they were relevant indeed, because in 1968, as now, what mattered most to TV executives was the getting and the keeping of highly rated shows. And since the audience was seen for the most part as an undifferentiated mass, the idea of airing polarizing material, which at that time any genuinely realistic show would necessarily have been, simply ran against the grain of network thinking.

Television, it will be remembered, was very much a product of the 1950s.[3] Although the primness of *The Adventures of Ozzie and Harriet* (1952–1966) had gone the way of vaudeville, the industry's moral principles circa 1950 were never repudiated. In 1967, for example, the National Association of Broadcasters revised their Television Code for the twelfth time. Though widely regarded within the industry as an absurd and unenforceable document, it still served as the NAB's official conscience.[4] Meant to be applied "to every moment of every program presented by television," its first article read, "Commercial television provides a valuable means of augmenting the educational and cultural influence of schools, institutions of higher learning, the home, the church, museums, foundations, and other institutions of education and culture." Among its commandments were:

> 5. Attacks on religion and religious faiths are not allowed. Reverence is to mark any mention of the name of God, His attributes

and powers. . . . The office of minister, priest, or rabbi shall not be presented in such a manner as to ridicule or impair its dignity. . . .

9. Law enforcement shall be upheld and, except where essential to the program plot, officers of the law portrayed with respect and dignity. . . .

16. Illicit sex relations are not treated as commendable. Sex crimes and abnormalities are generally unacceptable as program material. The use of locations closely associated with sexual life or with sexual sin must be governed by good taste and delicacy.

17. Drunkenness should never be presented as desirable or prevalent. The use of liquor in program content shall be deemphasized. The consumption of liquor in American life, when not required by the plot or for proper characterization, shall not be shown.

Other injunctions against impropriety, lewdness, disrespect for authority, hypnosis, astrology, and "the use of horror for its own sake" were also included among the code's pie-in-the-sky restrictions.[5]

It was, in short, a puritanical and wholly abstract document, bearing almost as little relation to TV circa 1968 as TV did to reality. What is significant is that even at this late date such lip-service to the civic pietism of the Eisenhower era was felt necessary and proper. Part of this was a reaction to criticism in the public sector and also in government that persisted long after the departure of President Kennedy's much-hated FCC chairman Newton Minow in 1964 and in fact persists to this day. Minow had railed against TV as a "vast wasteland" and threatened to revoke broadcast licenses unless the networks took responsibility.[6] In 1968, Senator John Pastore (D-Rhode Island) began a campaign against TV violence. In such situations, the broadcast industry tended to wrap itself in civic-minded pronouncements of similar spirit to the code, often made by its statesmen, like President Frank Stanton of CBS.[7] In 1968, in the wake of the Kennedy and King assassinations, the networks hastened to demonstrate the seriousness with which they took the senator's concern by sending notice to producers that violence had to be toned down. Aware that the heat must eventually pass, the producers and programmers obliged by reducing almost to nil the stylized shootings and fisticuffs that had filled so much of the airtime of Westerns and police dramas. A policeman might shoot a fleeing criminal and then inexplicably go over to him to confirm that he was still alive. As television historians Harry Castleman and Walter Podzarik note, "These strange new rules and illogical twists for action stories gave the 1968–1969 season the derogatory nickname of 'the one punch season.'"[8]

The recurring threat of government interference was one reason for conservatism in programming; a more significant one was the networks' working conception of their audience. "What we didn't have in the fifties and sixties," Mike

Dann says, "was the word demographics."[9] Although seldom articulated as such, the networks from the beginning worked under the theory of what NBC head of Audience Research Paul Klein called "least objectionable programming," or LOP. The theory behind LOP was a simple one. Since there were so many people in the audience, and since sheer volume of exposure was what advertisers paid for, it didn't make sense to alienate anybody. As articulated memorably by Klein in 1971, LOP arose from television's economics:

> Because of the nature of the limited spectrum (only a few channels in each city) and the economic need of the networks to attract an audience large enough to attain advertising dollars which will cover the cost of production of the TV program, pay the station carrying the program, and also make a profit, you are viewing programs which by necessity must appeal to the rich and poor, smart and stupid, tall and short, wild and tame, together. Therefore, you are in the vast majority of cases viewing something that is not to your taste.

In practice, that amounted to, in the immortal words of CBS standards and practices head William Tankersly, "a universal television that played to everyone and offended no one."[10]

For Klein, LOP was simple in practice: "Thought, that's tune-out, education, tune-out. Melodrama's good, you know, a little tear here and there, a little morality tale, that's good. Positive. That's least objectionable."[11] In 1951, the same sentiment had been voiced by Frank Wizbar, the director and host of one of TV's first dramatic series, *Fireside Theater* (1949–1963): "We sell little pieces of soap, so our approach must be the broadest possible."[12]

The LOP philosophy had been a bedrock assumption of all network programmers for most of television's history. It lay behind much of the great animus against "mass culture" that informed the debates in the 1950s in *Partisan Review* and elsewhere, where leading intellectuals such as Dwight Macdonald and Clement Greenberg vilified the new medium. The debate invariably drew on older art forms and media, usually to the disadvantage of television, although television's defenders often used history for the defense of "the most popular art." Gilbert Seldes, in *The Great Audience* in 1950, wrote, "The popular arts have always worried the moralist and the aesthete. . . . As each new medium comes into being, the intellectual shies away."[13] According to these apologists, television's low-grade appeal was a continuation, in the electronic age, of a genuinely "popular culture," which could be traced back to older popular forms. To its critics, it was, as Macdonald, Theodor Adorno, Clement Greenberg and others claimed, a corruption of that culture, imposed from above for crass or sinister purposes. Others considered "the boob tube" merely stupid.

What was seldom taken into account, at least explicitly, was the extent to which the whole argument about TV, and TV itself, was fueled by the intense anti-intellectualism of the Eisenhower era. LOP developed in an era when the opposition between "highbrow" and "lowbrow" was taken for granted by almost everybody.[14] (Seldes remains a notable exception.) This pervasive feeling afoot in the era contributed at least as much, if not more, than McCarthyism and the blacklist to the complexion of television. A practice that was defensible in business terms alone generally came cloaked in egalitarianism. "[Intellectuals] are not really reconciled," remarked President Frank Stanton of CBS in the late 1950s, "to some basic features of democratic life." Chairman Robert W. Sarnoff of NBC was more to the point: "If we listened to the eggheads we'd be out of business in six months."[15]

Beyond the anti-intellectualism of the 1950s, however (which, after all, was hardly confined to that decade as far as American business is concerned), the tendency of network programmers to avoid risk and offense made sense from a number of perspectives.[16] First of all, the networks were in the business of selling not to viewers, who would and did often surprise the TV industry with their choices, but to advertisers, who at this time bought according to millions of homes reached, as measured by the all-seeing statistical eye of the A. C. Nielsen Company. Those advertisers represent the bottom line, the sine qua non of success and failure in the industry. Since the job of every television executive is only as secure as the "numbers" allow, very few executives were or are willing to try new things, overestimate the taste of the public, or otherwise endanger themselves. As one remarked to Les Brown in 1970,

> It's a terrible thing, in a way. You begin to love the prestige and the authority, and the first thing you think about is how to preserve that and how to keep the money from stopping. Suddenly every new idea becomes a threat to you. It means you have to act on it, one way or another. You can't afford to be reckless. So you try to push the ideas down, make them go away or, if possible, make them someone else's responsibility.
>
> Listen, there is a technique, and I got wise to it right away. You learn to say no to everything. 'No' doesn't get you involved, 'yes' does. The company doesn't appreciate that you try to do right by it. So many boners and you're out. So you don't worry about doing right by the company. First you worry about doing right by yourself.[17]

A few titans might take a chance—William S. Paley of CBS, Sarnoff of NBC, or some lesser deity such as programming guru Fred Silverman during his Icaruslike ascent in the mid-1970s. But these men (and overwhelmingly, they *were* men) got to where they were through the stern discipline of safe bets. "In trying to satisfy most of the people most of the time," wrote President Oliver Treyz of ABC in 1960, "we are merely clinging to a time-honored show business tradition. . . . From Shakespeare to Barnum to Belasco to ABC—nothing's changed." Moreover, the nature of television series—as opposed to specials and "spectaculars"—depended on predictability. Two out of every three new shows failed, and therefore established series had to be held on to like gold. As with so much else in this period, mighty CBS led the way with its thinking: hire big stars because people like them and develop series with what Paley called "likable, intriguing characters who capture the imagination, interest or concern of the audience."[18]

But how were the networks to achieve this platonic ideal in a business where novelty was paramount and where each new season had to promise new excitement, new thrills? The answer was generally found in the reassuring duplication of existing trends and proven hits. Often, this meant the repackaging of old hits into (barely) new formats. Lucille Ball, for example, well into her fifties, was still getting into trouble, confiding in Vivian Vance, and performing the slapstick gags on *The Lucy Show* (1962–1974), which everyone remembered so affectionately from her *I Love Lucy* days almost twenty years earlier. If a private detective show like *77 Sunset Strip* (1958–1964) was a hit, half a dozen shows indistinguishable from it in form and often in content followed: *Hawaiian Eye* (1959–1963), *Bourbon Street Beat* (1959–1960), *Surfside 6* (1969–1962), *The Roaring Twenties* (1960–1962). This cost-conscious "recombinance," as television sociologist Todd Gitlin called it, is responsible for the clusters of shows that come to define TV for a few years at a time. Crippled or abnormal detectives, for example, filled the airwaves in the mid-1970s—paraplegic *Ironside* (1967–1975), fat *Cannon* (1971–1976), elderly *Barnaby Jones* (1973–1978), rumpled *Columbo* (1971–1977). A few years later, the vogue would be for "MTV Cops," *Miami Vice* (1984–1990) and its imitators. "Safety first is the network rule," wrote Gitlin in 1984. "The safest, easiest formula is that nothing succeeds like success. Hits are so rare that executives think a blatant imitation stands a good chance of getting bigger numbers than a show that stands on its own. . . . This hedging of bets also supplies them with ready made alibis in the frequent case of failure." Paul Klein agrees. "I don't think they tried to do anything but duplicate or replicate what had worked in the past. That was their job."[19]

There is no need to belabor the point. The status quo rules in television. And beyond this, the fact is that television's bottomless appetite for programming requires far more scripts, pilots, projects, and productions than can possibly be made with any sort of wit or intelligence. Then as now, TV shows were ground out with the uniformity of sausage links, and few writers in any case had any control over their work. Nearly all scripts were vetted by producers, directors, and executives with the care of a bishop examining a new catechism for hints of heterodoxy. Quality was not a high priority. "The shocking thing," said writer Ray Bradbury in 1967, "is that TV doesn't really want fine material."[20]

What kind of material, then, did TV want? To judge by the top ten Nielsen shows (for this was surely how the networks judged the issue), the stress was on a kind of burnished escapism. Producers had a vague idea that most of their audience was rural—and that, in any case, urban viewers were more likely to enjoy a rural show than the other way around. Two representative producers told Muriel Cantor as late as 1967 that "for their shows to draw large audiences in the cities, all American audiences must be 'rural, regardless of where they lived, unsophisticated, and uneducated.'"[21] Such attitudes were typical of television at the time. Most network buying and programming decisions were made in New York, by men with only the vaguest ideas about the flyover country. Well-educated, with cultivated tastes, many network executives spoke about rural viewers as if they were some kind of exotic being. In 1970, when *The Mary Tyler Moore Show* was being pitched at CBS, Marc Golden of Audience Research confidently announced, "there are four things America can't stand: Jews, men with moustaches, New Yorkers, and divorced women."[22] For CBS in the 1960s, the ideal, if not the reality, of rural America, continued to hold sway. And if there was any doubt, it was dispelled by the very biggest hit of the decade, *The Beverly Hillbillies,* which began a phenomenal sitcom run in 1962.

No sitcom, not even *I Love Lucy,* had ascended to the heights of the ratings in so short a time—six weeks. No sitcom was ever so roundly despised by critics upon its inception (David Susskind even asked his viewers to write to Congress in protest), thus proving yet again how irrelevant "the eggheads" were to popular tastes.

The basic premise of the show was, as they say, as old as the hills. Ozark mountain folk, after striking oil, find themselves living among the decadent rich in Beverly Hills. Hilarity ensues, as *TV Guide* might say. But in the case of *The Beverly Hillbillies,* concept was not all. *The Beverly Hillbillies* represented a departure from the current fashions in situation comedy. The sitcom, although divested of its all-knowing Dad and zero-sum suburban "adventures," in 1962 still relied on domestic settings, "normal" families, and at least the accoutrements of realism. The sitcom was not at this time in ascendance: only three of the previous year's top ten shows—*Hazel* (1961–1966), *The Andy Griffith Show* (1960–1968), and the *Danny Thomas Show* (1953–1971) at number 4, 7, and 8, respectively—had the honor of joining the Westerns, dramas, and variety shows that dominated the ratings that year, as they had every year in the 1950s. Of the three, only *The Andy Griffith Show,* with its small-town setting, seemed to reveal a market for huckleberryish humor of the kind *The Beverly Hillbillies* represented.

And even this was misleading—today, *The Andy Griffith Show* is remembered as a classic for its quiet humor and well-drawn characters. The other two sitcoms, *Hazel* and *The Danny Thomas Show*, were felt by many to be emblematic of the "vast wasteland" of early 1960s TV that had earned Newton Minow's wrath. The one show that viewers and critics, both then and now, regard as genuinely emblematic of the Kennedy years was as unlike *The Beverly Hillbillies* as one could get: the urbane *Dick Van Dyke Show* (1961–1966).[23]

The Van Dyke program was created as an alternative to the wasteland for upscale city audiences. "Seeking promotional platforms that were attractive to such viewers," remembers veteran demographer Ed Papazian, "advertisers let it be known they preferred vehicles focusing on the lives of more realistic characters—particularly comedies depicting the lifestyles of the professional-managerial elite that represented the pinnacle of vocational aspirations in our status- and reward-oriented society. The producers were happy to oblige, and the touchstone of the response became CBS's *The Dick Van Dyke Show*."[24] A workplace-based sitcom about the life of a television comedy writer, the show's humor was understated rather than zany, with a cast that included Carl Reiner, the Jewish comic Morey Amsterdam, and a young Mary Tyler Moore as the wife. Remembered Van Dyke, "there was never any attempt to be funny for its own sake. The relationship between the husband and the wife . . . it was very real, and everything that came out funny, came out of reality. There was never, you know, a blatant attempt to be funny."[25] It was perceived by some in the network, however, as problematic for these reasons. As a result, *The Dick Van Dyke Show* was, at least for the time, a dead end. It inspired no imitators or spin-offs.

Through a historical irony, however, the show did find success after a shaky start once *The Beverly Hillbillies* appeared on the scene as its Wednesday night lead-in. Few pairings could have been more incompatible in style and intent, and yet the vast audience garnered by the latter show built up exposure and familiarity enough among viewers to make the Van Dyke show a hit.[26]

The Beverly Hillbillies, on the other hand, needed no help. A monster success from the start, it led the way for a vastly popular new trend.[27] As per Paley's dictum, the characters were endearing. Boneheaded cousin Jethro, a strapping man-child after the Li'l Abner mold; crotchety Granny, always tending a still, distrusting city ways, and ready to grab her shotgun at the slightest provocation; unctuous, fawning banker Mr. Drysdale; his hypereducated spinster assistant Miss Hathaway, unrequitedly adoring Jethro. And of course, heading the Clampett family was the loose-limbed yet erect patriarch Jed Clampett, the personification of back-country virtue, sitting in front of his thirty-two-room mansion whittling.

It was a departure in a number of ways. First of all, *The Beverly Hillbillies* looked different than other sitcoms. Starkly artificial and stylized, it brought an

Cast of *The Beverly Hillbillies* in formal costume

element of theatricality to what had become an increasingly sterile genre. The characters were highly individuated but at the same time highly artificial and formalized, owing more to the stage and its iconic costuming than to the B-feature conventions of most filmed series. Mr. Drysdale is always wearing a different Brooks Brothers suit, and playboy Dash Riprock the era's flashy sportswear, but the Clampetts are always dressed exactly the same: Jed's torn felt hat, Jethro's rope belt and red plaid shirts, Granny's high-collared blouse. Like the Chinaman's pigtail or the Blimp's monocle, these are traditional identity tags of the kind familiar to stage audiences. (As amazing as it seems today, most suburban sitcoms of the 1950s were meant to seem realistic, not eerie and otherworldly as we regard them today.) *The Beverly Hillbillies'* artificiality inflamed critics still enamored of the realism of *Playhouse 90* (1956–1961), *Omnibus* (1953–1957), and the "golden age" of live drama. "Their assorted adventures," wrote the *New York Times,* "don't merely strain credulity, they crush it."[28] But to audiences, the show's fantastic element was liberating.

There was also a historical element to *The Beverly Hillbillies'* success. By the late 1950s, a critical literature had begun to accrue around the perceived consumerism and materialism of the postwar years. As it became clear that the economic perils of the 1930s and 1940s seemed to be safely behind, a kind of cottage industry developed. A large popular bibliography could be assembled from the mid-to-late 1950s of nonpartisan works that lamented the disappearance of American virtues. John Keats's *The Crack in the Picture Window* (1957) and *The Insolent Chariots* (1959) attacked the pursuit of homes and cars upon which so much of the postwar economic boom rested. Vance Packard's *The Hidden Persuaders* (1957) and *The Status Seekers* (1959) attacked advertising and consumerism, respectively, to wide attention and applause; the charismatic sociologist C. Wright Mills published several books, including *White Collar* (1951) and *The Power Elite* (1956), which were both class analyses of America with more than a little jeremiad in them. Novelist John Steinbeck, in a *New Republic* essay titled "Have We Gone Soft?" summed up the theme best: "If I wanted to destroy a nation, I would give it too much and I would have it on its knees, miserable, greedy, and sick. . . . On all levels American society is rigged. . . . I am troubled by the cynical immorality of my country. It cannot survive on this basis."[29] Most of these books, essays, speeches, and discussion were predicated, in one way or another, on the notion that Americans have declined from the virtues, Spartan and otherwise, of the forefathers (as, for example, David Riesman's famous comparison of the older "inner directed man," with his moral gyroscope, versus the modern "outer directed" man, antennae nervously atwitter).

It would be ludicrous to say that *The Beverly Hillbillies* shared the target audience of these high- and middlebrow critiques, but it clearly shares a longing for the world we have lost. "Jed Clampett was to be a tall man of simple, homespun honesty and dignity," Paul Henning, the show's creator, told the press upon its premiere. "The kind of Ozark mountaineer I knew as a boy."[30] This remark suggests an added appeal of the show, besides its use as a pastoral for the affluent society. Jed Clampett and his family are meant to represent pure American types, the sort of people Paul Henning remembered from his boyhood in Independence, Missouri, where as a soda jerk he served up phosphates to Harry S. Truman.[31]

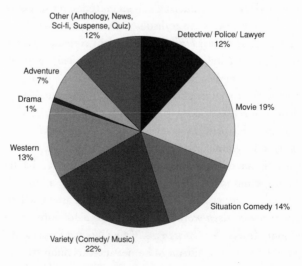

Distribution of Prime-Time Programming for 1968. The last hurrah for programming diversity. Programming would become far more streamlined in the 1970s.

Some observers took note of both elements, remarking that the show's success was not just due to artifice but also to social timing. Veteran TV writer and producer Sheldon Leonard, in a 1963 *Television Quarterly* interview, noted that

> The public appetite for comedy changes as the economic and political climate of a country changes. . . . We have been trying to make shows in our studio that present comedy situations which are not too far removed from the experiences of the people who are watching them. But there seems to be a taste for something a little broader— or even completely removed from reality. . . . Everyone thought *Hillbillies* would click, but it has had such great success that it points to a shift in the public taste again. For some reason, the broad social climate is making people look to entertainment in non-realistic areas.[32]

Leonard, who as the producer of *The Dick Van Dyke Show* understood this cultural fork in the road better than anyone, saw the meaning clearly. The 1960s were to be a decade of escapism, as the runaway success of *The Beverly Hillbillies* was to inspire what Eric Barnouw would later call "The Fortress" period of American TV.

As the world around it became increasingly bewildering and hostile, Barnouw suggests, TV became a "psychological refuge" for "the average man's view of the world. . . . It presented the America he wanted and believed in and had labored to be part of. It was alive with handsome men and women and symbols of the good life. It invited and drew him into its charmed circle."[33] Whether or not this was the case is impossible to say; Barnouw is extrapolating as all observers must from the Nielsen ratings and the character of the day's programming.

That having been said, Barnouw's point is well taken. By a kind of Darwinian trial and error, the networks in the early 1960s had discovered that escapism paid off. Throughout the decade, CBS president James Aubrey oversaw the development of feather-light entertainments, which he felt were the strength of CBS's winning prime-time lineup.[34] In some cases, this meant rural escapism, slavish knock-offs of *The Beverly Hillbillies'* winning formula. In Paul Henning's *Green Acres* (1965–1971), the formula is simply reversed: two high-society types, counterparts to the Drysdales, move out to "Hooterville," where they get caught up in culture shock and rural high jinks. (*Green Acres* also followed the *Beverly Hillbillies'* attention to stage conventions: at no time does erstwhile Wall Street lawyer Oliver Wendell Douglas pitch hay in anything other than a full three-piece suit, complete with watch fob and pocket square.) A third Paul Henning rural sitcom, *Petticoat Junction* (1963–1970), also took place near Hooterville and also did well in the ratings.

Although the rural sitcoms could not replicate themselves indefinitely (sub-genres, as a rule, bearing small litters), their escapist spirit came to dominate the decade. Although only a few actually had rural settings, all represented the kind of pastoral tranquility the countryside represented to the TV networks, or at least to their directing intelligences on the four-hundredth floor of the corporate head-quarters in Manhattan. As Harry Castleman and Walter Podzarik put it, "the aseptic peace of Fifties TV had been transported to the hills and nothing could disturb it."[35]

Thus, as the Vietnam War escalated, for example, audiences were treated to an odd subgenre of bloodless, playful war comedies: *Gomer Pyle, U.S.M.C.* (1964–1970), in which a dim-witted gas station attendant from Andy Griffith's hometown, inducted into the marines, clashes week after week with his crusty but benevolent drill instructor and a swell bunch of barrack mates who have never heard of Viet-nam; *Hogan's Heroes* (1965–1971), in which a motley group of POWs operate an undercover operation under the nose of bumbling Colonel Klink; *McHale's Navy* (1962–1966), in which Ernest Borgnine and his PT crew had zany adventures outwitting their commanding officer in the Pacific theater of World War II; and *The Wackiest Ship in the Army* (1965–1966), about the nutty crew of a two-masted schooner in World War II who, as Ed Papazian memorably puts it, "halted the merriment from time to time to gun down hordes of comic book 'Japs' who made the mistake of getting in their way."[36] Long-running Westerns like *Bonanza* (1959–1973) and *Gunsmoke* (1955–1975) and star-powered variety institutions like *The Ed Sullivan Show* (1945–1971) and Jack Benny's *Collegiate Comedy Hour* (1950–1965) helped to round out the Nielsens through the early and mid-1960s, with occasional police or medical dramas thrown in for good measure.

If such diversions, aired in the years of escalation (the Tonkin Gulf resolu-tion coming in 1964, Operation Rolling Thunder and the first combat troops in 1965) represented a pointed escapism, a comedy of containment, the suburban sitcoms of this period evidenced an even more legible desperation. The *Ozzie and Harriet* model having played itself out, programmers in search of nonconfron-tational suburban comedies turned to the fantastic. This became apparent by the 1964 season. Then, As Castleman and Podzarik put it, "in contrast to the fondly remembered high drama of TV's golden days, the networks' fall schedules of-fered country bumpkins, ridiculous settings, childish plots, witches, Martians, and pure soap opera. It all seemed deliberately designed to appeal to viewers who looked at television as a mindless escape tool."[37]

An escape tool, perhaps, but not necessarily a mindless one. Escapism implies pursuit, and it is the nature of any escapist vehicle, no matter how frothy, to re-flect indirectly the thing its audience wishes to avoid. So strenuous were the pre-mises of the most popular comedies in the 1960s that this thing must have been pretty disturbing indeed. Between 1962 and 1968, the shows listed in table 1.2 joined or displaced the Westerns and variety shows of the 1950s in the Nielsen top ten. And this list excludes shows with average ratings such as *Mr. Ed* (1961–1965, talking horse), *My Mother the Car* (1965–1966, talking car), *O. K. Crackerby* (1965–1966, *Hillbillies* clone), and *The Flying Nun* (1967–1970, self-explanatory), to say nothing of such youth fare as *Voyage to the Bottom of the Sea* (1964–1968), *Star Trek* (1966–1969), *Lost in Space* (1965–1968), and the prime-time cartoons *The Flintstones* (1960–1966), *Jonny Quest* (1964–1965), and the *Famous Adventure of Mr. Magoo* (1964–1965). The fantasy genre that dominated 1960s programming—the rural shows of Paul Henning, *Gilligan's Island* (1964–1967), *My Favorite Martian* (1963–1966), *Mr. Ed*, *The Addams Family* (1964–1966), *Bewitched* (1964–1972), *The Twilight Zone* (1959–1964), and others—had one thing in common. In no way did the outside world intrude. And this extended even beyond the plots and the premises, to the very nature of the productions themselves.

As the television industry developed through the 1950s, the economics of programming had made it easier and more feasible to simply buy filmed shows from subsidiaries of the big Hollywood studios, which by mid-decade had resigned themselves to the permanence of TV and decided to use the insatiable appetite of the new medium for grade-B products as a way to offset rising costs and declining revenues.[38] Live shows were culturally and aesthetically valuable, but they were also highly unpredictable and expensive. Moreover, they could be broadcast only once. The wave of the future, as television streamlined and standardized itself, and as the sums of money involved grew increasingly more intimidating, was clearly in filmed series. Initially, this involved transitional stages—first, what J. Fred Macdonald has called "vaudeo," the variety series, filmed before an audience, which was only to die out in the 1970s; and afterward, as the stakes became higher, a striving for greater predictability. By the time of shows such as 1965's *Get Smart*, catchphrases were inserted in the first season of programs even before they caught on. Eight shows were filmed, complete with the star's trademark phrases "Would you believe?" and "Sorry about that, Chief!" built right in.[39] The logical course of this evolution led inexorably to the elimination of the studio audience entirely, the one relic of the pretelevisual past and the sole nonstandardized element in the increasingly formulaic and sterile world of television comedy. This aim was accomplished by the use of the so-called Laff Box, invented by CBS engineer Charley Douglass in 1953. "I learned," *I Love Lucy* director Harry Ackerman remembered, "that Lucy was dead on a bare soundstage, so I insisted that we film in front of a live audience. It was for the performers' benefit at first, although of course we recorded the audience reaction and learned to 'sweeten' it when necessary."[40] Eventually, the audience was dispensed with entirely. Thus was invented the "canned laughter" that has been so symbolic of

Table 1.2

Situation Comedy Premises of the Mid-1960s

Program	Premise	Year of debut
The Beverly Hillbillies	Mountain yokels live among the wealthy, their folkways hilariously intact	1962
My Favorite Martian	Regular guy Bill Bixby lives with a Martian "uncle" who has magic powers	1963
Petticoat Junction	Rural matriarchy operating from country hotel	1963
Bewitched	Beautiful witch tries to fit in as suburban housewife	1964
Flipper	Intelligent, loyal dolphin saves the day—aquatic "Lassie"	1964
Gomer Pyle, U.S.M.C.	Backcountry yokel joins the Marines, folkways hilariously intact	1964
The Addams Family	Family of eccentrics/monsters living together happily	1964
The Man from U.N.C.L.E.	James Bond clone	1964
The Munsters	Family of bland movie monsters living together happily	1964
Batman	Comic-book superhero in camped-up serial adventures	1965
Get Smart	Spy-genre spoof with bumbling secret agent	1965
Green Acres	City society people move to the backcountry, folkways hilariously intact	1965
✓ *Hogan's Heroes*	Wacky POWS, bumbling Nazis	1965
Wild, Wild West	James Bond clone set in old West; more fantastic even than *Man from U.N.C.L.E.*	1965

the medium to critics over the years. ("Canned laughter is the lowest form of fascism," underground journalist Paul Krassner would later write. "Canned laughter is TV's ultimate insult to the audience.")[41] The machine insured that no comedy series, no matter how weak, would ever lack for howls of approval; in so doing, it arguably helped to ensure the decline of comedy on television. "We're manufacturing a reaction to our own creation," worried child-star turned producer Jackie Coogan. "It's the put on of all time."[42] Certainly, the fantasy sitcoms of the 1960s would have been impossible without it. Filmed on soundstages and requiring elaborate special effects (people appearing and disappearing, objects levitating, horses talking, etc.), the shows could not play before a live audience the way *I Love Lucy* or *The Honeymooners* did. And, once having heard laughter on televised comedy, the absence of it could only seem eerie or worse. Although the situation comedy had been abstracted from its roots—the stage first and then the studio stage of radio and early television—it had been given a protective coat of manufactured approval that would serve it well in its evolution.

In Sherwood Schwartz's *Gilligan's Island,* the machine was put to use in the service of "the program that showcased Aubrey escapism at its worst."[43] The show was highly conceptualized from the start. An assortment of nonethnic American types ("the millionaire and his wife . . . the movie star . . . the professor and Mary Ann") interact farcically on "an uncharted desert isle."[44] As with the Hillbillies, they all wear costumes, the same in every show, and no mention is ever made about the bottomless supplies of food, furniture, clothes, money, books, and so on. The plots, too, are highly conventionalized. Typically, a guest "castaway" washes up—Hans Conreid as Wrong Way Corrigan, Don Rickles as a thief, Vito Scotti as a Japanese(!) soldier—and offers the cast trouble and/or a chance to escape before he or she disappears at the end of the episode. More commonly, the castaways find a chance to escape (a raft, a jet pack, a carrier pigeon, etc.), and somehow Gilligan screws up the plan. Inevitably, the show ends with the castaways sitting around a radio, listening dispiritedly as the means of their rescue is welcomed back to the world. The Skipper hits Gilligan with his hat; the credits appear as the theme song plays. The show's reception was even more hostile than *The Beverly Hillbillies'* had been. Richard Dubrow of UPI was moved to note, "it is impossible that a more inept, moronic or humorless show has ever appeared on the home tube."[45]

If *Gilligan's Island* represented an all-purpose evasion of reality, other programs were more focused on particular vexations.[46] Take, for example, gender conflict. Premonitions of the Nixon-era's "battle of the sexes" might be gleaned from the preponderance of all-male preserves such as *Bonanza, My Three Sons, Flipper,* and so on among prime-time shows, along with the disappearance, in those years, of the harmonious household as a common sitcom setting. Of the top twenty-five shows between 1964 and 1968, only *Green Acres, The Dick Van Dyke Show,* and *Bewitched* had a nonmonster married couple at their center; and the marriage in *Bewitched* was more than a little problematic (as we shall see). From what had been the most idealized representation of marriage in the 1950s, television by 1964 had become almost entirely populated by widowers and singles. "Bachelor father" had been a novel enough premise in 1957 to name a show after. By 1964, every major sitcom, *as well as every major dramatic series,* had a single lead: *The Andy Griffith Show* (widower), *The Beverly Hillbillies* (widower), *Petticoat Junction* (widow), *The Fugitive* (widower), *Daktari* (widower and daughter), *The Lucy Show* (widow), *Lassie* (widow), *Peyton Place* (free love), *Daniel Boone* (unmarried), *The Virginian* (unmarried), *Family Affair* (widower), *My Three Sons* (widower), *Bonanza* (widower), *Wild, Wild West* (dashing lothario), *The Man from U.N.C.L.E.* (dashing lothario), *Get Smart* (would-be dashing lothario), *Hogan's Heroes* (unmarried), and *Batman* (asexual). *The Addams Family* and *The Munsters* both centered on married couples, but small comfort there—both families were by definition monsters who terrified any visitor who encountered them.

Even aside from this plague that visited married households in the 1960s, however, some of the most popular and/or enduring shows of the mid-decade showed fissure lines demonstrating why TV marriage was such a foundering institution.

For example, critics such as Susan Douglas, writing of CBS's successful series *I Dream of Jeannie,* have underlined the slavish relationship between the sexy genie and her "master," Major Nelson and the anxious haste with which he constantly orders her to go "back into her bottle." For Douglas in particular, this is plainly a fantasy for forcing the woman back into her "proper place," Jeannie's bottle being a metaphor for the home (or possibly the bedroom, since Jeannie's bottle, viewed from the inside, consisted mostly of pink, heart-shaped pillows).[47] Moreover, Major Nelson's behavior hearkens back to Ricky Ricardo's ongoing struggle to check Lucy's ambition to be more than a housewife, or later, Archie Bunker's injunction to his wife to "stifle yourself." One point most historians have seen clearly is the strange sexual tension at the show's core: Major Nelson is (until the last season, in which he and Jeannie married, and possibly even then) completely chaste, oblivious to the sultry beauty of actress Barbara Eden in her harem costume. NBC, on the other hand, was more attentive to Jeannie's sexuality, censoring the exposure of her navel as a matter of policy.

More to the point, *I Dream of Jeannie* was most revealing in what Jeannie did *not* do. Jeannie can change reality in any way she wishes, from bringing back the dead to sending Major Nelson back to the Old West. Her abilities have to be hidden, however, since Major Nelson, a colorless sketch of rectitude, fears only that Jeannie may ruin his image as a straitlaced officer. Her godlike ability to grant any wish he can think of goes unexercised for the simple reason that he is unable to imagine anything. Just as Sergeant Bilko always ends up where he started, and Ralph Kramden's get-rich-quick schemes invariably come to naught, Jeannie's powers are a threat to the status quo that has to be slapped down hard, every week.

This cruel trope appears again and again in the mid-1960s. The inability of magic powers or wishes to make people happy is a recurring message on American TV, even as the presence of such powers is used as a plot device, a "revoltin' development" that threatens the audience representative's middle-class life of Riley. In the highest-rated of all magic sitcoms, *Bewitched* (1964–1972), pretty young housewife Samantha Stevens is an all-powerful witch—a fact only her nervous husband Darrin knows.[48] Refusing to use her "powers," which are infinite and as easy as wiggling her nose, she works behind the scenes to support her go-getter husband, an advertising executive with strictly enforced bourgeois principles. The show's plots, at least in the early years, tended to revolve around how Samantha could resist the assaults of her mother Endora on her suburban existence or how she could use her powers, without Darrin's knowing, to advance his career.

The show was meant as fluff, but it reflected some of the sort of barely restrained tensions then running through the culture. As women became more and more aware of their own marginalization, and as what was at first known derisively as "women's lib" became a fixture of American life, the ideal of the perfect housewife—June Cleaver, Harriet Nelson—began to seem less appealing; the success of *Bewitched* may owe less to its negligible scripting and faceless characters than to the serendipity of its pregnant premise.[49] Barnouw, in *Tube of Plenty,* remarks on the similarity of these magical women to the housewives in commercials of the time who, by summoning Mr. Clean or waving a bottle of some potent cleanser, transform their homes with a gesture and a harp glissando into a paradise of antiseptic brightness.[50] But just as these products only empower women to be better drudges, so do Samantha's powers only increase her (and our) frustration with her domestic life.

The purported lightheartedness of the concept notwithstanding, *Bewitched* is filled with tension and potential animosity. Even on the plane of physical casting, *Bewitched* is unbalanced, a weighted deck. Samantha is a beautiful blonde, a model off the cover of *Look;* Darrin is cast not as her square-jawed counterpart but as a frightened-looking, angular, skinny nerd, the before man in a weight-lifting advertisement. Every week, her "powers" threaten to get out of control and belie his role, so precariously erected, of boss and breadwinner. In fact, Darrin Stevens's position as breadwinner is dismayingly realistic: unlike the patriarchs of *Fathers Knows Best* or even *My Three Sons,* his work is neither off-camera nor dignified but trivial and low—advertising.[51] Worse yet, he has a domineering boss, Larry Tate, the threat of whose displeasure is Darrin's greatest ongoing fear both

Bewitched's Darrin and Samantha Stevens: the cruelest coupling

at work and at home. (Servile company man that he is, Darrin insists on social-izing with Larry and his wife during his free time.)

Bewitched represents a culmination of assumptions informing network think-ing since *I Love Lucy*. The sitcom had to be an affirmation of the suburban way of life, because it had to take place in the suburbs (that being where the audi-ence was) and because it had to have a happy ending in which harmony was re-stored (it being a comedy.) Some other genres might skirt these necessities—road dramas such as *Route 66* or *The Fugitive,* for instance, having a different setting each week, or single-serving "guest star" characters whose lives could be changed without affecting a series' continuity. But the sitcom relied on stasis as a foun-dation for its very being.

What tension then, given its double burden! At the same time that it upheld the status quo, it was also required to provide viewers with escape fantasies, of normalcy shot through with magical possibilities. The magical sitcoms were the logical extensions of Lucy's frustrated attempts to enter show business or Sergeant Bilko's hopeless quest for unearned wealth.

Bound on one side by the "traditional" morality of the TV Code and the static conventions dictated by serial comedy, and on the other by the desire of the audience to be distracted and at least momentarily displaced, network entertainments stumbled onto a logic dictating greater and greater departures in plot, without ever changing the basic foundation: the situation comedy grew bigger tail fins throughout the decade.

TV Guide illustrates this in its summaries. Since at this time remote controls were not common, and there were only three or four channels to watch anyway, plot summaries were one way a viewer uncommitted to a certain show might decide what to watch. Choosing a night at random, consider, say, the night of 18 February 1965. Only the variations in the show are listed, the basic format of the series being presumably known to the reader.

TV Guide Listings for Night of 18 February 1965

8:00

Donna Reed—Comedy
Jeff finds things less than routine when he takes a part time job in an old fashioned gift shop. [guest cast follows]

Perry Mason—Mystery
Art student Betty Kaster's job as secretary to lecturer Philip Stark hasn't been a lark—she's become convinced that Stark plans to do away with his bedridden wife. [cast]

8:30

Dr. Kildare—Drama
"Make Way for Tomorrow." Because his Sarah needs the insurance money, elderly seaman Jamie Cousins decides to stop his heart—by using yoga. [cast]

My Three Sons—Comedy
When Chip suddenly gets sick, Steve has to cancel plans for his vacation trip to Hawaii—so the family brings Hawaii to him. [cast]

9:00

Bewitched—Comedy
Bored because Darrin's tied up at the office, Samantha agrees to go to lunch with her mother—in Paris. [cast]

Password—Game
Eydie Gorme and Frank Sinatra, Jr. play the word game. Moderator: Allan Ludden.

9:30

Hazel—Comedy
COLOR "Stop Rockin' Our Reception." George, confined to the house with a backache, planned to catch up on his viewing— until the family set went on the blink.

Baileys of Balboa
Sam and Buck have entered the Balboa to Laguna Antique Car Race—in an II MPH vintage auto. [cast]

Peyton Place—Serial
Leslie Harrington reveals astonishing plans to his son. [cast]⁵²

Leaving aside for the moment the evening's ten o'clock programming, in this official sketch of the evening's entertainments several things stand out. One is the extent to which each plot requires a twist of some sort, usually indicated by a dash. A *TV Guide* entry for a series ten years earlier would more likely have consisted of a single phrase, for instance, "Lucy loses her wedding ring" or "Tonto is accused of murder." In all but two of the above entries, such a summary phrase only sets up the twist. This is not to claim that there was some radical departure in the 1960s from the series dramaturgy of the 1950s; clearly, there wasn't. But as the decade progressed and television refined the formulae of the programs it bought, writers were forced into more and more unlikely plots, which depended for their humor on "guest stars" or elaborate devices such as split personalities, time warps, or suddenly emergent relatives or spouses. The most explicit case of this is *Gilligan's Island,* with its parodies, amnesias, and cosmonauts, but to some extent the same problem can be found in most mid-to-late 1960s programming.

Also worth noting about our evening of prime time is the extreme narrowness of the programming options presented. The same evening ten years earlier would have offered a much larger array of game shows, variety shows, religious programming, and dramatic anthology shows, all considerably less formalized in genre than the 1965 schedule. A typical night's programming from 1955, shown in table 1.3, demonstrates this. Not only does it show a much greater variety of programming formats, but those formats themselves tended toward more diversity. *Circus Time* and the two country variety shows both carried a large number of acts, both comic, musical, animal, religious, and so on within their discrete genres; and the dramatic series represent a different continuum altogether, the so-called golden age of high-quality live drama, often presented with a minimum of network control or production value and often dealing with socially meaningful themes.[53] Even among standard formats such as the quiz show, there was a certain looseness of format, as evidenced by Groucho Marx's *You Bet Your Life,* essentially a vehicle for the star's ad-libs. By 1965, only drama and comedy series, filmed in Hollywood and sold to exact specifications, could be found between 8 and 10 P.M. Even the variety show, which would continue for some years on the backs of aging superstars, was highly regulated and formalized and tended to take up big one-hour blocks. (In 1955, seven of the Nielsen top fifteen, almost half, were variety shows; in 1965, only one, *The Red Skelton Show,* made the list at all.) Only the taciturn Ed Sullivan avoided formalization, and only because he came prefossilized, a pretelevisual impresario whose sole function was to piece together eclectic, crowd-pleasing collections of acts.

Table 1.3
1955 Prime-Time Schedule, Thursday Night

8:00 PM	8:30 PM	9:00 PM	9:30 PM
Circus Time (circus variety)	*Circus Time,* cont.	*Wire Service* (news drama)	*Ozark Jubilee* (country variety)
Bob Cummings Show (sitcom)	*Climax* (live drama)	*Climax,* cont.	*Playhouse 90* (live drama)
You Bet Your Life (comedy/quiz)	*Dragnet* (police drama)	*People's Choice* (sitcom)	*Tennessee Ernie Ford Show* (country variety)

Thirdly, the 1965 schedule offers almost no point of contact with the outside world represented to viewers of the news. Without exception, the shows aired between 8 and 10 P.M. draw both their content and their form from earlier forms of TV. *Perry Mason* and *Dr. Kildare,* no less than *The Donna Reed Show, Bewitched,* and *Password,* are both dependent on appealing and trustworthy stars facing contrived situations; situations that, in point of practice, exist only to expose the stars to their audience in a predictable way. Only on *Peyton Place* is the plot proper of any real relevance to the show's appeal.

This gradual sealing-out process, by which the television programs of the 1960s became indistinguishable from their formats, resulted at least in part from the increased attention networks were paying to the great undifferentiated audience. The 1960s represent the era when television was fully rationalized; when the ad hoc quality of network decision making in the 1950s had finally passed into the hands of corporate executives and MBAs. "The idea," J. Fred Macdonald sums up, "was not to offer a wide range of shows and thereby please most people, it was to make the TV business more efficient and profitable by limiting the variety and increasing the similarity of productions."[54] The point, it was now clear, was to sell as many households as possible to as many advertisers for the least amount of money. It was inevitable in such an atmosphere that a process of standardization and risk-elimination, a kind of artistic Taylorism, would arise.

And yet, as much as standardization, escapism, canned laughter, and related developments were (and are) deplored by television's many critics, the observation has seldom been made that, in its attitudes and practices of the 1960s, television mirrored very basic attitudes within the larger sphere of American life. *Programming* may have represented a purposeful evasion of the sex war, racial tensions, Vietnam, and "the crack in the picture window," but other, less visible fault lines of the 1960s are revealed in the watermark of network decision making.

For example, a most significant issue, taken in the context of American society in the postwar era, was the ideal of standardization that informed television from top to bottom in the 1960s. This expressed itself in the practice of programming standard genres for mass audiences and measuring these audiences by means of a universal standard—the Nielsen rating. The Nielsens had existed since the days of radio, but their use as an absolute standard for gauging success and failure grew to religious proportions in the years of network oligarchy. For the purposes of the Nielsen sample, each household represents seventy-five thousand other viewing households. What that set has on is taken by statistical formula to represent the attention of three-quarters of a million people. Television is the preeminent mass medium in America, however, so even this high number is only a fraction of what a successful show should draw. The exposure of millions of viewers to TV is taken for granted, both by the network and the advertisers, who frequently in the 1960s and even afterward paid rates of four dollars per thousand viewers reached. Four dollars! The difference of one percentage point could mean a difference of hundreds of thousands of dollars in ad revenues, the loss of positions, and the fate of shows. Programmers Mike Dann and Paul Klein, at CBS and NBC, respectively, in 1970 lost their jobs despite sterling reputations and brilliant track records, at least in part due to a publicity-seeking war for ratings "dominance" that might well have been meaningless once statistical error was figured in.[55]

When Nielsen started a "Television Index" in 1950, the ratings appeared every six weeks and were only a partial factor in determining the fate of programs. In 1960, the process was shortened to sixteen days, a brief enough time to make judgments in the early days of a show's run; in 1967, it was shortened to nine days. (By 1973, the period would be a week, and *overnight* ratings would be available and hence required for every executive's desk first thing in the morning. "This is one of the few businesses," CBS's Steve Mills would say, "where a guy comes to work every morning and looks to see how he did the day before.")[56]

The networks' Nielsen fetish would not in itself be historically relevant except for what it tells us about television's conception of its audience. Such a presumption of statistical accuracy could not exist without a robust intellectual commitment to the idea of a vast, essentially homogeneous mass. In 1964, in an essay called "Nielsen Defends His Ratings," Arthur Nielsen himself wrote: "Did you ever watch someone start on a bowl of soup? He stirs the liquid, lifts the spoon to his lips and sips. He has just tasted a sample and rated it; whether he adds salt or not depends on that random sample."[57] Nielsen's metaphor is an interesting one, suggesting a view of America not as a "melting pot" in which people from all nations are cast into one vessel, there to intermingle their ethnic identities, but rather as a bowl of soup, all of whose ingredients are inextricably and immutably blended into one consistent whole. This view of American culture predominated after World War II. The racist ideologies of the Nazis had been discredited, and the truth of the motto *e pluribus unum* was taken for granted. The diverse "bomber crew" of war films was replaced in social discussion by other emblems of unity, such as the harmonious "triple melting pot" of Will Herberg's *Protestant-Catholic-Jew* (1955) or the sated "people of plenty" of David Potter's 1954 critique.[58] America, it was generally agreed, was "one nation, indivisible."

Nielsen reflected this view of America as an organic whole, any one part of which could be "sampled" to understand the others. He translated into terms immediately apprehensible to business what even at the time was highly problematic: the idea that American cultural unity was the result of democracy and in some way reflective of the free choice of the people. American cultural unity, as its critics often protested, was largely a result of enforced "mass culture" and hardly counted as a choice at all, given the lack of any alternatives. The networks always defended themselves from this charge by pointing out that shows like *The Beverly Hillbillies,* while abhorrent to critics, were hugely popular with audiences and that the homogeneity of programming represented the triumph of the *vox populi.*

Just as often, however, they admitted that, in Mike Dann's first of "seven basic scheduling rules," "in any given time period the success of a show will depend solely on its competition. In other words, you can have a hit at 8 P.M. Wednesday simply because your show is the best among three bad shows."[59] (This is what Paul Klein meant when he spoke of "least objectionable programming.") Shows like *The Beverly Hillbillies* or *I Love Lucy* were so highly exceptional in their ability to transcend their time slot that they informed the practice of television entertainment for years to come.

If network practice belied its official belief in free choice, however, that did not mean that the belief was completely disingenuous. (Their practice contradicted the preposterous Broadcasting Code, too, whose prescriptions many executives personally believed in.) The people might well be stuck with whatever the networks offered them. But they were still "the people." Arthur Nielsen's image of America as a bowl of soup served the networks very well over the years, and if to some extent it was a self-perpetuating delusion, that only put it more squarely into the mold of the times. The networks were hardly the only decision makers in love with statistics and the seductive abstractions they represented. One need look no further than Secretary of Defense Robert S. McNamara and his "whiz kids," processing the war itself through convincing-looking but wholly illusory data. False troop evaluations, make-believe "body counts," fudged statistics, and a hundred other sources of misinformation were channeled into the Pentagon's computers, producing results pleasing to the administration but with little correlation to the real world. "Garbage In, Garbage Out" was the shorthand for this process, and as the war dragged on in spite of all official assurances of victory, the patent falsehood of the process became well known to the public.[60]

But even setting aside the familial relation between Nielsen thinking and Pentagon disinformation, a more elemental connection existed between the networks and the larger society whose attention they bought and sold. Both were dominated by "the cult of consensus." The 1950s, it will be remembered, was a decade whose critical discourse was marked by cries of alarm over the dangers of conformity.[61] This trend played itself out most starkly in the HUAC interlude, where the refusal to genuflect before the House Un-American Activities Committee constituted prima facie evidence that one was in league with traitors. But beyond the HUAC melodrama was a concern by intellectuals that Americans had lost their individualism.

Formerly, wrote David Riesman in *The Lonely Crowd,* the American had been "inner directed," guided by a moral gyroscope oriented by the Protestant work ethic and the mores of the growing republic. Today's American, on the other hand, was "outer directed," a cipher who depended on antennae to navigate "the personality market." C. Wright Mills, in *White Collar,* wrote of a vast middle class that behaved like "cheerful robots" who had lost themselves completely in the world of self-effacing middle management and corporate bureaucracy. Mills's work was highly influential, as was William H. Whyte's *The Organization Man,* which made the same point in less inflammatory language.

These and many other writers filled the pages of the important magazines and newspapers with alarums over the cookie-cutter mentality of the new suburban America of the 1950s and early 1960s. Lewis Mumford made this charge most memorably in 1961, describing the vast housing development of Levittown as

> a multitude of uniform, unidentifiable houses, lined up inflexibly, at
> uniform distances on uniform roads, in a treeless command waste,

inhabited by people of the same class, the same incomes, the same age group, witnessing the same television performances, eating the same tasteless prefabricated foods, from the same freezers, conforming in every outward and inward respect to a common mold manufactured in the same central metropolis. Thus the ultimate effect of the suburban escape in our time is, ironically, a low-grade uniform environment from which escape is impossible.[62]

For these critics, television was both a symbol and a cause of this body-snatching conformity that robbed Americans of their souls. It was "mass culture," and as Dwight Macdonald remarked in 1957, "it thus destroys all values, since value judgments imply discrimination. Mass Culture is very, very democratic. . . . All is grist to its mill, and all comes out finely ground indeed."[63]

And television in this period was actually more diverse and eclectic, and less processed, than it was to become! In the 1960s, with the ubiquity of filmed shows featuring canned laughter and scheduling that was based entirely on "counter-programming," that is, what (equally formulaic) shows the other networks were broadcasting, television by 1968 had reached a point where such corporate tautologies had almost come to define the totality of TV.

Thus "the business behind the box" said much about the times. That the most popular communications medium the world had ever seen was entirely willing to ignore what was happening before its Argus eyes speaks volumes about the mind of the 1960s. The decision to streamline and rationalize TV programming, predicated on profit and the idea of a single audience, created the great disconnect between TV and America in 1968. It was utterly typical of the time, and utterly hopeless, given what was going on in America. Television's corporate culture in 1968 was in a state of stasis, institutionalized insularity, and attenuated denial. And it was about to run headlong into the cultural, economic, and statistical power of the baby boom.

2
The Demographic Imperative:
Culture and Counterculture, 1968–1970

Looking back, it's hard to understand why so many people took "the counterculture" seriously. Yale law professor Charles Reich, the author of *The Greening of America* (1968), suggested that the human race, or at least that part of it with the good fortune to produce hippies, was about to enter into a third phase of its existence—a state portentously named "Consciousness III" by its author. Historian Theodore Roszak went Reich a step further, opining in *The Making of a Counter Culture* (1969) that "the primary project of our counter culture is to produce a new heaven and a new earth so vast, so marvelous, that the inordinate claims of technical expertise must of necessity withdraw to a subordinate and marginal status in the lives of men."[1]

A mere decade later, when every city had an organic co-op and every rock band its own jet, such pronouncements sounded ridiculous. This is unfair but understandable: taken as a social movement on its own, the counterculture now looks merely sanctimonious. Its articles of self-identification, like smoking pot and attending rock concerts, are entitlements for every able-bodied youth in America. The easy talk of revolution is grating, too, particularly given the subsequent conversion to plump capitalism of so many hippies, including many holier-than-thou radicals. And shorn of its historical context—cold war civics, the Johnson administration's "credibility gap," the civil rights movement, awakened minority consciousness, and so on—the outrage of sheltered college students and suburban adolescents seems now merely petulant and fatuous, willfulness masquerading as civic disobedience.[2]

For these reasons, it is easy to underestimate the seriousness with which the adult world took the counterculture. While few observers were as credulous as Roszak or Reich, the counterculture impacted on the Establishment (as it was called) far more than it might today. It seemed to spread out of nowhere, appearing on unprecedented scale, self-aware and disproportionately huge.

Its demographic bulk is still underappreciated. "Beginning in 1964," Landon Jones points out in his study of the baby boom, "the cutting edge cohorts of the boom generation—those babies born in 1946 who had absorbed the first shocks of their size—began turning 18. In the next six years, more than 20 million of them entered the 18–24 period in which most people leave home and make decisions that will affect them the rest of their lives."[3] Jones quotes the Princeton demographer Norman Ryder, who pioneered cohort theory, to the effect that in each generation this life stage has been the one during which children challenge their elders, acting as "cultural insurrectionaries, agents provocateurs with no allegiance to the past." This may or may not be true, but Jones cites the census figures shown in table 2.1 to demonstrate (at the very least) the potential for mischief this youth wave represented.[4] Even under the most tranquil of conditions, such numbers would be impossible for mass-communication industries like advertising and television to ignore. But these were not the most tranquil of times, and in fact the mass-communications complex had not ignored this generation at any point in their lives.

Table 2.1
Demographic Impact of the Baby Boom

Year	Size (in thousands)	Percent change within population
1900	10,307	—
1910	12,748	+23.68
1920	13,018	+ 0.02
1930	15,463	+ 0.19
1940	16,616	+ 0.07
1950	16,075	- 0.03
1960	16,128	+ 0.003
1970	**24,687**	**+53.07**
1980	29,462	+19.34
1990	25,148	- 0.15
2000	24,653	- 0.02

A good part of the baby boom's collective identity arose from the media. The advent of transistor radios in the 1950s had made them independent of their parents' culture: dying radio stations, starving under the pressure from television, were only too happy to convert to "youth music" formats and service the teenaged owners of these radios with rock music, which in turn created a niche on television, which in turn alerted hundreds of thousands of other teenagers to "their" music. The baby boomers, assiduously courted by radio, television, and print advertisements, soon came to think of the youth culture as ground zero, a new world for a new generation, one with even less regard than usual for its predecessors.

World War II had re-created the country; America was rich and secure; and the young, taken as a class, had only the vaguest notion of what an America of privation, austerity, and sacrifice was about. What Abbie Hoffman would call the "Woodstock nation" had its birth in the 1950s. Just how much of it derived from the economic boom of the Eisenhower years is still underappreciated.

"Hail, hail, rock and roll / Deliver me from the days of old," sang Chuck Berry in 1956, getting to the heart of the matter.[5] Part of the baby-boom credo, after all, was that they had emerged full blown, outside of history. "It's a sad fact," wrote critic Greil Marcus in 1969, "that most of those over thirty cannot be a part of [rock and roll], and it cannot be a part of them. I don't want to talk about the ability of adults to 'enjoy the Beatles' or to 'think Dylan has something to say,' but about the rock n' roll era as the *exclusive possession of our generation*, about what our love for it and our immersion in it might imply for our consciousness and vision" (italics mine).[6] Rock music is not an arbitrary choice here. Among students of boom culture, the music is almost universally acknowledged as the binding element in the baby boom's formation and the bedrock upon which the subsequent counterculture was formed; however, it is seldom acknowledged just how much the birth of rock music owed to canny cynics in suits and ties. Leonard Bernstein would later call Elvis the "greatest cultural force of the twentieth century," and John Lennon would claim that "before Elvis there was nothing."[7] But the inspiration for Elvis was less exalted. "If I could get me a white boy that sounded like a nigger, I could make a million dollars," Sam Philips, Elvis's discoverer, is reported to have said wistfully in 1954.[8] Producers like Philips and disc jockeys like Alan Freed and Murray "the K" Kaufman were middle-aged men with little emotional investment in rock.

This is not to say, as some critics have, that rock and roll's emancipatory promise was a swindle from day one; the mere fact that the music was vigorously opposed in the 1950s and identified with lawless youth until well into the 1970s belies that claim. But it is equally true that from its inception, a vast and entrenched business confederation had a strong stake in "youth culture."

As with most media, the motive behind it was the sale of commodities via advertising. The advertising industry had a huge influx of business after the war, owing to the sudden expansion in the number of brand names on the market. "The big statistical thing," remembers Paul Klein, "was the number of brands that expanded exponentially."

> Right after the war, the number of brands on the market [because of] the competition with P&G [Proctor and Gamble] and Colgate,

Lever . . . and P&G having seen that was afraid to lose shelf space, and so they expanded the number of brands they had on the market, and in order to advertise those brands they bought a lot of television. And they knew who were brand conscious . . . you know, [with] an old person, it was difficult to change his brand, but a new person who wasn't yet in the market you could establish brands with. Or you get him to switch brands, because he wasn't that baked-in yet.[9]

A further appeal of advertising targeted at youth was youngsters' ability to direct their parents buying. "An advertiser who touches a responsive chord in youth," wrote marketing consultant Eugene Gilbert in 1950, "can generally count on the parent to succumb finally to purchasing the product."[10] Throughout the 1950s, television's sales pitch was relentless and stark: even on children's shows like *Howdy Doody*, kids were advised by host Buffalo Bob to "have your Mom or Daddy take you to the store where you get Poll Parrot shoes, and ask for your Howdy Doody cutout!"[11]

By the 1960s, advertisers understood that the youth market was a kind of marketing nirvana. Even the preteen market represented sales of $50 billion in 1965.[12] Teenagers accounted for 55 percent of all soft drink sales, $120 million worth of male toiletries, 20 percent of the cosmetics and female toiletries sold in America, plus God only knew how many second cars, TV sets, and other durable goods.[13] "It was natural that [advertisers and marketers] began to say, do we want to target our current, old, customer, or go with the younger, more trendy, image-shaping type?"[14] Advertising copy-testing had just become a wide practice in the late 1950s, and brand managers using "scientific marketing" techniques, "whiz kids" of the advertising world, had begun to think more in terms of targeting than ever before.

This was good news for ABC, the perennial third-place network. ABC had been the unquestioned leader in youth programming, or "kid-vid" as it was called, into the mid-1960s. Cornering the market on young viewers came, paradoxically, largely as a result of the network's overall ratings weakness. Since at the time the Nielsens only measured household use, without breaking down viewership any further, ABC needed something to boast about. "ABC was lower rated," remembers Jerry Dominus, a CBS sales executive who has also worked for J. Walter Thompson, "but they invented the story about the younger audience and the big city profiles. Because that's where their audience was and a function of where their stations were."[15] Unlike CBS and NBC, which had affiliated stations in all the major cities, ABC at this time was a relatively new company, with less exposure. "It was as if *Newsweek* competed with *Time* but couldn't be on the stands in Miami, Boston, Phoenix, and half the other cities," according to Dan Melnick,

ABC's program developer in the early 1960s. "I decided the only way to make my mark was to do shows completely unlike those on other networks. . . . our entire fare had a different, younger look. We did shows which, in retrospect seem like the Establishment. But in those days shows like *The Fugitive, Ben Casey, Maverick,* and *77 Sunset Strip* were very innovative, totally different from what was available on other networks."[16] ABC learned to counterprogram against the CBS and NBC shows, putting a private eye against an old-guard situation comedy, or a Western against a game show in order to attract a younger audience. Thus, ABC found itself a niche. CEO Leonard Goldenson remembers his moment of clarity: "We should build programs around casts of young, virile people . . . and create programs with stories that younger people could identify with. This was a lighting bolt to us. We began programming for the young families of television, and in so doing revolutionized television."[17]

But not right away. What ABC in fact had done was to establish a specialized appeal in an artificial marketplace where even the weakest of the three networks couldn't help but make money. All the rules applied—least objectionable programming, package deals with producers, the Nielsen fetish—and innovations, as a rule, were few. There was one major exception. ABC's breakthrough, both stylistically and financially, was *Batman,* a program that had tested at record lows in the network's early previews.[18] *Batman* went on to become both a cult phenomenon and a huge ratings success, inspiring a number of imitators during and after the years of its original run (1966–1968).

The success of *Batman,* like all breakthrough series, owed little to precedent. Earlier superhero series had been wooden, tendentious, and utterly unbelievable. The faceless hero squared off each week against equally generic gangsters, to a foreordained conclusion marked by a pantomime fisticuff and waiting paddy wagon. Superman was particularly bad this way—the middle-aged hero standing arms akimbo as other middle-aged thugs shot cap pistols at him.[19] *Superman* (1952–1957) was a pill; for the 1960s, particularly for 1960s youth, something less ridiculous was needed. The moral authority of the becaped, square-jawed hero was old hat, an invitation for satire. *Batman* avoided such mockery through the expedient of anticipating it.

In her 1964 essay "Notes on Camp," Susan Sontag noted, "When something is just bad (rather than Camp), it's often because it is too mediocre in its ambition. The artist hasn't attempted to do anything really outlandish. ('It's too much,' 'It's too fantastic,' 'It's not to be believed,' are standard phrases of Camp enthusiasm.) The hallmark of Camp is the spirit of extravagance."[20] *Batman* was a program invariably described as "campy"; that is, its over-the-top sensibility communicated an awareness of its own style, an archness that both entertained and disarmed audiences. *Batman* was an even bigger pill than *Superman,* the Man

Against Crime, Matt Dillon, and so on, but wore his solemn uprightness as a kind of commedia dell'arte mask, in this case with pointed little ears and brows artistically penciled over the eyeholes. ("The whole point of Camp," Sontag wrote, "is to dethrone the serious.")[21] The camp elements of Batman were laid on triply thick, as if to make plain to even the densest viewer that he was watching a send-up. Comic book sound effects like "BAM!" and "WHAP" were superimposed over fight scenes. A voice-over would end each episode with the same old-time radio portentousness Gary Owens would later mock on *Laugh-In*, telling the viewer to "Tune in next week, same Bat-time, same Bat-channel!"

All of this served a needed function. The crowd of people who originally tested *Batman*, developer Edgar Sherick recalls, were "in one universe, and our show is in another. We've got to promote this show so when the audience comes to it on the air, they won't be jarred out of their conventional expectations."[22] An unprecedented mass-media promotional campaign followed, and what it accomplished was the enlightenment of *Batman*'s viewing audience. Instead of the usual advertisements in *Variety* and *TV Guide,* the show was hyped as something radically different. *Batman* was to be a full-bore entertainment assault, not another action show that just happened to be eccentrically made. The villains were even more interesting than the heroes, or certainly more grotesque. Producer William Dozier was even invited to discuss the aesthetic of his new show in the *New York Times*. "He must be flamboyant, humorous, bigger than life, bizarre," he said of the *Batman* villain. "He must convince us that he is a potential killer. He must suggest humor but he must not be a comedian."[23]

"He must suggest humor but not be a comedian": that was the key to understanding the new show. Although played very broadly, *Batman* was not comedy. It enjoyed the attraction of comedy—that is, people watched it expecting to laugh—but at the same time, it was able to play as an action show. Added to this was the patina of intelligence granted the show by its excess, which differentiated it from such puerile youth fare as its Wednesday night competition, *Lost in Space*. It was not the same old dreck, but a new and better kind of dreck and one that pointed the way for television's future; in the meantime, it was "something new and different," the most prized of television commodities—when successful. As such, it inspired imitators.

The mid-1960s were filled with tongue-in-cheek adventure shows, programs that seemed to mock the conventions they wholeheartedly employed. *Batman* was merely the culmination. The popular *Man from U.N.C.L.E.,* which had been based on the James Bond movies, altered itself stylistically to copy *Batman*, as did such programs as *Honey West* (1965–1966), *Wild, Wild West* (1965–1967), *I Spy* (1965–1968), and *T.H.E. Cat* (1966), which all used the camp formula of protective self-mockery to various degrees. (Two other spy shows, *Get Smart* (1965–1970) and *Mission: Impossible* (1966–1973), found success with straight farce and earnest intrigue, respectively.) Most got good ratings, and all were considered "youth-oriented" shows.

But however important ABC's early youth-programming was in the long run (it would triumphantly return ten years later), it didn't begin to suggest how TV would handle the emerging force of the new counterculture. The reeling sensibilities of Reich and Roszak were echoes of what had been felt by the mid-1960s by business leaders and advertising agencies. It was not merely that, as a common rule of thumb had it, half of the population was, or soon would be, under the age of twenty-five. More to the point, it was felt that the world belonged to the young; and the more conspicuously rebellious young people were, the more the business establishment wanted to appeal to them. Cultural historian Tom Frank has described vividly, in *The Conquest of Cool,* how the mass society critique of the 1950s found its most expressive impulse in the "creative revolution" of the advertising industry in the 1960s. "Youth was a posture available to all in the sixties," Frank writes. "Admen clearly believed that the marketing potential of youth culture far transcended the handful of people that were actively involved in the counterculture. . . . Youth was the paramount symbol for the age, whether in movies, literature, fashion, or television."[24] And beyond youth, the counterculture—or rather an *idea* of the counterculture—beckoned for businesses seeking the future of capitalism. For many sales, marketing, and advertising executives, the counterculture was exactly the shot in the arm American consumerism badly needed. At the time, according to Frank,

> The counterculture seemed to have it all: the unconnectedness which
> would allow consumers to indulge transitory whims; the irreverence
> that would allow them to defy moral puritanism; and the contempt
> for established social rules that would free them from the slow-moving, buttoned-down conformity of their abstemious ancestors. In the
> counterculture, admen believed they had found . . . a cultural machine for turning disgust with consumerism into the very fuel by
> which consumerism might be accelerated.[25]

The problem, of course, was getting through to the counterculture on something approaching its own terms. It seemed unlikely. None of the ABC shows were considered breakthrough material. Even *Batman* itself was seen as a fluke, a "kid-vid" fad that played itself out after a mere three seasons. In any case, programming for youth per se was still a subspecies of the established practice of "escapism" and in any case not any of the networks' main concern. Despite the allure of the counterculture, big, established ratings hogs that could produce for years and years remained the goal of every network. *Bonanza* was one such prize sow. This all-male Western, in which patriarch Ben Cartwright lived with his three sons on a prosperous ranch, had been NBC's Sunday night keystone, holding the line against all comers, from Perry Mason to Judy Garland. Although something of a departure from the traditional Western, with its reliance on character conflict and sitcom-style relationships as opposed to Colt-wielding lawmen and sweaty, whisky-swilling heavies, *Bonanza* was the definition of Establishment TV fare. One son, Adam, was a leading-man type; another son, the bluff, overgrown "Hoss" was a typical source of comic relief; a third son, Little Joe, was a male ingenue, providing sex appeal. The series was stable, appealing, and formulaic in the most prized way, and any program sent in against it faced impossible odds.

Imagine the surprise of CBS, then, when the midseason replacement series they threw against *Bonanza* in the winter of 1966, a variety vehicle for a mildly popular brother act known mostly for comic folk songs, dethroned the Cartwrights from their ratings perch within a matter of weeks. And this success was due, at least in part, to the ability of the Smothers Brothers to attract a younger, hipper audience than variety shows could usually count on.[26]

Of course, this feat would weigh but little without Nielsen success, which the brothers also had. The *Smothers Brothers Comedy Hour* produced exactly those kinds of Neilsen ratings that advertisers most craved. To take as an example our randomly selected night of 18 February, this time of 1968, *Bonanza* weighs in with a 24.7 rating, compared to the *Smothers Brothers*' potent 27.7. Better still, the *Smothers Brothers* didn't take its ratings entirely from 18–34-year-old viewers. The ratings were spread out relatively evenly between groups 18–34, 35–49, and 50+, as opposed to *Bonanza*'s retiree-heavy demographic. The *Smothers Brothers*' success gave CBS the best of both worlds.

The *Smothers Brothers* appealed to the young without alienating their parents or grandparents. Clean-shaven and crew-cut, Tom and Dick played generic folk music in red blazers and exchanged comic patter along the lines of "Mom always liked you best." The brothers were not new to television. CBS, true to form, had tried to use them first in a fantasy sitcom in which junior executive Dick is visited by his dead brother Tom, now an angel. The show lasted only one season, after which the brothers went back to their lucrative touring. As Tony Hendra remembers, "to that vast majority of student bodies west of the Delaware and east of the Rockies—who had heard that there was something blowing in the wind but were nervous about booking it lest it turn out to be too scruffy or too Jewish—the Smothers Brothers were perfect."[27]

When *The Garry Moore Show* (1958–1967) left the air in 1964 on the command of William Paley, another variety show was needed. The process went through the usual channels: Mike Dann picked up the telephone and called the William Morris Agency. "I said I need a variety show," Dann recalls. "They said, 'We've got the Smothers Brothers.' I said, 'Who are they?' They said, 'Oh, two guys, they do variety, jump around. They're different.' I said, 'Gee, they've got kind of a young appeal, too. I like it.'"[28]

The Smothers Brothers Comedy Hour (1967–1970) debuted to glorious ratings in 1967, and the reason for their success, as Mike Dann had intuited, was the swing vote of younger viewers. Sunday night was traditionally family night, and such an orderly cosmos as *Bonanza*'s Ponderosa ranch had always been dominant there. Variety shows had been counterprogrammed against it, but these were invariably gas-guzzling, heavy-treaded affairs, overseen by some Friar's Club elder and thus presented no real choice, in generational terms, for the huge but fickle youth audience.[29]

The Smothers Brothers, for all their clean-shaven appearance, were from a different environment. They were "young" and mettlesome. They had been outside of New York and Burbank and had picked up the new ideas, new forms, and the new solidarity coalescing in opposition to the war and the Establishment. Most of all, they had found themselves suddenly buoyed by the wave of baby-boom numbers who deserted the Ponderosa for their show. It was their show that broke the intellectual stranglehold of the 1950s corporate consensus on programming; and it did this because, alone of all the "youth shows" of the period, it was true to its core audience on their own terms.

How so? The key to understanding the *Smothers Brothers*' breakthrough success lay in a remark made by Les Brown (for one) in *Variety:* "For the first time in history," wrote Brown, "popular culture is not being handed down to the younger generation but handed up by it."[30] The most successful youth shows of the 1960s, like *Batman* or *The Monkees* (1966–1968) had tapped, however obliquely, into something discrete in late baby-boom culture. But there was not a long-term appetite for "camp" in the grown-up mind, nor did the *Hard Day's Night*-inspired slapstick of the Monkees do much for viewers much past pubescence.

These programs were facile exploitations of the boom's numbers and immaturity and reflected only so much of the times as can be gleaned impressionistically by the costuming, the plot devices, and so on.[31] The Smothers' innovation, on the other hand, was in producing a show whose youth-appeal came not as a result of smoke-filled deliberations in the boardroom but as a direct result of its makers' own youth and exposure to the antiwar movement, antiauthoritarianism, and the "cultural insurrection" of Norman Ryder's demographic theory, now writ large by the sheer bulk of the boom. "We reflected the same consciousness that was occurring in the country at the time," Tom Smothers recalled to Tony Hendra.[32]

But not at first. As Aniko Bodroghkozy has pointed out, the first season of the show was a balancing act, in which every gesture of defiance was defused by a broad skit or an easygoing ballad by Tommy in his cardigan sweater.[33] "From the angle of the network," writes Hendra, "the brothers were unconventional but airworthy performers, reacting out to attract a new and dynamic segment of the audience. From the brothers' angle, on the contrary, they were the champions of that audience fighting for its right to be heard, for its fair share of the nation's attention."[34] It had been noticed even by CBS that something was in the air, and by 1967, its most conspicuous precipitates, in Haight-Ashbury and elsewhere, were a topic of humor and concern. "Hippies" generally showed up on police shows and other moralistic dramas, usually as confused kids who, after an earnest talk with an elder, cut their hair and announced their intent to change "the system" from the inside.[35] On a memorable episode of NBC's *Star Trek,* 1969's "The Way to Eden," for example, the crew of the starship *Enterprise* encounters a group of wandering space hippies, replete with body paint and love beads.[36] Led by the sinister Dr. Severin, they search for the mythical planet of Eden, where they can escape the corruption of the System. "Stepping into Eden, yeah brother," they sing,

> No more trouble in my body or my mind!
> Gonna live like a king on whatever I can find!
> Eat all the fruit, and throw away the rind . . .
> Gonna live, not die! Gonna live, not die!
> Hey, Brother!

The space hippies don't really mean any harm, but they cause much trouble for Captain Kirk, the ship's impatient commander, whom they call "great white captain" and "the man." Mr. Spock, the half-alien second officer, is more to their liking, since he inexplicably knows their customs. Spock approaches Adam, a particularly obnoxious space hippie, and makes a triangular hand gesture.

> *Space hippie:* One.
> *Spock:* One is the beginning.
> *Space hippie:* Are you one, Herbert?
> *Spock:* I am *not* Herbert.
> *Space hippie:* He's not Herbert! (making triangular hand gesture).
> We *reach!*

Spock even sits in on an interstellar jam session with his Vulcan harp. In the end, of course, after they take over the ship and go to Eden, the space hippies are shown the folly of their way. Their leader is a madman, their utopia a deathtrap. When Adam dies after eating a poison apple, Mr. Spock is quick to underline the irony: "his name," he points out with a raised eyebrow, "*was Adam.*"

Although real hippies did not watch much TV, in many ways they represented the direction the youth culture was taking. Far more young people, particularly in college, were sympathetic to the hippie project of free living and moral ascendancy than actually moved to Golden Gate Park; these were the *Smothers Brothers'* core audience, and they came to inform the humor of the show more and more as the show prospered. A kind of "in humor" came to mark the program's writing: the older viewers who found Tom and Dick likable and unthreatening were amused by their banter, or at least amused enough to not bother changing the channel; and the younger, "hipper" viewers could get jokes unintelligible to their elders.

"Dig," wrote Harlan Ellison in his column in the *LA Free Press,* "this is somewhere near where it's at, I think. . . . the hip folk are watching the show religiously (or irreligiously, depending on where your Valhalla is located)."[37] "A Little Tea with Goldie," for example, became an ongoing skit, in which (viewed from one angle) a San Francisco hippie girl hosted a ladies' daytime show in her far-out idiom; and (viewed from another angle) a hippie mole filled a TV-show monologue with covert reference to marijuana ("tea") and other hippie folkways.[38] Such parallax was the secret to the show's bimodal audience of young singles and older viewers and was moreover not a unique phenomenon: Jack Webb's *Dragnet '67,* for example, with its solemn tales of acid-crazed hippies corrupting society, was also a ratings success with both groups. ("It was the poetry of polarization," David Marc called it in *Demographic Vistas.* "The 'unhip' applauded the statement for decency; the 'hip' laughed their heads off.")[39] Unlike *Dragnet '67,* however, *The Smothers Brothers Comedy Hour* did not depend on polarization, for the most part; there was still enough common ground between the generations to keep the humor from turning divisive and exclusionary, as it had in the underground improv companies such as San Francisco's Committee, from which came actress Leigh French, who played Goldie.

What really got the show into trouble was its antiwar orientation. A conflict like this was bound to happen if the show was to continue to draw for its spirit on the younger generation. The generations who still ran the country did not, in most cases, have any particular animosity for youthful idealism, and tended to find the hippies rather laughable than threatening. Even President Johnson, "the Man" who incarnated in his being everything objectionable about the old to college students, had great sympathy for the ideals of the young, being an idealist himself when all was said and done. He liked high-minded young men like his protégé Bill Moyers. Tommy and Dick Smothers fit this mold too. Therefore their gentle mockery, early on, of the American political system and implicitly of the war was not objectionable to either the audience or the network. In fact, they were thought by one and all to be just what TV needed. The brothers, wrote the *New York Times,* were "forerunners of the next generation of artists who must be brought along if the medium is to protect itself against the inevitable obsolescence of the oldtimers who currently dominate so much of television comedy."[40]

On the subject of explicitly political humor, however, the network was more touchy than even on the subject, usually paramount, of ratings and sales. Chairman William S. Paley was a prominent Republican, as was President Frank Stanton, and both men were used to criticism from the White House on what the Johnson administration saw as its "biased" news reporting of the war in Vietnam. This was not merely a matter of party loyalty, either, or of Paley's jockeying for the position of ambassador to the Court of St. James, as Tommy Smothers has suggested. Though these may have been factors, more important still was the presence of the FCC and the ability of the government through it to create havoc in the business of broadcasting. It had done so once after the quiz-show scandals, had threatened to do so again in the "vast wasteland" screed of Kennedy-era chairman Newton Minow, and would actually do great damage to the networks a few years down the road, with the Prime Time Access rule. The Nixon administration was not above leaning on the networks, and although even Paley, with his Jovelike vision, could not have foreseen the alliterative attacks on the media that Nixon's vice president would loose, the atmosphere even in 1967 was marked by paranoia, threats, and corporate anxiety. "There were calls from the White House after the show [over the *Smothers Brothers*]," Dann recalled years later.[41]

The connection between this authoritarianism was clearly of a piece with the peremptory official attitudes to protest, a fact not wasted on Tom Smothers. A certain playfulness had marked the Smothers' early essays at the Generation Gap: George Burns appeared with Herman's Hermits, Kate Smith as a Salvation Army singer performing "Sgt. Pepper's Lonely Hearts Club Band." As the show became increasingly politicized on behalf of the antiwar campaign, however, these differences soon ceased to be funny. Why couldn't the brothers leave well enough alone? They had one of the most successful shows on television, with a huge rating. More importantly, they were drawing the baby-boom audience to TV in unprecedented numbers. ("*The Smothers Brothers*," CBS programming executive Perry Lafferty later marveled, "was one of the few shows that brought people to television who were not viewers. Now that's a hell of a thing to say.")[42]

But since the show drew for its basic energy on the feeling "out there" among the awakened young, it could not settle into a Red Skelton-like routine of weekly good feelings. It was attractive because it was dynamic; that dynamic led to trouble. "We were definitely headed for more confrontation," recalled producer Ken Fritz. There were constant battles with the network over the content of comedy sketches, particularly with the network's Office of Standards and Practices. Since these objections were invariably couched in questions of taste, however, they could not be written off as completely political. As the east coast's leading underground journal, the *East Village Other,* wrote at the time, "The Smothers' presentations were certainly not radical but CBS still felt them a threat to honky culture."[43]

The booking of Pete Seeger in the fall of 1967, on the other hand, was a political bait to the network. Seeger had been blacklisted since 1950, and his appearance on the show was to be doubly provocative. Not only was he to appear, but he planned to sing a new song of his own composition, "Waist Deep in the Big Muddy," which was a thinly veiled attack on Johnson and the war. Seeger was allowed to appear, but the song was cut; the relationship between CBS brass and the brothers torqued up one setting. "We're getting nasty letters now," Perry Lafferty, Mike Dann's subordinate at programming, said. "And now you want to put this Pete Seeger on? We don't want him!"[44] Seeger did appear in censored form but attracted notice in the *New York Times*.[45]

In early 1968, Seeger appeared again on the show. This time he sang "Waist Deep in the Big Muddy," and CBS relented. The song was sung, in its entirety, as the culmination of a medley of American military songs that reflected the ambiguities of American wars—the fierce jingoism of "Damn, Damn, Damn the Filipinos," the less-than-heroic "I Don't Want No More of Army Life." "Waist Deep in the Big Muddy" took place in World War II but was clearly about the war in Vietnam. The bullying commander orders his troops to ford a river, and as they begin to sink he accuses them of being "nervous nellies," one of Johnson's signature folkisms. The penultimate stanza leaves little doubt:

> Now every time I read the papers
> That old feeling comes on
> We're waist deep in the big muddy
> And the big fool says to push on![46]

Throughout the next two years, a death struggle was fought between CBS and one of its most popular shows. Harry Belafonte sang "Lord Please Don't Stop the Carnival" over footage of the Democratic Convention in Chicago; CBS cut the segment in toto and sold five minutes of the resulting time to the Nixon for President Committee. By the spring of 1969, CBS was canceling whole episodes; in April, the new president of the corporation, Robert Wood, pulled the plug on it entirely, on the pretext that the brothers had voided their contract by delivering a show two days late.

The fallout from the cancellation was at least as significant, if not more so, than the show itself. The news made the front page of the *New York Times,* whose television writer, Jack Gould, had been one of the show's champions.[47] The last thing the industry needed was political friction. Senator Pastore was very much on the networks' minds. The popular Democratic senator chaired a senate subcommittee that had brought pressure on the networks for being too violent. With the election of Richard Nixon, the only politician in America more hostile to the media than Lyndon Johnson, Pastore's regulatory fervor seemed more menacing.

The cancellation of the show was seen by many inside the industry as a peace offering to the government after the Chicago convention debacle.[48]

Thus ended TV's first real foray into youth culture. Both sides were mystified and hurt. Why would a network whose interests were being served so well take such a fascistic attitude toward the content of the show? And the network, in turn, asked itself why would two talented young men like the Smothers Brothers, who had everything they could want—including full artistic control of their show—deliberately force the network's hand with what they knew to be material offensive to the affiliates and to William Paley? The conflict resembled nothing so much in its essence as the famous scene in Bob Rafelson's film *Five Easy Pieces* (1970) in which Jack Nicholson and a waitress drive each other crazy. Nicholson, the first great countercultural movie star, sits down in a diner with his friends and attempts to order a chicken salad sandwich, on whole wheat toast, with tomatoes instead of potatoes on the side. The waitress tells him there are no substitutions. He has to order what's on the menu. Why can't I get what I want, Nicholson asks? The waitress repeats the rule. The argument escalates until Nicholson explodes, and he leaves without eating. Both sides feel angry and insulted. It's obvious that to Nicholson, the waitress is an authority figure, imposing arbitrary rules on him for no reason other than because she can. To the waitress, she is just trying to do her job, and Nicholson is giving her a hard time. Why? She doesn't make the rules. And anyway, what does he expect? This isn't his kitchen. It's a restaurant. Both sides feel put upon and persecuted, and the conflict ends without resolution or enlightenment.

The pattern of spiral escalation between the sides continued throughout these years and never more lucidly than in the *Smothers Brothers* debacle. And yet, for this reason, it is unrepresentative of the relationship between TV and the counterculture, the proverbial exception that proves the rule. Seldom would the networks indulge in outright censorship; seldom would programming intended for youth have such an identifiable point of view. Far more illustrative, though less often told, is the short history of *Laugh-In* (1968–1973), the *Smothers Brothers*' most meaningful rival for the hearts and minds of the baby-boom audiences.

The similarities between the two shows appear striking, at least in retrospect. Both are counterculturally charged variety shows, featuring "with-it" humor, oddball continuing characters, and a general air of electrical irreverence. Both enjoyed immediate popularity and a meteoric ascent in the ratings before flaming out. The two shows were seen even by many at the time as being of a piece: "[*Laugh-In* hosts] Rowan and Martin, and the Smothers Brothers," wrote the *New York Times*, "could represent the deepest change of the current season."

> The sacred cows of today's society no longer are immune to the irreverence of the newer school of comedians, and it will be important to see how far their influence and ingenuity may spread. . . .

Alan King, the comedian, suggested that one reason some viewers might be turning away from TV was its isolation from the realities of the surrounding world. The restless humorists ironically may be the instrument for gradually and subtly bringing TV into the mainstream of modern concern. And the Establishment may possibly have more to fear in the long run from the contagion of laughter than from the more publicized stern protest.[49]

Jack Gould, the *Times'* reviewer, erred in conflating two very different approaches. Although Tom Smothers and the show's staff welcomed the arrival of *Laugh-In* not only as kindred spirits but also as a check on CBS censorship practices, *Laugh-In's* humor was different in tone and intention from theirs.[50]

George Schlatter, the show's producer, had created in *Laugh-In* a new form of television comedy, one that for the first time since Ernie Kovacs attempted to exploit the technical possibilities of television. It had been Kovacs's innovation to pioneer a highly visual style of comedy that depended on quick cuts, special effects, montage, and so on. A finger would pop out of the center of a telephone dial and start dialing; a used-car salesman would slap a car's hood, causing it to fall through the floor; snapping celery stalks and slamming drawers played the "1812 Overture." No joke lasted more than a few seconds before being replaced by another, completely unrelated one: the resulting "blackout humor" provided a kinetic, nonlinear pleasure for its viewers. *Laugh-In* resuscitated the formula, substituting Las Vegas-style one-liners, double entendres, and non sequitur catchphrases for Kovacs's brilliant visuals.[51] The "joke wall" featured a dozen or more doors that would swing open for a gag and then close. Similarly, there was "the party" sequence in which the cast would dance the frug and then freeze every few seconds as one of their number told a joke. Most of the show consisted of blackout sketches. One featuring Lily Tomlin's feisty operator Ernestine would conclude and be immediately followed by Arte Johnson's peering Nazi, saying "verrrry interrresting" into the camera. As Castleman and Podzarik note, "the material went by so fast that if there were three good jokes in ten, the laughter from these blotted out the seven flops. If none of them clicked, there would soon be more flashing by anyway."[52]

The show was nothing if not dynamic, and it soon caught on. Unlike the *Smothers Brothers,* however, it caused no controversy and presented no threat. *Laugh-In* was anchored by Dick Rowan and Dan Martin, another Las Vegas smart guy/dumb guy act of the sort always to be found on *The Dean Martin Show, The Tonight Show,* and other slick showbiz venues. (Rowan, the smart guy, held a pipe in his hand as a badge of sensibility.) Its "flower children" were just crazy kids, out to have a good time; likewise with its satire and topical humor—it was all in good fun, as the speed with which it moved away from any one joke attested.

Where the brothers had been pointed and polemical, even didactic, in their support of the antiwar cause, *Laugh-In* took only the trappings of the youth culture—its jargon, its irreverence, its energy. After a few short years, the show had burned itself out, even its name having become an anachronism. The impression it made on the networks, however, was longer lasting.

First of all, *Laugh-In* demonstrated that "hippie" or "countercultural" humor was a controllable commodity, one that could be deployed whenever the network wanted to pull a youthful demographic. The *Smothers Brothers'* experience to the contrary, "hip" humor was not synonymous with politics. In fact, none of the substance of the counterculture—its ideology, its origins in the civil rights and antiwar movements, its dependence on drugs and communal living—were needed to maintain what appeared, at least to the network brass, to be countercultural form. *Laugh-In*'s most visible successor, in fact, used its trademark blackouts, one-liners, continuing characters, and frenetic pace in a program that flourished in American prime-time television for twenty years: CBS's most enduring rural hit, *Hee Haw* (1969–1971; syndicated, 1971–1989). The joke wall reappeared as a cornfield, with various bumpkins popping up and sitting down. Minnie Pearl was plugged in for Ruth Buzzi. Buck Owens and Roy Clark took over the anchoring duties from Rowan and Martin. The show was identical in form and could not have been more different in content. It could not have been more different, that is to say, if *Laugh-In* had had any content; it didn't, which is precisely what made it so popular with both audience and network. *Laugh-In* found a way around the charge of "escapism" that had bedeviled so many straitlaced sitcoms: it removed all formal connection to older genres and relied entirely on kinetics and the borrowed energy of the youth culture. The fact that its hosts were two middle-aged Vegas lounge lizards did not hinder this project in the slightest.

What was most important about *Laugh-In* was that, above all else, it was new. It was clearly ahead of the curve, and in the end, that mattered more than whether it was funny or faithful to the ideals of youth. The young, the networks had intuited, took TV for granted, were immune to its "spectaculars" and tired acts. So they would be accommodated. The young were a minority, but they screamed for attention. They existed in such numbers, with such buying power! As one marketing research association put it:

> By 1970 almost one out of every three persons in the U.S. will be under the age of 25. During the 1970s this youth market will control over $45 billion in spending power annually (and it is growing at a phenomenal rate). Because of this, companies in the 1970s who continue to use today's marketing strategies will almost surely suffer a reduction in market share or, more seriously, total company extinction. . . . fads must be pursued, youth buying-behavior must be analyzed.[53]

Nor should one look only for bottom-line motives. Youth culture was where the action was, culturally speaking—it represented the cutting edge, and more and more the ineffable quality of hipness was becoming important to people in the media business. No one wanted to be caught behind the times. Everyone wanted to be part of the future.

But the youth culture, that most visible precipitate of the baby boom, was not overly concerned with their future, any more than they were constrained by tradition or a sense of continuity to the past.[54] The Grass Roots fixed this disdain for a scorned posterity with their hit song of 1967, "Let's Live for Today":

> When I think of all the worries
> People seem to find
> And how they're in a hurry
> To complicate their mind
> By chasing after money
> And dreams that won't come true
> I'm glad that we are different,
> We've better things to do!
> Let others plan the future,
> I'm busy loving you!
> Sha la la la la la live for today![55]

Television was served in different ways by this attitude. The counterculture's pleasures tended to be ones that did not advertise on TV—sex, drugs, rock music, and free association. The exclusion of all of these from the official culture helped to give youth its own fortress mentality circa 1969–1970, and even the celebrated "death of hippie" marked by a funeral in the Haight did not diminish it. Nor, despite many protestations, did a series of disasters. Hippie capitals became magnets for runaways, criminals, violent "speed" addicts, and worse, but these demoralized the culture without extinguishing it. The Altamont debacle, in which a murderous riot erupted at a free rock concert while the Rolling Stones sang "Sympathy for The Devil," killed the Woodstock buzz. Soon after Altamont came the Manson murders, in which solid youngsters from the suburbs were seemingly transformed by drugs and communal living into kill-crazed psychopaths who wrote rock lyrics on walls with blood. Finally, the deaths of Jimi Hendrix, Jim Morrison, and Janis Joplin cast a pall over the rock world.

Throughout all this, television served the youth culture by focusing the entire official adult world into one flat plane. TV's consistency made it easy to characterize, and its ubiquity made it convenient to condemn. The endless stream of commercials imploring the consumer to buy, buy, buy were perfectly illustrative of people "in a hurry to complicate their mind" by running after "dreams that won't come true." The Establishment was a shadowy entity, and the counterculture more or less reflexively turned to television as a symbol of the mass society whose mores they were abandoning. For anybody who contemplated "dropping out," television was at best laughable; at its worst, television was sinister propaganda, a weapon in the hands of "the man." "Back then," Mark Crispin Miller has written, "TV had seemed to us as something alien and unbelievable, like enemy propaganda—the smiles too broad, the music all wrong."[56] Writing in the *LA Free Press,* TV critic Harlan Ellison warned his readers,

> You ought to be frightened. You ought to be scared witless. They've got you believing all you're seeing is shadow play, phosphorescent lunacies sprinkled out of a clever scenarist's imagination. Clever of them. . . . They've taken the most incredibly potent medium of imparting information the world has ever known and they've turned it against you. To burn out your brains. To lull you with pretty pictures. To convince you nothing is going on out there, nothing really important.[57]

This is the countercultural attitude in its extreme form, and it would be a gross exaggeration to portray it as representative. But even when the progressive young did watch, they were not the loyal, immobile viewers craved by networks but rather skeptical occasional viewers, popping in and out, and never staying with one show for long. For one thing, young people had so many things to do. They had been brought up on television, and would return to it when they had children of their own; but in the meantime, the 18–24 age range (particularly the "young marrieds") were the most sought-after audience on Madison Avenue, and they had little use for television—at least by television advertising's demanding standards.

By 1970, over $3.5 billion in ad expenditures were flowing into the network coffers, and only a relatively small part of that ($704 million) was local advertising.[58] (And in the biggest cities, which did the most business, the affiliates were often owned and operated by the networks.) Ninety-seven percent of American households now had TV sets, so they were reachable. But the majority of the TV sets in use were being watched by older and younger viewers.

Set against such rock music and the excitement of being young in America in 1970, television inevitably looked tame, and worse still, manipulative. As Les Brown notes in his study of the 1970 television year:

> Not all [young people] were indifferent to television, but most no longer depended on it as they had when it was their electronic mammy. For many . . . TV was the window on the Establishment; and for those who had dropped out of the mainstream, it was the meretricious huckster of the plastic world they were rebelling against.

Basically unchanged in either content or form from what it had been when they were growing up, television came to symbolize the dry surrogate parent with nothing important to say, the one-eyed Polonius relentlessly pushing a single precept: Want Something and Buy It. To idealistic youth, returning to TV was regressive.[59]

Luckily, the networks had a trump card. Everyone had to settle down sooner or later; and the hippie pleasure principle, with its attitude of "live for today," suited consumerism right down to the ground. Pleasure as a way of life was not conducive to communal living, cooperative farming, or any of the various social alternatives being proposed. On the contrary, these were austere and demanding environments, requiring specialized knowledge and much hard work. The lifestyle of baby boomers depended more on the possession of luxury items: stereo sound systems, "hip" clothing, cars (for independence), single "pads" that required furnishing, and of course plenty of brand-name toiletries and staples.

All this had become crystal clear, thanks to more sophisticated market research. Both the advertising agencies and the networks now had a number-by-number breakdown of who watched what shows. At NBC and ABC, they liked what they saw. The fragmentation of the culture was reflected in the fragmentation in the market. The "most" no longer equaled the "best"; ABC's foothold in youth programming, once thought a consolation prize, now pointed the way to the future. Following ABC's lead, NBC and even stodgy, rural CBS, with its vast and faceless overall lead in Nielsen "households," all set out to lure buyers with the virgin soil of youthful demographics.

Demographic marketing represented the business version of Reich's and Roszak's conversion experiences and had the same damascene force. The A. C. Nielsen Company in the early 1960s began to supplement its Audimeter ratings, which had merely told what a given TV set was showing, with a separate sample supplied with diaries. These diaries served as a check on the ratings, but more importantly, they supplied the company with information about who lived in the house, who watched what program, and other specific data about the household members' sex, ethnicity, educational status, and so on.[60] By 1970, the ratings categories had gotten increasingly segmented. Originally, a category of 18–49 had sufficed; then 18–35 and 35–49 had helped ratings harvesters. Now, viewers from 18–34, 18–49, and 25–49 were represented, along with the bookend categories of 12–17 and 50+. Who was to say how far the trend might go? Given the marketing imperative of reaching out to the baby boom, such information was a revelation to marketing firms and advertising agencies. Having before them a precise statistical picture of who was watching what, it now became possible to target the most desirable audience, and by paring away the attention of less attractive consumers (blue-collar workers, old people, blacks, etc.), to present a trimmed bouquet of baby-boom viewers to prospective advertisers.

The cultural impact of this in terms of television was enormous. Television was one of the first facets of the Establishment to redefine itself in response to baby-boom culture, and other media, such as magazines, would follow suit for similar reasons.[61] The rise of demographic marketing drove the changes in American television during the Nixon years; it caused a realignment of the televisual cosmos, but not right away. Red Skelton, for example, was by the late 1960s a television institution, an elder of the medium. *The Red Skelton Show* (1951–1971) was the anchor of CBS's Sunday night lineup, and his comic characters seemed timeless and ageless, the essence of TV comedy at its best. Skelton was paid accordingly, following William Paley's proven but exorbitant policy of maintaining a star stable at all costs. Freddie the Freeloader, Clem Kadiddlehopper, the Mean Widdle Kid, and other characters were icons, and the show routinely placed in the Nielsen top ten. But the show was not doing for the network's business what it did for the viewers; former CBS sales executive Jerry Dominus remembers sitting down at some point around 1969 and figuring out what Skelton was earning the network. Between the difficulty of selling advertising and the show's high costs, it turned out to be nothing.[62]

As early as 1967, the reason behind those sales problems was obvious: it lay in the nature of Skelton's audience. The survey broke down the ratings across a half dozen lines of cleavage: blue-collar versus white-collar, South versus Northeast, grade school education versus one or more years of college, annual income under $5000 versus income over $10,000, and most important of all, adults 18–34 versus adults over 50. The Skelton show was fourth in the overall top ten and high on the lists of blue-collar, Southern, grade school education, and annual income under $5000. *But he did not even appear* on any of the other top tens.[63] A huge line of cleavage demarked the TV audience now; the question was only who could exploit it first.

The problem with attracting younger audiences, however, was that neither the networks nor their favorite producers were at all sure what young viewers wanted. There were no more *Laugh-Ins* in the wings. Most had a vague sense of "young" as a show-business adjective—Mike Dann's first perception of the *Smothers Brothers* comes to mind—but most were by age, position, and frame of reference quite removed from youth culture. A few things could be divined. Even if only a small minority of young people were out-and-out hippies, there was a general antiestablishment sentiment among the young that was tinged with a tone of civic piety borrowed from the civil rights and antiwar movements. Campus protesters, like hippies, were a minority, but they were influential and magnetic among college students, even the most conservative of whom seemed to feel some need for change. (A 1971 *Playboy Magazine* survey taken after the Kent State debacle found 88 percent of responders in favor of "large-scale alterations of the U.S. system of government.")[64] Therefore, it was thought that a patina of politicism might help interest younger viewers. Television would henceforth strive for "relevance," a phrase coined by incoming CBS president Robert Wood—about whom more later.

There was precedent for "relevance" in the "serious" dramas of the 1950s and 1960s, both in live drama and also in highly regarded, low-rated series such as *East Side/West Side* (1963–1964) and *The Defenders* (1961–1965). On the randomly chosen night of 18 February 1965, in fact, *The Defenders* came on at 10 P.M. and dealt with a genuinely cutting-edge topic: a suicide committed under the influence of LSD. The juxtaposition, however, between such programming and what preceded it made shows like *The Defenders* the exception that proved the rule.

The success of two shows in the 1968 season demonstrated the power of "relevancy" once and for all. Aaron Spelling's *The Mod Squad* (1968–1973) was the first full-bore attempt by network television to create a show expressly flattering rebellious youth. Pete was the troubled scion of a wealthy family, driven to petty crime by existential angst; Julie was a poor white runaway; and Linc was a black rebel who wore an afro and sunglasses, full of righteous rage. (Preseason ads identified the three undercover cops who made up the squad as "One black, one white, and one blonde.") The three were recruited by a crusty but benevolent police captain to infiltrate the dark side of the urban/drug/minority subculture and to purify it of evil "from within." Remembers Spelling,

> It proved to me there was an audience out there for a young show if we honestly depicted what was happening. I tried to build up the contrast between our show and the older model of a cop show, the one where I got my start, *Dragnet,* which had returned with a new version called *Dragnet '67,* with Jack Webb and Harry Morgan. They were right wing, we were liberal. They thought everybody under 25 was a creep, we thought everybody under 25 was misunderstood.[65]

The show was highly tendentious in its hipness, however, subordinating subversive impulses week in and week out to the aims of traditional law enforcement. The tight-lipped centurions who guarded Los Angeles against its baser impulses in Jack Webb's "youth show," *Adam-12,* were in fact doing the same job as Pete, Julie, and Linc. They didn't say "man" or "groovy" and were as solemn as deacons; but they were "law-and-order" men all the same, in President Nixon's phrase, and thus on the same side as the Mod Squad. Nor for that matter was the squad any less pure in spirit than Matt Dillon or Perry Mason. As Castleman and Podzarik point out, the fact that "the three young demigods" worked for law enforcement was key in the series' ability to attract older as well as younger viewers: "With Pete, Julie, and Linc involved in cases as timely as the evening's headlines, ABC could exploit current issues such as youth rebellion, drug abuse, and racial tension while making sure the legitimate authority always triumphed in the end." "Now *this* was TV reality," the two add mordantly.[66]

The Mod Squad performed beyond Spelling's wildest expectations in the ratings: it attracted a very large youth audience, as expected (nearly double such rivals as NBC's *Star Trek* and ABC's *Laugh-In*); but it also performed well among all the other age groups, especially the 35–49 segment. It continued to perform in syndication: a 1973 *Variety* ad selling the show in syndication boasted, "because of its 'Young Appeal' *Mod Squad*, with contemporary plots and dynamic young stars, will deliver the right demographics . . . young adults, teenagers, and children."[67]

The Mod Squad gaze into the future: "One black, one white, and one blonde"

The other "relevant" innovation was *Julia* (1968–1971), a warmhearted family series about a widowed black nurse raising her son. Though conventional and saccharine, *Julia* was a far more daring experiment than *The Mod Squad*. It was, in fact, a genuine about-face on television's part, since TV had for many years been something of a Jim Crow enterprise, Linc notwithstanding. After the controversy attending the televised version of *Amos 'n' Andy* (1951–1953), in which the NAACP sued CBS, the networks washed their hands of blacks, along with all other ethnicities. In the fifteen years that followed, very few series characters other than menials were black.[68] A thaw in the mid-1960s allowed for black characters, usually functionaries of some sort, in dramatic ensembles—*Star Trek*'s communications officer, Lieutenant Uhura, who served as Captain Kirk's receptionist; explosives expert Barney Collier on *Mission: Impossible;* George C. Scott's secretary on *East Side/West Side*. Occasionally, black characters would emerge in conspicuous guest appearances, usually as put-upon slum dwellers, wrongly accused men, and the like on "think" episodes of popular dramatic programs. Bill Cosby was a dashing secret agent on the successful *I Spy*. But like Sidney Poitier, his success was applauded without being acted upon. "Negroes rarely get the opportunity," complained one black actor to *TV Guide* in 1968, "to portray human beings on television. They are usually cast in the role of auxiliaries to white people. Their only reason for existence . . . is for the benefit of white people in the story."[69]

Julia was Paul Klein's idea. NBC was being beaten badly by Red Skelton on Sunday, and it occurred to Klein that a black series might earn the network prestige.[70] Since the slot was considered a ratings graveyard anyway, NBC could afford to be less concerned about its Nielsens. Contrary to all expectations, however, *Julia* proved to be a hit. It was progressive without being pedantic; Diahann Carroll was beautiful and charismatic; the writing and direction were of a uniformly high quality; and it went without saying that there was no mention of civil rights, black power, or riots.

This last took some doing. Race has always been a primal conflict in the public life of this country, but 1968 may have been the most racially divided year in America since the Civil War. Part of it was disappointment. Optimists among liberals had come to believe, just a few years earlier, that a dark age was indeed ending in American history. After nearly a century of oppression and segregation, the power and piety of the civil rights movement had won black citizens equal rights at long last. A generation of black intellectuals and writers had become prominent. Lyndon Johnson, himself a Southerner, promised more, and did more, for blacks than had any president in history, possibly excepting Lincoln. And although the decade-long process of integration had met with the "massive resistance" of a recalcitrant South, in the end it was accomplished.

But by 1968, intergration as an ideal was battered. Many American blacks, especially younger ones, had grown impatient with the infinite forbearance enjoined by Dr. Martin Luther King Jr. and other religious leaders. Charismatic and combative leaders such as Malcolm X and Eldridge Cleaver had by this time replaced King, and their message was sweet nectar to many of their audiences. "I don't see an American dream," said Malcolm. "I see an American nightmare."[71] Black intellectuals were especially caught up in the excitement. James Baldwin, who had been the star of the *Paris Review* and one of the most articulate of black public intellectuals, had come to a defiantly radical stance by the mid-1960s and was joined there by other black intellectuals, such as the poet LeRoi Jones, who in 1968 would take the name Amiri Baraka. Black rage became a regular spectacle on the news, which covered race riots in Newark and Detroit as if they were happening in foreign countries.

Many whites were astonished by this turn of events, and Southerners in particular felt vindicated. The federal government, because of the South's extreme recalcitrance to accepting change, had been forced to take an unmistakably authoritarian position where civil rights were concerned. Now the South saw the rest of the country reaping the whirlwind and felt justified in its opposition. So strong was this feeling that Richard Nixon adopted a "southern strategy" aimed at the once-unthinkable task of breaking the Democratic party's hold on the region. He might well have broken through, too, had not the South produced its own third party candidate, George Wallace, who ran for the presidency on an explicit anti-integration platform. The assassinations of Dr. King in April and Robert F. Kennedy a few months later gave the awful racial climate a kind of grim air of permanence. "The assassin's bullet not only killed Dr. King, it killed a period of history. It killed a hope and it killed a dream," wrote Cleaver in *Ramparts Magazine*.[72]

Julia, then, would be escapism at its best. Relevant programming might have been on the ascent, but escapism was still enjoying its last hurrah. Table 2.2 shows the Nielsen top ten in 1970.[73] CBS continued to dominate the top ten, but its presence was grounded on long-burning stars from the 1950s, such as Red Skelton, Lucille Ball, and Doris Day, rural comedies such as *Mayberry R.F.D.* (1968–1971), and Westerns such as *Bonanza.* Rounding out the Nielsen top twenty-five were another seven CBS shows, representing more of the same; among them, *Hee Haw, The Dean Martin Show* (1965–1974), *The Beverly Hillbillies,* and *The Glen Campbell Goodtime Hour* (1969–1972). Word was getting through to the network high command from the sales department that it was increasingly difficult to sell time to advertisers on these shows, despite their stellar ratings, because the rival networks had made advertisers aware of demographics. CBS was the number one network; but now its strength was drawn almost entirely from the "C and D counties," the hinterlands where viewers were loyal, predictable, and, as it happened, older and poorer then the younger urban/suburban viewers who were the quarry of so many campaigns.

The fragmentation of the culture had finally obtruded itself into network thinking, through the back door of ratings and the front door of advertising sales. Television was no longer a unified field: as Ed Papazian puts it, "By twisting this way and that in response to the divergent forces that were emerging, television's mass appeal facade was rent asunder in the 1960s."[74]

Table 2.2
Nielsen Ratings, 1970

Program/Network	Rating
1. *Rowan and Martin's Laugh-In*, ABC	26.3
2. *Gunsmoke*, CBS	25.9
3. *Bonanza*, CBS	24.8
4. *Mayberry R.F.D.*, CBS	24.4
5. *Family Affair*, CBS	24.2
6. *Here's Lucy*, CBS	23.9
7. *The Red Skelton Show*, CBS	23.8
8. *Marcus Welby, M.D.*, ABC	23.7
9. *Walt Disney's Wonderful World of Color*, NBC	23.6
10. *The Doris Day Show*, CBS	22.8

This was not the first time a fault line had been drawn between old and young, particularly in the 1960s, but now CBS decided to switch sides once and for all. It was a moment that mattered. Television is by default a reflection of America. A hit show like *I Love Lucy* or *Batman* becomes a national subject of conversation, a nearly universal reference point in a country whose vast spaces often preclude more tangible commonalities. Add to the atomizing effect of vast space the demographic rifts and the fragmentations of the 1960s, and television remains one of the few constants in an unraveling universe—the "fortress" that Eric Barnouw wrote of.

But something had to give, and it would be age and attenuated genres like the pastoral and Western. Thus, television, the most formidable resistor to social change throughout the 1960s, finally threw in the towel. Such a decision inevitably meant accelerating social change in America ever further, but TV is only an intermediate cause, and in any case the networks don't pay their executives to be social workers. Ratings alone are the Darwinian engine of survival, and it would be ratings that would doom the older shows.

The incoming president of CBS, Robert Wood, had been a manager of the big-city stations owned by the network for many years and had seen firsthand CBS's struggles keeping up in the big-city markets. At the hugely profitable "O & O" stations, those owned and operated by CBS, the network seemed to be the enemy in many ways. Most local TV stations were independent businesses, run in partnership with one of the networks. But many of the largest big-city stations were run by the network and yet still had to answer to a local marketplace—thus creating a tension between the corporate-national perspective and the local one that was all too familiar to affiliates in flyover country.

That tension tended to be resolved the same way every time. "The interest that always will prevail," Wood told Todd Gitlin, "will be that of the network. My interests were obviously insular, or reduced to the welfare of our stations. I recognized that *Gunsmoke* and all these rural shows were doing terrifically nationally. It just wasn't doing much for the [primarily urban] company-owned stations division."[75] The fact that Wood was in touch with the earth, as it were, was a large part of the reason for his promotion to president of the network. Frank Stanton, Paley's lieutenant, hired Wood because of the skills he would bring to what had become a rarefied and abstract position, a corporate summit with little connection left to the realities of affiliates. The O & O stations would make the best training ground for network executives, Stanton believed. "They were closer to the ultimate consumer. What the hell did I know? I was like an oblong blur suspended from Los Angeles to New York."[76]

Upon ascending to the network presidency, Wood began to move for "relevancy," for "updated, contemporary" programming. One didn't need sales reports to tell that CBS was becoming ludicrously disconnected, even more so than it had been a few years earlier. On the evening of 4 May 1970, the day the Ohio National Guard opened fire on student protesters at Kent State University, CBS aired the following lineup: at 7:30, *Gunsmoke;* at 8:00, a middle-aged Lucille Ball wearing a blonde wig over her ruby-red dyed hair, as yet another layer of artifice was laid over the ossified *Here's Lucy* series with a plot about Lucy having to impersonate a gum-chewing secretary; at 9:00, the cast of *Mayberry R.F.D.* visiting Palm Springs, in one of those "vacations" with which dying sitcoms dried to milk a few more ratings; and at 9:30, Doris Day having a comical encounter with a computer on *The Doris Day Show.*[77] Wood called for change.

Programming head Mike Dann was opposed to the plan, which began with a purge of some of CBS's most successful veteran series. Dann was a network player through and through—he wanted to win every season, and he didn't much care what went on at Sales or outside the network. If CBS was number one, sales would take care of themselves. The question was decided when Paley approved Wood's plan.

"Mr. Paley," Wood had told him at the critical meeting,

> you can sit on your front porch on a rocking chair collecting your dividends on what you've created. A parade will be coming down the street and you may watch it from your rocking chair, collecting your dividends, and it will go by you. Or you might get up from that chair and get into the parade, so that when it goes by your house

you won't just be watching it you'll be leading it. Mr. Paley, CBS is falling behind the times, and we have to get back in step.[78]

The plan was a daring one: for starters, Wood intended to cancel *The Jackie Gleason Show* (1952–1970), *The Red Skelton Show,* and *Petticoat Junction* (1963–1970), three proven hits. The former two shows were in the top ten, and the latter had a loyal audience. Moreover, both Gleason and Skelton had been on the air for so long that they were signature stars for CBS. But costs had become prohibitive on both men's shows, as each year renewal triggered an automatic 8 percent raise for the star.

It made economic sense to release Gleason and Skelton, but it didn't seem to make cultural sense. Or did it? Attitudes that had once been linked with decadent enclaves of hippies were now showing up everywhere. The antiwar movement had come to include working-class people, the elderly, suburban homeowners, and even a significant portion of Nixon's silent majority, who were sick and tired of the war and its costs.[79] An X-rated movie, *Midnight Cowboy,* had won the Academy Award for Best Picture. The most popular quarterback in the NFL, Joe Namath, wore long hair and funky fur coats. Even Richard Nixon himself appeared on *Laugh-In,* saying "Sock it to *me?*" in puzzled tones. Wood's sense of something in the air was ridiculously late in coming, but it was a measure of the inertia at CBS that even at this late date his message was received with incredulity.

Wood's sales background served him well, however. As a former affiliate manager himself, he appeared before a national convention of affiliates in May 1970 and spoke of "starting down a new decade."

> The winds of change are at gale force. Everything is being tested and challenged. . . . For television to stand still while all this is happening is to be out of touch with the times. . . . The days are gone when we can afford to be imitative rather than innovative. Indeed, if we are not only to lead but to survive, we must be responsive to the forms and concepts of today. We . . . have to attract new viewers, viewers who are part of every generation, viewers who reflect the growing degree of education and sophistication that characterizes American society. . . . We are taking a young fresh, new approach to programming. We're not going to be afraid to try the untried.[80]

This was the man who had canceled the *Smothers Brothers* just a year earlier. Wood was a conservative by inclination; he was a radical only when the zeitgeist forced his hand.

The first products of the CBS turn reflected the uneasiness of this conversion. Labored, didactic, and polemical, the first "relevancy" programs were all commercial and critical failures. *The Storefront Lawyers* (1970–1971), for which CBS had very high hopes, posited three idealistic young lawyers splitting their time between a high-rise Century City firm and a ghetto storefront, where they could assist those in need. The plots were hardly more realistic than *Petticoat Junction*'s. For example, in the debut episode, the lawyers defend an old man who has been bilked out of his house by a corporate cheat, whom he has shot in retribution.[81] Although there are many witnesses, the Storefront Lawyers try the entire community for the crime, so moving the judge that she spares the maddened oldster the death penalty, instead remanding him into the care of a mental asylum. Their work done, the young interns link arms and skip down the street in triumph. The show was a disappointment in the ratings: its measly 17.3 rating for January 1971 showed its strongest audience being those over fifty years old.

Still, once the Pandora's box of relevancy had been opened and its topical contents loosed upon the broadcasting world, it was not long before all three networks got into the act. The summer of 1970 was filled with the phantom voices of network promotional claims: "We're putting it all together this fall on CBS!" "Let's get together on ABC!" "It's happening on NBC!"

A number of copycat series followed *The Storefront Lawyers*' clumsy formula. *The Interns* (1970–1971), *The Young Lawyers* (1970–1971), *The Young Rebels* (1970–1971), and *Matt Lincoln* (1970–1971) all featured casts of young, handsome people, invariably featuring a girl, usually blonde, and one or two blacks. The plots and premises were equally ludicrous—*The Young Rebels*, for example, featured young idealists in colonial garb fighting the Revolutionary War with countercultural rhetoric. Most shows featured a crusty elder against whom the principals were defined—a gruff, dense sort played by veteran gangster/policeman types like Broderick Crawford and Lee J. Cobb. Beyond their patent silliness, however, the shows all revealed to even the most casual observer the unchanged form and substance of conventional TV drama. "Back then . . . ," Mark Crispin Miller has written, "TV kept trying earnestly to 'reach' us, offering us laughable descriptions of the way we weren't: the stiff bell-bottoms, the calculated bangs, the nice faces solemn with 'commitment' and everybody saying 'man' and 'groovy.'"[82]

Inevitably, each episode ended with the Establishment chided, but with a moderate viewpoint winning the day. Even Andy Griffith was drafted into the relevancy brigade, starring in ABC's *Headmaster* (1970) as the principal of a private school whose students encountered some form of timely trouble each week— drugs in one episode, campus revolt in another. The kids were always treated to a homespun lecture and invariably came around—or if they didn't, ended up in a hospital ward or jail.

One reason for this conservatism was purely pragmatic. Series depend on the same characters in the same place, always doing more or less the same thing. You can't overthrow the system one week and be back on the job the next. The rebellious heroes of the films these shows meant to emulate, such as Dustin Hoffman in *The Graduate* (1967) or Elliot Gould in *Getting Straight* (1970), could drop out of the system with dramatic finality because the rolling credits relieved them of their onscreen existences; it is the melancholy fate of TV characters to repeat themselves endlessly until their audience grows sick of them.

But an equally significant reason was political. "Let's face it," one anonymous executive told Les Brown of *Variety,* "the squares have always been the network audience and always will be. If you don't play it their way, you're out of business."[83] And as the *Smothers Brothers* debacle had demonstrated, while controversial politics might not be bad for ratings, they could be very bad for business. Senator Pastore was still threatening to legislate TV violence out of existence, and now television had a much more powerful enemy in the White House.

Richard Nixon had despised the media for years, memorably vowing upon his first exile that they wouldn't "have Nixon to kick around anymore." Even more than most politicians, he considered any coverage of his administration or its entanglements that was not explicitly favorable to be "biased," the product of a liberal coterie. This policy was not unique to Nixon's paranoia, particularly where Vietnam was concerned: President Kennedy had in fact asked the *New York Times* to recall David Halberstam from Vietnam. Neither had Lyndon Johnson been reticent to bully the media, particularly the broadcast media, into following the administration's line. ("I thought you were my friend," he once told Frank Stanton after CBS failed to promote the Vietnam war on the news. "I thought you and Walter [Cronkite] were my friends and look at what you and that boy Rather do to me.")[84]

But Johnson's animosity tended to be personalized, aimed at specific individuals and decisions. (With considerable effect: networks often tried to comply—sometimes killing stories and assigning "friendly" reporters upon request.) LBJ, however, refused to use the FCC as a whip to keep the networks in line, preferring personal intimidation instead. The Nixon-Agnew administration, on the other hand, had it in for the media en masse and used all the power at their disposal.

This became clear on the evening of 13 November 1969. At a Republican meeting in Des Moines, Iowa, Vice President Spiro Agnew spoke scathingly of "a little group of men who not only enjoy a right of instant rebuttal to every presidential address, but more importantly, wield a free hand in selecting, presenting, and interpreting the great issues of our nation."[85]

"Is it not fair and relevant," Agnew went on to pointedly ask, "to question the concentration of power in the hands of a tiny enclosed fraternity of privileged men . . . *enjoying a monopoly sanctioned and licensed by the government?*" [italics mine]. What act of persecution had marked this latest incursion, for which

Nixon's personal hatchet man, Agnew, was so successfully deployed? After the president's 3 November address, in which he hoped to talk the antiwar moratorium movement out of existence, ABC had had the temerity to allow W. Averell Harriman rebuttal time. Harriman was a preeminent diplomat and at the time was involved in the Paris peace negotiations, but he was also a Democrat and a dove and hence a Nixon "enemy." Giving Harriman the right of rebuttal was equivalent to collaboration, and it was not in the president's nature to pull punches in fighting back.

The Des Moines speech sent a chill through all three networks. The affiliates, run by small-town conservatives almost exclusively, supported the president. Worse—and here was the real meaning of Agnew's message—the chairman of the FCC, Dean Burch, remarked after the speech that it was "thoughtful and provocative," deserving "careful consideration by the industry and public." The FCC had immense power to disrupt not only the networks but the affiliate stations themselves, who depended on federal licensing for their existence. All three networks immediately knuckled under—all three, for example, refusing to cover a mammoth Vietnam War Moratorium march on 15 November 1969. (The president, for his part, claimed to have stayed inside the White House watching a football game on TV.)

Furthermore, the speech gave Agnew immense prominence on the very media he excoriated. All three networks broadcast his remarks live, with enthusiastic applause from the Republican crowd working like canned laughter to underscore Agnew's performance. They also allowed it to air without rebuttal, and a new thing was born—a negative media star, a man who excoriated the media full time as one of its brightest stars.

It was in these years, after all, that Agnew began to carve a career out for himself as the alliterative champion of the "silent majority," who went hither and yon scourging "nattering nabobs of negativism" and "effete corps of impudent snobs." Agnew, in the terms of the business, made for "good TV." He was ugly and hostile but also weirdly charismatic.[86] His phrases made good sound bites and were immediately taken up by the industry for the sort of token self-examination with which television, then and now, periodically tried to lend itself credibility.

Agnew's greatest value, however, both politically and televisually, was his unmitigated divisiveness. Unlike the president, who had to at least appear to be looking out for all Americans, Agnew was free to bait the left in the service of "that silent majority" of conservatives who were the administration's power base. The hostility and anger of the time generated Agnew full-blown: what had been merely laughable a few years before were becoming in 1970–1971 force fields of intense emotional power. This is reflected even in the fun-house mirror of late 1960s programming. Young idealists had appeared sympathetic if misguided and their differences with their elders vaguely comical. ABC even broadcast a prime-time game show called *The Generation Gap* in the latter part of the 1969 season, in which a team of elders were quizzed on teenage slang and folkways, and a team of youngsters on such musty topics as Carmen Miranda, the Edsel, and Senator Claghorn.

Increasingly, however, the baby boom was generating strife in proportion to its great numbers. The older generation seemed less likely to regard the oppositional culture of youth as a portent of utopian possibility—seeing instead rancor, privilege, and threat. Civil rights had ended with black power, "burn, baby, burn," and race hatred on an epic scale. Hippiedom, which had apotheosized itself as the "Woodstock nation," was shown to be as bad as its worst enemies had claimed by the Altamont debacle. Even *Rolling Stone,* the leading underground newspaper, thought the concert a moral disaster, and Ralph Gleason, one of the leading rock critics, wrote that it marked the end of rock music's moral claims. A few months later came the Manson family murders. Neither occurrence was in any way typical, but it was a black mark on the youth culture nonetheless. "Not so long before," remembered Todd Gitlin, "long hair had portended good." Now, the counterculture, Gitlin saw, was in many ways a recrudescence of the "yahoo streak" in American culture.[87] And so it went throughout the youth culture. Campus protest had devolved into uprisings and riots; the New Left, which had begun in the rarefied language of the Port Huron Statement, ended with the anarchic terrorism of guerrilla groups such as the Weathermen and the Symbionese Liberation Army. So inflammatory and divisive had the protest movement been that when My Lai war criminal William Calley was pardoned by President Nixon, the news was greeted with widespread approval.

The war was in many ways the linchpin of the conflict. Most galling of all to the older generation was the juxtaposition of protest with the endless growing death rolls of the war, death rolls that were disproportionately filled with the names of working-class youths. "Here were those kids, rich kids who could go to college, didn't have to fight," one construction worker remembered. "They are telling you your son died in vain. It makes you feel your whole life is shit, just nothing."[88] Liberals at the time identified such sentiments with "hardhats"— silent-majority types who represented bourgeois prejudices and the bad old days before the baby-boom enlightenment. They were "reactionaries," members of an Establishment that reflexively resisted the abrogation of its old privileges.

Imagine their surprise, then, when hardhats declared themselves minorities, "white ethnics" who wanted a piece of the rhetorical pie. Borrowing the ideology that had empowered gays, Hispanics, Indians, blacks, and women, the white ethnics declared that they, too, were an oppressed people, that they, too, were being done a disservice by being identified with a WASP elite from which they had been historically excluded. The very title of the movement's manifesto, Michael Novak's 1972 book *The Rise of the Unmeltable Ethnics,* seemed to deny the assimilationist principle of "the melting pot" that had defined American society for so long.[89] Like the Silent Majority, the white ethnics were a bloc of fragmented America. They coalesced in response to social and political effects of the baby boom, and so the division often ran across generation lines, which by 1970, at times seemed like battle lines.

The lines never seemed more clearly drawn than on 4 May 1970, when National Guard troops opened fire on protesters at Kent State University, killing four students. The event was widely seen as epochal by the young and their sympathizers, a sentiment amplified and immortalized in Crosby, Stills, Nash, and Young's "Ohio":

> Tin soldiers and Nixon's coming
> We're finally on our own
> This summer I hear the drumming
> Four dead in Ohio! Four dead in Ohio![90]

Two days after the shooting, Mayor John Lindsay of New York declared the coming Friday to be "a day of reflection" and ordered the flags lowered to half-mast. The gesture was meant to appease the gathering storm of protesters who were expected to paralyze parts of the city; instead, it precipitated another violent skirmish, as an army of two hundred construction workers descended upon protesters in front of a downtown federal building, beating them with their tools before marching down to City Hall and forcibly raising the flags to full height. Nor did the uprising subside: rather, it grew into a movement: in coming weeks, the city would see a parade of one hundred thousand construction workers and longshoremen carrying patriotic placards. Construction union leader Peter Brennan journeyed to Washington to present President Nixon with an honorary hardhat—a gift the president described as "a symbol, along with our great flag, for freedom and patriotism to our beloved country."[91] The release two months later of the Pentagon Papers exacerbated the situation.

Such discord was probably inevitable, but the election in 1968 of Nixon and Agnew had guaranteed it. Nixon, unlike Johnson, was neither surprised nor hurt by the disdain with which young people of liberal bent held him; their scorn, like that of minorities, radicals, and other "impudent" upstarts, was the very engine of his success. Nor, unlike LBJ, was Nixon particularly uncomfortable with the television cameras, despite his physical and temperamental unsuitedness to them. Nixon threatened the industry through Agnew, forced the networks to preempt prime-time coverage for his addresses and pseudoevents, and would end up presiding over legislation that would cripple the industry in 1971. Nor would

Nixon's downfall come as a result of television, but rather his own misdeeds and the reportage of the *Washington Post*.

But Nixon's mastery of television, not to mention Agnew's short-lived career as a media star, demonstrate the extent to which television by 1970 had become a thoroughly politicized medium. LBJ had been angered in the 1960s by the networks' refusal to voluntarily provide war propaganda, as they had willingly done for FDR. But the news aside, television had attempted to provide light entertainment for a nation; as it abandoned that mission, programming for youthful audiences and attempting to ward off the image, so dangerous for any media, of being out of touch with the world, its mission fragmented like so many demographic audience segments. TV was, for the most part, *still* broadcasting banal entertainments in the hope of attracting huge audiences, but now there were increasing troubles from the affiliate stations, from advertisers, from Congress, and the White House.

The wake of discord had finally broken over TV's bow, and trouble loomed on the horizon as the next generation, so affluent and immense, seemed to be abandoning it in its hour of need. Their experiment with youth programming had failed. New technologies such as the VCR and cable loomed. And now the government seemed to have turned against them. Congress had decreed that cigarette advertising would, as of 2 January 1971, be verboten on TV. This alone was worth $220 million to the networks, and other even more threatening legislation loomed beyond: a law to divest the networks of part of prime time, an antimonopoly law to break up ownerships of multiple media outlets in a single market.

Of all the times to have viewership problems! The networks found themselves in the same unimaginable predicament the auto industry had a few years earlier. Here they were, the width and breadth and depth of commercial television, as it was known at the time, and all of a sudden their core market of young people turns against them! The network high command wore the same bewildered expressions as Detroit had worn, when they first saw the sales of Volkswagen Beetles to customers whom automakers had assumed were Chevy buyers from birth. And too, the same pained feelings of persecution when a government that had always, with a few exceptions, cheerfully served their interests, up and regulated them, as Congress had been forced to do to the auto industry in the wake of Ralph Nader's *Unsafe at Any Speed*. In such an atmosphere, the need for new solutions took on an urgency not uncharacteristic of an age marked by Weathermen on the one hand and Agnew on the other, of Gloria Steinem and Pat Nixon, of George Wallace and George McGovern, a time of aging centers of power and gathering centrifugal forces. Who had thus upset the cosmos? There could only be one culprit.

It was the young, the baby boomers who had thus reordered the constellation. They had the money; they were the arbiters of taste; they were the force behind the leftward policies of the ever-pragmatic Nixon administration, who even as he championed big business and the silent majority politically, actually presided over one of the most liberal administrations of any modern president. Even in his own, highly sensitive electioneering, Nixon in his late career is a product of the baby boom, if only for the aplomb with which he rode the backlash to its sentiments and ideology.

But the networks, unlike Nixon, did not have the luxury of appealing to a vast and inert mass. Even if such a thing had been possible, as it perhaps had in the 1950s, the advertisers would not stand for it. Business continued to be done, commercials continued to be sold, ratings for the top shows continued to be high—but an atmosphere of alarm had set in. The fragmented audience had become a given, and the experiment with "relevancy" having failed miserably, there seemed to be no way in sight to bridge the gaps between the competing minorities who now made up the viewing audience. Some way had to be found to bring television back the interest and acclaim that it had had once and badly needed again. The "great audience" needed to be rebuilt if television was to remain the center of American society.

3
"The Church of What's Happening Now": The Great Shift, 1970–1972

"**Y**ou know a man you can depend on," said Vice President Agnew, describing the Forgotten American, "he's sitting right there and his name isn't 'the third' anything."[1] Clearly, he knew what he was talking about. Having been thrust into the national spotlight as the cultural point man for the Nixon administration, Agnew displayed a far surer grasp of the culture than had any of his predecessors. In the fall of 1970, Agnew was a ubiquitous media presence, appearing in print, on television, in hundreds of jokes and comedy routines, and on uncounted editorial pages. Invariably, his subject was culture and his tone apocalyptic.

Two typical examples suffice. Red Skelton, banished from CBS for his silent-majority demographics, was snatched up by NBC and introduced into the fall lineup with an appearance by the vice president, who used his role as midwife to the beloved clown's new show as an exposure-garnering pseudoevent. Some weeks later, in Las Vegas of all places, Agnew inveighed against a "drug culture" that "brainwashed" youth through such songs as the Beatles' "I Get By with a Little Help from My Friends" and the Jefferson Airplane's "White Rabbit" and through such movies as *Easy Rider.*[2] In Agnew's view, there was only one side or the other to be on: "squares" and "bumpkins" versus "the drug culture" and "the so-called intellectual community."[3] This view was echoed throughout society, as the "Woodstock nation" and the "silent majority" settled into armed camps.

As far as the broadcast industry was concerned, the split was profoundly problematic. Consensus was their bread and butter; programming for two different audiences was to them like squaring the circle. "Narrowcasting," as it would later be called, went against the grain of television's economics. Older audiences might no longer call the shots; but they couldn't be abandoned entirely. Every American needed to do his or her part if the networks were to make money. "Relevancy" had seemingly failed: the with-it dramas of the previous year had fared badly, as had ABC's venture at a *Laugh-In* imitation, *Turn-On* (1969). *Turn-On,* in fact, was one of the biggest disasters of all time; it had been so abrasive, its one-liners so awful ("The capital of South Vietnam is in Swiss banks!"), and its tone so confrontational that a hurricane of viewer and affiliate objections caused it to be canceled after one show, the shortest program run in network history.

There were some encouraging signs. A few attempts to cross-pollinate proven TV formats, such as the situation comedy and the variety show, with domesticated rock music had found some limited success. *The Partridge Family* (1970–1974) was a Van Trapp-style family singing group. They traveled from episode to episode in a not-so-magic bus decorated with psychedelic colors—but meticulously laid out in Mondrianesque squares and bricks. The band sang bubble-gum music so convincingly that eldest son David Cassidy became TV's first teen pop idol since *Ozzie and Harriet*'s Ricky Nelson, achieving several top ten hits. *The Sonny and Cher Comedy Hour* (1971–1977), a husband-and-wife variety show, featured mod outfits, Vegasized rock hits, and much derisive patter between the stars. But the future lay in other directions.

It certainly didn't look like an auspicious time to be tinkering with programming. The arrangements by which a new series was commissioned suddenly changed, however. On 4 May 1971, the administration's long-held threat to bend the networks' news divisions to its will via pressure from the FCC materialized. The Prime Time Access Rule restricted the amount of evening time the networks could control by half an hour: poof, in a puff of smoke, went one-seventh of every night. Worse still were the Financial Interest and Syndication Rules. The "fin-sin" decree called firstly for the networks to divest themselves of all financial interest in the shows they broadcast. So great had their monopoly become over commercial television that all three networks by 1970 held stakes in 98 percent of their programming.[4] The networks had producers over a barrel, but the good times, the FCC ordained, were at an end. The other end of the arrangement, by which the networks played middleman in all syndication arrangements after shows' initial runs, was likewise derailed. These practices were plain kickback arrangements and as such did call for some curbing. It was a victory for affiliate stations, who could use the extra time to show local advertising, and for independent producers, who were being frozen out of the schedule. But to the networks, it amounted to politically motivated restraint of trade. Some felt the threat was from the left, in the form of longhaired radicals such as Nicolas Johnson on the FCC Board; others, that is was from the right, in the Nixon White House.

The latter were probably closer to the truth. A memo from Nixon aide Jeb Magruder to H. R. Haldeman reveals the strategy with a subtlety characteristic of the Nixon White House:

> The real problem that faces this administration is to get this unfair coverage in such a way that we make a major impact on a basis in

which the networks, newspapers, and Congress will react to and begin to look at this somewhat differently. . . . [We can] utilize the antitrust division to investigate various media relating to antitrust violation. Even the possible threat of antitrust action, I think, would be effective in changing their views in the above matter.[5]

Also at this time, Congress banned cigarette advertising on television, cutting out a major part of the networks' revenue base—just as syndication rights were being amputated, along with half an hour each night of prime-time advertising.

It was in the shadow of this dark hour that Wood was attempting to reinvent CBS. Fortunately, things were not as bleak as they seemed. The Prime Time Access Rule actually turned out to be a blessing, as the trimmed-back schedule meant that the network now only had to supply eight new shows to replace the thirteen that had been canceled in the great purge.[6] And one of these seemed especially promising. Upon his ascension to CBS's presidency, Wood found a project that had already been approved and that suited his purposes perfectly: a series to star Mary Tyler Moore, Dick Van Dyke's TV wife. Moore seemed a good bet, particularly since she and her husband, Grant Tinker, had already been given an independent production entity, MTM, with creative control and thirteen episodes ordered up in advance.

This creative control was to be extremely important, since much of what Tinker, Moore, et al. wanted to do was modern and realistic in a way CBS had not yet tried. *The Mary Tyler Moore Show* (1970–1977), as it came to be called, was far less consciously, didactically "relevant" than the faddish series of the previous year, such as *The Storefront Lawyers*.

But, on the other hand, neither would it resemble *The Doris Day Show* (1968–1973), *That Girl* (1966–1971), or any of the other "girl on her own" series of the time. "At the time we started in 1970, every other show was restricted to plastic, Protestant, virginal people. . . . We wanted to do something that was about the real world," said series cocreator James Brooks.[7] The show was to revolve around Mary's life as a single working woman in Minneapolis, where she would work in a TV station. Neither of these premises seem particularly daring, but both were significantly of the moment at the time. Mary was originally to have been a divorcée, restarting her life in the brave new world of an America in which there was life outside of marriage for a grown woman. "I said I like that," Moore later remembered, "because that's kind of progressive."[8] The idea was rejected by CBS programming executive Perry Lafferty, an old-school executive who believed the audience to be so stupid that they would think Moore had left Dick Van Dyke. Mary was therefore remade as a young woman coming off the breakup of a long romance. "It tells you something," remarked Brooks, "about our own lack of awareness of the women's movement at that time, which was just starting, but our feeling was that if a girl was over thirty and unmarried there had to be an explanation for a freak of nature like that."[9]

A real city was chosen (why *not* Minneapolis?) to add a layer of realism: the one-season glow of the Los Angeles soundstage would be exchanged for sleet, snow, and changes of season. And Mary was given a job that had come very recently into the public eye: she was to work in a TV newsroom, as a foot soldier among the very "corps of impudent snobs" against whom Vice President Agnew had fulminated. Remembered Moore later: "As for the idea of the TV newsroom, that came about at least partly from Spiro Agnew, of all people. We really have to give him some of the credit. When television news came under Agnew's scrutiny, suddenly everyone became aware of the people involved."[10]

Thus did art and politics blend, in a far smoother manner than they had in the relevancy series. The last and perhaps most important innovation had nothing at all to do with the real world but was purely formal. The show was to have an ensemble cast. Rather than a boyfriend, a neighbor, and a boss, *The Mary Tyler Moore Show* would feature six or seven major characters, all of whom would be individuated personalities, as opposed to types. The humor would proceed from their characters as much as from the wit of the script. This was a difficult feat to accomplish, then as now, but Tinker, Moore, Brooks, and cowriter Allan Burns were willing to try. They cast dramatic actors such as Ed Asner in comic roles and paid minute attention to character development and motivation. Although the least topical or controversial of the series' innovations, and not much noted at the time, it was to have the greatest long-term influence.

The Mary Tyler Moore Show began with moderate success in the ratings, and by the end of the year had climbed into the twenty-second position overall in the Nielsens. The show was praised as "the best-written sitcom in the business."[11] It had not, however, made the kind of major waves its fresh approach seemed to augur. It was not even CBS's most controversial situation comedy that season. That honor belonged to a new show called *All in the Family*.

The pilot for the show had been turned down once already. ABC, still sufficiently traumatized by the *Turn-On* fiasco, had had first crack at a new series about a bigot who was forced to live with his liberal son-in-law. At first, this seemed supremely "relevant," and when Norman Lear approached them with a pilot for the show, to be called *Those Were the Days,* they had been interested enough to give Lear the go-ahead to make a second pilot; in the interim, however, *Turn-On* had turned them off. Lear took the pilot to CBS.

Norman Lear had been a successful comedy writer, a TV producer, and even, with his partner Bud Yorkin, a successful movie producer. Neither man particularly needed to be involved with weekly television. The two had recently coproduced the hit movie *The Night They Raided Minsky's*. But then Lear read in *Variety* of a British series entitled *Til Death Do Us Part*. The show centered on a bigoted father who was forced to live under the same roof as his leftist son-in-law, making for heated battles over the day's politics and social issues. The concept struck a chord with Lear: "if that could happen on American television!" he later recalled thinking.[12]

Lear was, like many Jews in show business, a man of liberal sensibilities who sympathized with the movement against the war, and agreed with critics who felt that television was one great missed opportunity. Discussing the show in retrospect many years later, Lear described the context of what would become *All in the Family*'s debut. "I didn't know this when I started with *All in the Family*, but that show was the first to make social issues integral to evening television sitcom. . . . We followed a whole bunch of shows like *Father Knows Best, Leave It to Beaver, Green Acres,* and other shows of the '60s. They were all fine shows, but you would think by watching them that America had no blacks, no racial tensions, that there was no Vietnam."[13]

Word. And yet unlike the producers of "relevant" dramas like *The Storefront Lawyers,* Lear felt that a genuine relevancy need not be laid on superficially, as a gimmick, but could work as the engine behind a comedy series, one that drew on conflict for its humor. "I've always considered that an audience laughs hardest where they're concerned most," Lear told Todd Gitlin in 1983.[14] The *All in the Family* pilot found a receptive audience in President Wood, who thought the show would represent the sort of leadership he had spoken of to Chairman Paley. "I really thought the pilot was very funny," Wood told Gitlin. "And it was in the vanguard. . . . How do you get in that parade and how do you get in the front of the parade? I thought, Well, it may be too far in front of the parade. You never know until you put the thing on the air. The jury, after all, is the audience. But it sure seemed to be a terrific way to test this whole attitude about the network."[15]

Lear faced an uphill battle, however, getting his vision of the show onto the air. Standing squarely in his way was the incarnation of television propriety, CBS's standards and practices head William Tankersly. As the chief censor of the network, Tankersly stood for the consensus aesthetic that had defined television throughout the 1950s and 1960s: in his words, "a universal television that plays to everyone and offends no one."[16] This position was diametrically opposed to the whole idea of *All in the Family,* which while not meant to offend, certainly intended to stir up trouble. Tankersly was mollified by a few minor concessions on sexual matters, such as an opening scene in which son-in-law Mike is seen coming downstairs zipping his fly. Lear gave in these points, which were in all probability put in solely as bargaining chips with Tankersly in mind. No political material was removed.

The show was introduced to the public in what had come to be known as "the second season," programs that debuted in winter as replacements. Everything about its debut reflected the mixed feelings CBS seemed to have about the show. Was it comedy, or was it commentary? How might viewers respond to a "relevant" sitcom, particularly one that featured such incendiary language from its star? "The defining tone of prime time television during these years," points out Ella Taylor, "was consensual and integrative, reflecting the prevailing political and cultural temper . . . committed to holding the middle ground and avoiding controversy in its construction of the social world."[17] The clumsiness with which the debut was handled reflects this. Dann put the show on directly after *Hee Haw* and directly before *60 Minutes.* This seemingly perverse act of scheduling was actually of a piece with Dann's programming philosophy all along, one in which content matters but little and all audiences are equivalent. The prevailing sense that audiences might not be ready for *All in the Family* came out in other ways as well. The network hired extra switchboard operators and stationed them at consoles across the country in preparation for a deluge of angry calls. Interviews and press releases with the entertainment media intimated that something revolutionary was in the works. Finally, at 9:30 P.M. on the evening of 12 January 1971, just before the show was to air, a disembodied voice informed viewers, in the solemn tones normally reserved for tests of the Emergency Broadcast System: "The program you are about to see is *All in the Family.* It seeks to throw a humorous spotlight on our frailties, prejudices and concerns. By making them a source of laughter, we hope to show—in a mature fashion—just how absurd they are."[18] The now-familiar sequence of Archie and Edith, singing at the piano, then appeared. A white-haired, pugnacious-looking man holding a cigar sits next to his wife at a piano. Eyebrows raised, he begins to sing: "Boy, the way Glen Miller played. . . ." She joins him: "Songs that made the hit parade. . . ." He again: "Guys like us, we had it made!" Together: "Those were the days!" So familiar is this sequence to many Americans today that its impact is irrecoverably blunted. Although to an audience inured to war and riot on the evening news (that very day, Father Philip Berrigan had been indicted on conspiracy charges), the sight of a man sitting at a piano with his wife could in no way be considered shocking, it represented a departure from viewing norms. Sitcoms tended to be filmed on lots in Hollywood; because the sets were anonymous and artificial, a convention had arisen of not specifying where a given family lived. (Hence the archetypal vagueness of *Father Knows Best's* Springfield, *The Dick Van Dyke Show's* New Rochelle, or the generalized "New York" of so many other shows.) *All in the Family* was highly localized, its setting—the row houses of Queens—displayed underneath the title credits. Furthermore, it was not filmed at all but rather videotaped on a live stage set. Thus was the "filmed before a live studio audience" boast by which the more enlightened sitcoms of the 1970s set themselves apart from their canned predecessors. The live audience, however, was not the most significant formal departure *All in the Family* made; another convention of videotape, much less remarked upon but much more significant in terms of the show's "look," was the deep-focus effect the video camera brought. In the *All in the Family* frame, you can see a lamp or closet door in the background as clearly as the speaking figure in the foreground. This brought a greater immediacy to the action, which was very much in keeping with the series' realistic ambitions. "You seem to be right there in the room with them," pointed out one industry observer.[19]

None of these innovations would have had any impact, however, without the conflict-riddled teleplays for which *All in the Family* became known. The first episode set the mold for these. Son-in-law Mike, or anyone else who tilts against Archie in political or social argument, is automatically right, as measured by how angry they become with Archie. "Anger in a Norman Lear comedy," critic Michael Arlen would point out when *All in the Family*'s runaway success had generated half a dozen other Lear hits, "isn't something isolated and set apart. . . . it has become part of the spirit of the occasion, like music in a musical comedy."[20]

This anger, though, all derives from one source. The characters aren't angry with each other: they are generally angry with Archie, or reacting to Archie's anger, or both. The tension in *All in the Family* all radiates from him. The show's cast is a constellation of one-dimensional characters who only exist for purposes of comparison, like the cat a paleontologist sets next to the rendering of a dinosaur. Lionel Jefferson patronizes Archie, Edith one-ups him in a saintly and bemused way, Mike engages him head on, Gloria rolls her eyes or pouts. Even when no one steps into the breach to put Archie down, the chorus of derisive laughter from the studio audience reassures us that he stands for wrongheadedness.

The nostalgic theme music is not merely scene-setting: once we realize what Archie is, his idyllic reverence of a past in which "guys like us, we had it made," can only be interpreted ironically. Archie's a relic of the past, the show reassures its audience. As a popular ad campaign for Benson and Hedges cigarettes told women, "you've come a long way, baby." Archie is a creature of the past, lingering into the present as an unquiet spirit, a ghost who has outlived the era that created him. Norman Lear knows that. You and I, the audience, know it. Mike and Gloria know it. Even Edith, for all of her servility, knows it. The only one who doesn't know it is Archie, and it is this very indomitability of the character, and Carroll O'Connor's gifted rendering of it, that elevates him above traditional TV heavies and bigots. They "learn their lesson" at the end of every episode. That Archie *never* learns his lesson is the source of his great iconic power. He was the Sisyphus of the hardhats, constantly attempting to roll Meathead, Gloria, Edith, Norman Lear, his neighbors, the scriptwriters, and the political climate of the 1960s generally back up the hill of vanished time.

All in the Family's Archie Bunker: The
hardhat apotheosized

This cultural power of Archie went a long way toward earning the show its
fabulously wide audience (by the 1974–1975 season, an *average* episode was viewed
by a fifth of the total population).[21] But the real key was that the older, put-upon
Americans whom Archie represented enjoyed him far more than they might have
been expected to, given his full-time status as butt and buffoon. "What's great
about that show," a railroad worker told *Life Magazine* "is that it *is* biased. What
I mean is, it's just like you feel inside yourself. You think it, but ole Archie, he
says it, by damn."[22] For all Archie's malapropism, Lear gave his antihero sentiments that were extremely potent at the time. Consider this exchange, from the
first episode, "Meet the Bunkers."[23] "I just want to learn how to help people,"
Mike tells Archie, explaining why he is studying sociology in college.

> *Archie:* Your mother-in-law and me is people. Help *us* and go to
> work!
> *Mike:* I know what's bothering you. You're upset because I was nail-
> ing you on that law and order thing.
> *Archie: You* was nailing *me?*
> *Mike:* Yeah, that's right, and now I'm going to tell you something. I
> know I promised, Gloria, but I feel I got to say this. You know why
> we have a breakdown of law and order in this country, Archie? Be-
> cause we got poverty, real poverty. And you know why we got that?

Because guys like you are unwilling to give the black man, the Mexican American, and all the other minorities their just and rightful hard-earned share of the American dream!

"The black man," "the Mexican-American," "just and rightful share": Mike has fallen into the grammatically formal idioms of political writing, which is explicitly nonparochial—the language of ideals, not the language of narrow parochialism. Contrast Archie's response:

> *Archie:* Now let me tell you something. If your spics and your spades want their share of the American dream, let them go out and hustle for it, just like I done.

The tension between Mike and Archie's language mirrors their political positions. The sentiment that Archie is voicing here, however, is not so easily dismissed. Because the show drew on reality for its conflict, rather than on plot contrivances (as in traditional "situation comedies"), the conflict is charged, animated from within. The twilight of "the American dream" was no joke. And what may have made Archie even more appealing was the lengths to which his makers loaded the deck against him. Norman Lear certainly doesn't talk about "your spics and spades," any more than he shares Archie's broad working-class Queens accent, his malapropism, or his general burden as unmeltable ethnic and forgotten man of American politics. Founded on the rock of real, if illiberal, feelings, Archie remains the unmoved mover, the figure whose wrong opinions, put-downs, and vulgarity put every other character comparably on the side of the angels. As such, he became embedded in the national mind, the symbol of an age if ever there was one. But in the early going, the show often amounted to little more than bear baiting.

> *Mike:* Now I suppose you're going to tell me that the black man has had as much opportunity in this country as you.
> *Archie:* More, he's had more! I didn't have no million people out there marching and protesting to get me my job!
> *Edith:* No, his uncle got it for him. (huge laugh from audience)

Was this then aimed at a liberal audience? Why then did it debut in the time slot directly after *Hee Haw*, that bastion of square demographics? Audiences were either unaware of or baffled by *All in the Family*. Ratings were so disappointing in the early going that it was not until May, when word of mouth had given the show a lift, that CBS decided to renew it, eventually giving it the prime lead-in spot before *The Mary Tyler Moore Show*. And critically, opinion was mixed. Although the show, as a midseason replacement, did not attract large audiences, the critics had been alerted to its debut. "Unless there is a third world war," critic Clarence Petersen wrote on the day of the premiere, "double ax murder in a convent or one heck of a storm in the next 24 hours, there seems little doubt about what the chief topic of conversation will be tomorrow morning: the new CBS-TV comedy *All in the Family* which debuts tonight."[24]

The function of the TV critic is a dubious one; for the most part, it is his or her melancholy lot to praise shows with low ratings and to take critical stances against hugely popular programs and thus appear curmudgeonly or effete. In the case of *All in the Family,* however, the critics were as divided as the audience and the Bunker household. Most of the major press outlets whose opinion the industry valued—the *New York Times,* the weekly *Variety,* and *TV Guide*—praised the show. A number of others, including the *Washington Post,* daily *Variety, Time,* and *Life,* despised it. The split between the two editions of *Variety* was especially egregious: the weekly version hailed the show as "The best TV comedy since the original *The Honeymooners,*" while its daily counterpart saw "nothing less than an insult to any unbigoted televiewer," remarking that it was "too bad this bundle from Britain wasn't turned back at the shoreline."

Perhaps the most carefully reasoned split appeared in the form of two editorials in the Sunday *New York Times* during the fall of 1971. On 12 September, Laura Z. Hobson, the author of *Gentleman's Agreement* and *Consenting Adults,* both highly regarded fictional indictments of prejudice, wrote an essay entitled "As I Listened to Archie Say Hebe." Archie Bunker, Hobson maintained, was a comic, likable figure who made bigotry more attractive. Language such as *hebe* and *spade* were themselves euphemisms for *kike* and *nigger,* she pointed out, epithets that would have made Archie look considerably less sympathetic. Moreover, she asked, could it really be assumed that everyone would receive Archie's notions ironically? Could not some members of the audience see the presence of formerly taboo expressions and attitudes as a legitimation? Hobson's case was lucid and, as it turned out, prescient in a number of ways. Norman Lear pooh-poohed her alarm in a wry response a few weeks later on 10 October entitled "As I Read How Laura Saw Archie . . ." Archie Bunker was indeed a lovable bigot, Lear claimed. That was exactly the moral of *All in the Family:* the banality of evil. Furthermore, as a Jew, Lear had been on the receiving end of bigotry and so had the moral credentials to create and air a bigot. Finally, Lear claimed, reaching for the oldest weapon in television's arsenal, Hobson was an elitist, whose editorial displayed a bias against the undereducated.[25]

This exchange, which dates from the earliest months of the show's decade-long run, lays out the essential controversy not only about *All in the Family* but about all the realistic programming that would define television's mainstream in the show's wake. Other criticisms filled in the edges—Richard Burgheim in *Time* sidestepped the entire issue by noting that "the show proves that bigotry can be as boring and predictable as the upthink fluff of *The Brady Bunch*"—but they did not address the central issue. Was the new realism a step forward, an emancipation from the see-no-evil escapism of 1960s television, or was it a step backward, an introduction of potent toxins into the main artery of American social life? Both sides had valid points to make, and what's more, both sides could point to the audience response for evidence. Both conservatives and liberals, hawks and doves, seemed to love the show. One formal study taken by a pair of social scientists showed that both liberals and conservatives came away from *All in the Family* with their perspectives completely intact.[26] Opinion seemed to be divided everywhere. Tony Brown, an important black TV journalist, called the show "shocking and racist," while other blacks felt it was "unoffensive and realistic," as Archie's "rantings serve a purpose."[27] Carroll O'Connor himself was taken aback. "You think you're kidding the character," he said of Archie years later. "You are really playing to a crowd out there who are, indeed, Archie Bunker. . . . there were many people who thought Archie was 100 percent right on everything."[28]

By May, the ratings had begun to pick up. The show earned a surprise Emmy award as the best situation comedy of the year, which no doubt earned it some new viewers. Much of the competition was now in reruns, word of mouth was working its unseen magic, and the gale of discussion the show generated earned viewers as well. Just before the show exhausted its season run and went into the limbo of reruns itself, it was able to achieve the impossible: it attained the top position in the Nielsens. Wood's gamble had paid off. More significantly, it had given "realistic" conflict-based comedy the beacon glow of proven success; as with *The Beverly Hillbillies* earlier, pilots by the hundreds and series by the dozens attempted to emulate it. None had the transcendent success of the original; but by then, they didn't need to.

Emboldened by *All in the Family*'s success, Wood that summer undertook a massive housecleaning. Gone, finally, would be the great rural-appeal fixtures, *The Beverly Hillbillies, Green Acres, The Jim Nabors Hour, Hee Haw,* and *Mayberry R.F.D.,* all CBS's signature sitcoms from the 1960s. Gone, too, would be *The Jackie Gleason Show* and *The Red Skelton Show,* both institutions, both stale and expensive, having outlived their usefulness to the network's corporate bottom line. It was a bad time for older viewers, all of whose favorite shows were being offered up for sacrifice on the altar of youth. (ABC had pulled the plug on *Lawrence Welk*'s bubble machine in September.) The worst blow to the audience as a whole, however, was Wood's decision to end, after twenty-three years, the run of *The Ed Sullivan Show.*

Jerome Kern once remarked that Irving Berlin didn't have a place in American popular song, because "he *was* American popular song." If Berlin had a counterpart in television, it was surely Sullivan, who embodied television by the late 1950s, and whose weekly variety show continued to represent the apex of mainstream success right up until the moment of its passing. Along with Walter Cronkite (also of CBS), Sullivan was one of the two men who defined American television for most of its existence up to that point. Compared to him, Milton Berle was a flash in the pan, and Lucille Ball a nostalgia act. (Lucy continued to be a popular TV presence, but her shows of the 1960s could not begin to compete with *I Love Lucy*'s popularity.)

It was Sullivan's unique gift to stay up with the times by never having belonged to them. Even in the mid-1950s, he had been stilted and awkward, an unlikely TV presence whose only function was to present the most popular or entertaining acts then on the scene. As television became the central locus and measure of national attention, his show became the great imprimatur of success, the place where you knew you had arrived. As John Leonard has remarked, "Ed's emblematic role was to confirm, validate, and legitimize singularity, for so long as the culture knew what it wanted and valued, and as long as its taste was coherent."[29]

Sullivan's own tastes were not identical with his audience, being in many ways more upscale. He certainly would not have presented Elvis Presley or the many rock acts that followed him but for their demonstrated appeal. (Sullivan had sworn that Presley would never appear on his show. When Steve Allen had Presley on, however, and beat him by six ratings points, he immediately called up Presley's manager and spent a small fortune on a three-appearance contract.) For Sullivan, "public opinion [was] the voice of God."[30] The success of the Sullivan show, as it was called, was predicated on Sullivan's ability to present something for everybody: it was the ultimate show that "plays to everyone and offends no one." It represented in the limited field of show business a working model of the "consensus" ideal propagated in the abstract by political scientists and historians such as Louis Hartz, Daniel Bell, and Daniel Boorstin in the 1950s.[31] Sullivan did this, and did it successfully for over twenty years of violently transitional American history.

This fact made its passing even more lamentable. Unlike *I Love Lucy*, or for that matter, *All in the Family*, the Sullivan show was able to provide a singular continuity through the changing eras. The acts might change, a Kate Smith dying, a Cass Elliot being born, but the format of the show stayed utterly the same: the same wooden gait, stiff neck, and expressionless face provided the connective tissue between expressions of what might appear to be wholly different cultures. The show never stopped presenting an act because they had gotten old; on any given show in the late 1960s, one could see a borscht-belt act such as Jackie Mason or Myron Cohen, or the ventriloquist Señor Wences, or any number of animal acts (Animal acts! On prime time!) along with the latest British Invasion rock band or afroed R&B singer. (As Larry Gelbart once observed, "vaudeville may have been dead, but television was the box they buried it in.")[32] Thus were not only disparate demographic groups but also regions, religions, and even continents bridged under the glare of a weekly "variety" show.

The cancellation of Sullivan, therefore, represents a final definitive break from the cultural assumptions of 1950s television. TV had been refining or "streamlining" itself, in Fred Macdonald's phrase, all throughout the 1960s—reducing its genres, making shows more alike and predictable, homogenizing its product generally. Sullivan, with his background as a Broadway gossip columnist and his feeling for popular entertainment, personified the older grab-bag approach, the New York showbiz ideal, as compared to the ideal of programming as commodity, of filmed series from Hollywood, equipped with canned laughter and syndication kickbacks. Whether or not the audience any longer enjoyed Sullivan is unimportant; Wood felt his time had passed, and Wood was president of CBS. It was his vision of television that would hold sway, both then and afterwards.

As of early 1972, that vision seemed to be proving itself. Once *All in the Family* had arrived as a huge hit, it came to dominate the society outside of television as few TV shows had since the days of *I Love Lucy*. Despite the enormous popularity of *The Beverly Hillbillies,* for example, its success was almost entirely in the aseptic context of ratings success. But a kind of Archiemania broke across the landscape in the early to mid-1970s, a time (1972–1976) when *All in the Family* was the number one show in television for five straight years, a feat not equaled before or since. T-shirts, buttons, bumper stickers, and other merchandise capitalized on the show's currency. Archie's favorite expressions—"Meathead," "Dingbat," "stifle yourself," and so on entered the popular lexicon. Facetious "Archie Bunker for President" campaigns were even held in 1972 and 1976, with the silver-haired patriarch actually receiving a vote at the 1972 Democratic nominating convention.[33]

Audiences came together to watch the Bunkers come apart. The networks could hardly believe it. For one thing, it had always been assumed that a show that was too tendentious in its politics would alienate millions of potential viewers. Politics and religion were simply off the table. *All in the Family* changed that; it was the first program to use extratelevisual conflicts as the wellspring for comedy. Later, this became the norm. Todd Gitlin wrote in *Inside Prime Time:*

> TV entertainment takes its design from social and psychological fissures. That is the deep, unspoken reason why writers always look for conflict at the heart of the tale. If the messages are susceptible to divergent interpretations, that is no failure for television. On the contrary, a show that couldn't be interpreted variously would slide into what [*M*A*S*H* creator] Larry Gelbart calls "electronic pam-

phleteering.". . . . Producers and writers as well as network executives normally don't deliberate about how to market a show to diverse audience segments, but the successful ones claim to know in their bones how to do it.[34]

Gitlin is here writing about television post-Archie; in the antediluvian period before *All in the Family,* it was the constant complaint of producers that such fault lines were *not* being exploited. "We try not to do anything controversial," one told Muriel Cantor guiltily as late as 1970. "Because of this we are a success." Another agreed, telling Cantor, "[most] shows are Mickey Mouse and I do them for the network and the Nielsen Families. I know the audience is smarter, more intelligent than they think it is."[35] It was Norman Lear's single most significant breakthrough that, with the help of President Wood, he was able to break through the straitjacket of consensus that had constrained earlier television. Dwight Macdonald had lamented in 1953 that "a mass society, like a crowd, is so undifferentiated and loosely structured that its atoms, in so far as human values go, tend to cohere only along the line of the least common denominator; its morality sinks to that of its most brutal and primitive members, its taste to that of the least sensitive and most ignorant."[36] Macdonald's jeremiad has to be understood in the context of the blacklist-ridden, egghead-hectoring, pietistic culture of the early 1950s, when dissent seemed to be relegated to intellectuals and other marginal types. But now things were opening up. The credit cannot go to Lear and Wood alone; the Smothers Brothers, too, deserve credit for their work in breaking ground for the robustly politicized comedy of the early 1970s.

Because *All in the Family,* unlike *Laugh-In, Batman,* and so many other "breakthrough" shows of the mid-to-late 1960s, was not a one-time phenomenon. Its conception of the audience as politically fragmented, but able to unite at the comedy of conflict, reshaped television. The format turned out to be marvelously replicable. A year almost to the day of *All in the Family*'s premiere saw the debut of another Lear series, *Sanford and Son* (1972–1977), on NBC. Based like *All in the Family* on a British series, the show centered on a curmudgeonly black junk dealer and his son, who lived together in Watts. The setting could not have been accidental; in relocating the series to America, Lear had his choice of all locales real and fictional, and he chose the site of one of the most famous televised race riots in recent memory.

Unlike Archie, however, Fred Sanford was not an ideologue. Full of bluster and get-rich-quick schemes, he was an old-time sitcom character embroidered with political consciousness—a few racial epithets, as likely to concern Hispanics as whites; a few wisecracks about inflation and the government; and constant references to items of black culture such as *Jet Magazine,* Lena Horne, soul food, and the like. Most of the actual conflict onscreen arose from traditional in-house sitcom relationships. Young son Lamont is embarrassed to bring his new girl-friend home. Bible-thumping Aunt Esther wants Fred to come to a church func-tion. Puerto Rican neighbor Julio buys a goat. The critical response was consid-erably less guarded than it had been for *All in the Family,* Fred Sanford being neither a full-time bigot nor a white man. And audiences, once having discov-ered the "realistic" situation comedy, immediately made *Sanford and Son* a hit.

By the time the Nielsen ratings for 1971–1972 came out (see table 3.1), they revealed a changed face of television. This list is interesting in a number of ways. The most controversial and potentially divisive program of the previous season sat in the number one spot, followed at number two by the new variety show hosted by the young black comic Flip Wilson. *Sanford and Son* debuted at number five, giving Norman Lear two of the top five shows and Wilson the first success-ful black variety show in TV history. (Like *Sanford and Son, The Flip Wilson Show* was not entirely benevolent in the way it derived humor from black culture. As J. Fred Macdonald has noted, "it . . . became riotously funny to joke about skin color, hair texture, race riots, poverty, welfare checks, and minority social cus-toms. Inhibitions disappeared, and writers and comedians seemed to ignore ra-cial sensitivities. It now became a mark of fashionable outspokenness to deliver jokes based on old bigoted slurs. In bringing this new type of humor to popular video acceptance, the transitional series was *The Flip Wilson Show.*"[37]) The rest of the top ten were veteran audience-gathering machines, all designed to the speci-fications of the 1960s. *Marcus Welby, M.D.* (1969–1976) was a medical soap op-era, with a benevolent father figure for the oldsters and a handsome young resi-dent for the ladies. *Gunsmoke* by this time had evolved into a kind of dramatic anthology series, in which social and psychological conflicts were played out under the guise of a Western. Marshall Dillon still represented the one true way, how-ever, having become only more of an authority figure as he grew into his emeri-tus years. *Mannix* (1967–1975) was a private-eye series of the Mike Hammer mold, with the tough-guy hero beating his enemies senseless at every turn. (Senator Pastore had faded from view somewhat, liberating the networks to return vio-lence to its rightful place on the airwaves.) *Funny Face* (1971) was a youth show for old people, about a pert and wholesome small-town girl studying at UCLA. *Adam-12* still centered on two stern young centurions, patrolling Los Angeles on the lookout for violators of the social contract. And *Here's Lucy,* most attenuated of all, still offered Lucille Ball, her hair brightly dyed, bustling around sitcom limbo accompanied by her real-life children, now grown to adulthood.

Few of these shows had what might be considered attractive demographics, but all were very high ratings earners, and in a business in which success is mea-sured as much by relative viewer share as by ad revenues (in the hearts of execu-

Table 3.1
Nielsen Ratings, 1971–1972

Program/Network	Rating
1. *All in the Family,* CBS	34.0
2. *The Flip Wilson Show,* NBC	27.9
3. *Marcus Welby, M.D.,* ABC	27.8
4. *Gunsmoke,* CBS	26.0
5. *Sanford and Son,* NBC	25.2
6. *Mannix,* CBS	24.8
7. *Funny Face,* CBS	23.9
8. *Adam-12,* NBC	23.9
9. *The Mary Tyler Moore Show,* CBS	23.7
10. *Here's Lucy,* CBS	23.7

Note: The ABC Movie of the Week, at number six, is omitted.

tives, if not on the bottom line), they were invaluable. Nonetheless, watched today alongside *The Mary Tyler Moore Show* or even the early Lear programs, they appear to be of a piece—unwatchable, repressed, stilted, banal. The canned laughter is grating, the moralizing egregious. What had mostly kept these shows alive by this time, after all, was sheer force of inertia, the continuity of years of routine TV watching during a time when very little was expected from TV. These shows were the holdovers from the golden age of least objectionable programming, built for low expectations.

The new shows, on the other hand, are recognizably modern; they would not be out of place at the time of writing, a time whose standards and conventions about television programming still largely derive from the period under discussion. As shows emulating their form and style would take over the Nielsens in the years to come, it would become apparent that all the networks won in 1971–1972, not just CBS. Nonetheless, Robert Wood had transformed CBS, garnering six of ten of the top shows, including the crown jewels of his modernization drive. *The Mary Tyler Moore Show,* the ninth most popular series, had been his first risk and his first success, and although overshadowed popularly and critically by the Lear shows, it surely represented a sweet triumph of entrepreneurial courage.

There would continue to be plenty of old-fashioned shows produced. But they were now recognizable as such. By ventilating television entertainments with outside issues, the swirling whirlwinds of discontent and social unrest had blown the stale air right out. After the introduction of *All in the Family,* the space between the news and entertainment divisions of all three networks no longer represented a gulf of denial.[38] The outbursts and "disturbances" of the 1960s were now understood to be neither transitional nor exceptional but rather the state of the union: the fact that so pragmatic a man as Wood was impelled to give new programming the green light attests to the changes afoot in America.

More significant still, surely, is the overwhelming success these shows found. A more guarded optimism might have hoped that they would secure desirable market niches for themselves—Mary among the young women who are the most desirable target for the great ad buyers such as Proctor and Gamble, *All in the Family* among the kind of upscale, sophisticated viewers who had watched socially meaningful TV movies. Instead, *Mary Tyler Moore* went to a place where only Lucille Ball had been before; and *All in the Family* helped America define itself for half a decade.

Take just the latter case. (More on Mary later.) *All in the Family* came along at exactly the right time. Archie Bunker and Mike Stivic represented opposites sides of a yawning gulf, sides that had literally come to blows under the polarized atmosphere of the Nixon administration. *All in the Family* milked this polarization for sitcom laughs, which is to say that it domesticated it, shrank it, rendered it harmless and devoid of content. Neither Mike nor Archie would be convinced, and as Archie was at all times written as an ignoramus and a bigot, his position on such issues as affirmative action, gay rights, Watergate, and the war in Vietnam was usually a sounding board for Mike's (Lear's). Thus did volatile issues go to the Bunker household to die of philosophical starvation, and good riddance. As *Newsweek* noted in 1971, "[the show] does have fun—flaws and ill omens notwithstanding—by transforming our preoccupations into comic fantasy. . . . *All in the Family* cuts every which way, turns everything it touches into burlesque."[39]

In truth, there may not have been far to go. It might have been argued, in that fall of 1971, that just as the entertainment side of television was coming to resemble the outside world, so was the outside world coming to resemble television ("Archie Bunker for President"—"He is.") The politics of guerrilla theater, wiretapping, the lunatic fringe, the terrorist left, and the silent majority and their alliterative spokesman had all combined to help create a circuslike political atmosphere in America—one that did, in fact, seem in many ways a burlesque of order.

Even by the late 1960s, what had been legitimate issues of public debate had seemed to spiral out of control, with the civil rights movement morphing into black power, to take one example, or feminism growing from a grass-roots activist movement into a national one and from there into bra-burning, antimale iconoclasm. To some extent, all of these perceptions were unfair. Inequality was hardly negated by the existence of H. Rap Brown or sexism by Valerie Solanas.

But by the early 1970s, enough was enough. Todd Gitlin, in *The Whole World Is Watching,* narrates the downfall of the new left as it fell in love with television; its excesses grew more freakish and self-destructive, more marginal and less concerned with actual political change.[40] Leftism no longer had a sympathetic public or a national constituency. Gesture, sloganeering, and received truths were all that was left of an exhausted insurgency.

Gitlin's radicals, though, did achieve one thing. Their excesses drove liberals back toward a kind of working consensus. This was true not only of old-time centrists like Arthur Schlesinger Jr. but even, to some extent, former hippies and counterculturalists now overwhelmed, like so many other Americans, by the discordant legacy of the 1960s. In 1975, Robert Crumb, the most prominent of all the "underground comix" artists of the 1960s and one of the leading lights of the counterculture, published a pungent commentary in the form of a strip from his "Let's Talk Sense about This Here Modern America."[41] Crumb's famous misanthropy extends as fully to "slogan chanting radicals" as it does to "big bizness" and the other established villains of the counterculture—the "I'm glad that we are different, we've better things to do" theme of the mid-1960s has almost disappeared, leaving only the hippie folkways as what would later be called an "alternative lifestyle," and not a very bold one at that. As Nicholas Lemann has noted, "Although sixties radicals (cultural and political) spent the early seventies loudly bemoaning the end of the revolution, what was in fact going on was the working of the phenomena of the sixties into the mainstream of American life."[42]

The Right, too, had come into disrepute. Richard Nixon's administration presided over one of the most liberal Congresses in our history, as the president, always more interested in his own political survival than in any ideology, presided over increased spending on social welfare programs, the creation of the Environmental Protection Agency, and a host of other liberal programs.[43] Opposition to these would have marked Nixon as a reactionary, a loser proposition more recently occupied by George Wallace and Barry Goldwater. The "vital center" espoused by leading cold-war liberals such as Bell, Boorstin, and Schlesinger had also disavowed the right in the 1950s; despite occasional bursts of hysteria, America even in the most polarized periods of the 1960s seldom embraced an articulated conservatism (as opposed to the unconscious, temperamental conservatism bred in the country's bones). John Birchers, segregationists, and other hostile types had outworn their welcome by the early 1970s, when it was a hardy soul indeed who had not had his or her fill of vituperation, accusation, and discord.

By spinning these evils into comic gold, *All in the Family* served the nation well. In this way, despite Lear's liberalism, the show was essentially conservative. To that degree, Laura Hobson and the other leftward critics of the program were

Cartoonist Robert Crumb's vision of fragmented America, from "Let's Talk Sense about This Here Modern America," *Arcade: The Comics Review,* no. 2 (summer 1975): 8. Copyright © R. Crumb, 1975.

correct; *All in the Family* did trivialize serious issues. Once the novelty of dinner-table discussions of war and Watergate wore off, *All in the Family* came more and more to use topical issues merely as springboards for character-driven humor. Edith discovers that her cousin Liz is a lesbian, but rather than a heated discussion of lifestyle choices in a free society ("Archie, this is a free country! Aunt Liz had a right to live as she chose." "Not if she chooses to be what you call an unnatural actor, there," etc.), the occasion is one for long double takes for Edith ("Oh . . . Oh!") as the audience roars in the background. Despite Mike's increasingly rare sermons, Archie's and Edith's mute reactions and double takes often received the biggest laughs, and both characters became increasingly complex and sympathetic as the show went on. This trend reached its apex in an episode broadcast in October 1976, in which Edith took Mike to task for his hostility to Archie. "Mom, Archie hates me!" he tells her.

> *Edith:* No-o-o, Mike, Archie doesn't hate you.
> *Mike:* Then why does he always say, "get away from me, Meathead!"
> when he comes in the door?
> *Edith:* Mike, Archie is jealous of you.
> *Mike:* Of me?!

Edith tells Mike that for five years Archie has supported Mike, feeding him and giving him a roof over his head, so that he can fulfill his ambition of graduating from college. "When you owe someone so much, you begin to think you'll never be able to pay them back. And that makes you resent them even more," Edith says sagely. Moreover, she tells him, he should try to understand Archie's point of view. "He'll never be more than what he is now, even though he had dreams once, like you. He had to drop out of school to help support his family. He never will go to college. You have your whole future ahead of you, but most of Archie's life is behind him. So you see, he's jealous of you, Mike." The camera fixes in a close-up of Edith as she says this, and she holds the screen dramatically. Mike and the audience are both moved, and Mike greets Archie when he enters with "it's all right, Archie, I understand!" and a big hug. Archie gives one of his trademark double takes, as the show fades out to laughter and wild applause.[44]

Thus, although the series continued to provide Archie with fodder for his stage bigotry in the form of comical situations, admirable blacks, manly homosexuals, strikes, menopause, and the like, *All in the Family* by 1974 had settled in to a highly affectionate family sitcom, a sort of "Father Knows Least."[45] The topical theme played less and less a part as the show enjoyed season after season of immense popularity.

Lear's other shows followed the same pattern. In the wake of his great successes with *All in the Family* and then *Sanford and Son,* Lear was able to sell executives on a whole stable of "spin-off" shows, separate series vehicles for subordinate characters from established shows. In his position as the author of the biggest series on TV *and* a successful spin-off, Lear was about as safe a bet as any programmer could possibly hope for—a quality that, as we have seen, is prized above all else by television executives.[46] Thus, he was in a position to put the following shows into desirable time slots:

Maude (1972–1978). Like *Sanford and Son,* this was another reverse image of Archie, in this case Edith's "limousine liberal" cousin from Connecticut. Maude was working on her fourth marriage, was twice as smart as Mike Stivic, and three times as caustic as Archie. The show was Lear's most defiant of television conventions, and *Maude* had episodes dealing with abortion (which Maude had, with *Roe v. Wade*-inspired verve), menopause, alcoholism, and other taboos. The show inspired much protest but also much attention: it was a top ten show for three years running (in number four, six, and nine, respectively in 1972–1975).

Good Times (1974–1979). Itself a spin-off from *Maude* (and hence a grandchild of *All in the Family*), *Good Times* revolved around the home life of Maude's black maid, Florida. Florida lived with her family in a rough Chicago housing project, in which the indignities of poverty enumerated in the theme song ("temporary layoffs . . . easy credit rip-offs") put the family through endless trials. *Good Times* was also a hit, although for reasons highly displeasing to both Lear and series star Esther Rolle. The show had been intended as a positive portrayal of the black household, which, as the Moynihan Commission had reported, was in a state of decay. Older son James Jr., played by Jimmie Walker, meant as a comic relief, quickly became the star. As critics have noted, however, "Jimmie Walker's sudden rise to cult status was the perfect example of the shaky status of television's newly found social conscience."[47] With his bug-eyed antics, womanizing, and especially his mindless catchphrase ("dy-no-mite!"), "JJ," as he was called, was perceived by the TV intelligentsia as an unmistakable descendant of the Kingfish and other old-time showbiz "coons."[48] Ratings were unhurt by this revelation.

The Jeffersons (1974–1982). The Bunkers' neighbors on Hauser Street, the Jeffersons were again mirror images of the Bunkers. Husband George, the owner of a successful dry-cleaning chain, was a truculent bigot who disliked white people as much as Fred Sanford did. His occupancy of a luxury high-rise apartment ("a dee-luxe apartment in the sky," as the show's theme told) was meant therefore to give rise to hilarious culture-shock possibilities, as if Archie Bunker were to move to Watts. The show was a late entry into the Lear derby, however, and by this time racial comedy had been leeched of its ability to shock. *The Jeffersons* was the most formulaic and listless of the Lear shows. George Jefferson was surrounded by broad-minded, urbane neighbors and family, all of whom took turns humbling him for his bad attitude. A sassy black live-in maid provided a calculated infusion of ethnicity to the deracinated cast, and the tame confrontations that followed were enough, under the immutable laws of least objectionable programming, to keep the show a hit for several years in the mid-1970s.

Lear would have several other interesting projects before the 1970s ended, but these were the shows that carried his flag in the decade's first half.

Wood, meanwhile, had one more major project left in his modernization drive. Robert Altman's 1970 film *M*A*S*H* had made a major splash by setting two antiestablishment figures into a Korean war setting that unmistakably resembled Vietnam. The movie starred two of the era's characteristic stars: Elliott Gould, who excelled at playing Jewish (and crypto-Jewish) wise guys, and Donald Sutherland, a talented young character actor who had made a career of playing oddballs. Premiering the same year as *Patton,* a more traditional war epic embraced by President Nixon, *M*A*S*H* was a perfect counterpoint. It represented war as seen by Nixon's adversaries, the antiwar left and the young. To doctors Pierce and McIntyre, the army surgeons whose antics the movie chronicles, the war is pointless, contemptible, and cruel, something to be endured through individualistic bravado, irony, and furtive hedonism.

The "war comedy" genre had been in much evidence in the previous decade, from the POW-camp mirth of *Hogan's Heroes* to the zaniness of *McHale's Navy.*

M*A*S*H took the genre a step further, giving these high jinks a moral validity. Hawkeye Pierce was to become Sergeant Bilko with a halo. Under a thin patina of playboy abandon, Pierce was a true "ladies man" who became the epitome of the "sensitive guy" of the 1970s. He was also a hard-drinking prankster redeemed by his bottomless compassion for innocent GIs caught in the idiocy of war. (Gung-ho soldiers of the Calley type were noticeably absent from the show's ten-year run; only stuffed-shirt officers and martinets were allowed to speak up for the war, and were inevitably punished for it in one way or another.)

The concept of an antiwar war comedy, a *Hogan's Heroes* with countercultural credentials and a presold youthful public, was too inviting for CBS to resist. Wood's underlings contacted Twentieth Century-Fox; Larry Gelbart, a veteran comedy writer living abroad, agreed to return to America to write it, having been lured back to television by the promise of an unprecedented opportunity to do something substantial. "I wasn't very active about expressing my feelings about the war," Gelbart remembered years later, "except for the odd demonstrations in Grosvenor Square, which hardly counts. So I think perhaps I was drawn toward something that would let me get this sort of tardy negative vote in." Nor by this time could much harm come to one's career from such a project, at least politically. "It was chic to be antiwar. You couldn't offend anybody."[49]

Thus, *M*A*S*H* was introduced to the network lineup on the evening of 17 September 1972. It was not an immediate hit, largely owing to the black hole of a time slot it had been assigned to. It was mismatched in between the gray-powered *Anna and the King* (1972) and *The Sandy Duncan Show* (1972) and against powerful competition—NBC's *The Wonderful World of Disney* (1965–1983) and ABC's *The F.B.I.* (1965–1974), all of which brutalized it. By its very nature, *M*A*S*H* mocked Disney's thrice-bleached oldster appeal and *The F.B.I.*'s cryptofascist authoritarianism; people who liked these shows were unlikely to be won over by it. Once the show was moved to Saturday, however, and sandwiched safely between *The New Dick Van Dyke Show* and the two-fisted *Mannix*, *M*A*S*H* did considerably better. The following year, CBS's new programming head, Fred Silverman, elected to give it the royal treatment, sandwiching it between its hugely popular siblings *All in the Family* and *The Mary Tyler Moore Show*. *M*A*S*H* also benefited from *All in the Family*'s production-code transgressions. "*M*A*S*H* capitalized on Norman [Lear]'s expanding network approval," Gelbart has said. "We were able to capitalize on the new spirit that [*All in the Family*] created."[50] Between the new freedom and the boffo lead-in, *M*A*S*H* became a runaway success.

That success ran a strange road. What started out as a vaguely black-humored lark became one of the most self-important shows ever. Over the course of the first two years, *M*A*S*H* changed its emphasis from the playboy doctor theme

("Doctor, I thought you wanted to study Gray's Anatomy, not mine!") to more sober, self-conscious portrayals of men and women under difficult circumstances. ("All I know is what they taught me at command school. There are certain rules about a war. Rule Number One is that young men die, and Rule Number Two is that doctors can't change Rule Number One.") It received wild critical praise as a bastion of humanism on the tube. And it still packed an hour's worth of jokes, one-liners, sitcom goofs, double entendres, and comic double takes into each half-hour episode. How was such a thing possible? The show accomplished it through a simple shift of gears, a tonal transition that transformed banality into irony.

"We joke to keep from crying": such was the justification for the stream of gag lines that passed over the (unseen) bodies upon which the surgeons of the 4077th operated. The camera invariably shot the surgeon from the waist up, his hands working away on what we knew theoretically to be a patient. The gag writing on *M*A*S*H* was first-class, produced as it was by veteran jokesmiths and delivered by Alan Alda with a flippancy that suggested great pain. Irony was his native tongue.

But this was a different species of irony than the bald-faced camp of *Batman,* however, and it is worthwhile to make some distinctions here. *Irony* is defined by Samuel Johnson's dictionary as "a mode of speech in which the meaning is contrary to the words." The grossest example of this would be speech in the stilted, sarcastic manner, with invisible quotation marks hovering around each utterance—for example, the use of phrases like "good men and true," "truth, justice, and the American way," and other old-fashioned pieties by hipsters. *M*A*S*H* had more than its share of this kind of irony, too:

> *Hawkeye:* I just don't know why they're shooting at us. All we want to bring them is democracy and white bread, to transplant the American Dream: freedom, achievement, hyperacidity, affluence, flatulence, technology, tension, the inalienable right to an early coronary sitting at your desk while plotting to stab your boss in the back.[51]

But that wasn't really the irony the show would thrive on, and in fact it grew infrequent after the first season or two. The *M*A*S*H* mode was to write jokes and comic situations that on a less meaning-laden show might be considered pedestrian but that, in the context of a strenuously established premise—"we laugh to keep from crying"—are made to sound brave or even noble.[52] Thus, wrote *Newsweek:* "M*A*S*H is the most moral entertainment on commercial television. It proposes craft against butchery, humor against despair, wit as a defense mechanism against the senseless enormity of the situation."[53] *M*A*S*H* was simultaneously a comedy and also a homily.

The early 1970s needed both. *M*A*S*H*, it will be remembered, premiered in the fall of 1972, at a time when the war was already seven to ten years old, depending on when you chose to date its beginning. It was Vietnam, not Korea, that supplied the setting for *M*A*S*H*, and it was Vietnam, with all its well-known horrors and futility that supplied the moral underpinnings of this slightest of commercial artworks. The standard structure of the series soon became comedy interrupted by the arrival of helicopters bearing the wounded, at which moment all differences and plot problems would be dropped as the cast turned earnest and converged on the landing pad.

Moral *M*A*S*H* was; but never political. Its Korean setting allowed the show to avoid making explicit anti-Vietnam War statements after the fashion of the Smothers Brothers, or Mike Stivic. Its antiwar stance could be inferred easily enough, but who, other than George C. Scott's Patton, was in favor of war? *M*A*S*H* early and often took pains to point out its disengagement from all 1960s-style political protest. Said Larry Gelbart years later, "We wanted to make war the enemy, without ever really saying who was fighting." His favorite line, Gelbart said, was when Corporal Klinger, the cross-dressing clerk, says under fire, "Damn Truman, damn Stalin, damn everybody."[54]

A vague and angry indifference: this apolitical reaction, the aftershock of the 1960s, was to become a dominant theme of the 1970s on TV as throughout American society.

4
"Love Is All Around": Uneasy Footing in the New America, 1972–1974

Of the sweeping political and cultural changes that overtook the country as a result of the great upheavals of the 1960s, none was more immediate or enduring than the newfound status of women. "Women's Lib," as it had come to be known, had emerged as a political factor in the 1960s when, following the example of the civil rights struggle, women began to lobby for their inclusion in societal reforms. Feminism had a long and noble history in America, of course, dating back to the 1840s; but after achieving the vote for women in 1922, the movement had been very quiet for a very long time.[1] Now it was awake again and powerful.

Betty Friedan's *The Feminine Mystique* (1963) had been a spark. The atmosphere of protest and progress had helped greatly as well. By the early 1970s, feminism had affected a sea change in American culture. The subservient place of women within traditional family structures may not have been perceived as stifling by Edith Bunker, but that's only because she had been brainwashed. Everyone knew things had to change—or so it seemed to a vast number of middle-class women. In professional life, too, conditions required redress, as women tended to get the least desirable jobs and those for an inferior wage. Nor were women, like blacks, a minority that could be pacified or repressed. They represented half the population, and their influence, in the private sphere at least, knew no geographic or economic bounds. Naturally, this meant that the support of women was absolutely essential for both parties—there could be no "southern strategy" predicated on the writing-off of women's votes, as President Nixon had done with blacks. Furthermore, the country had been morally galvanized by the civil rights struggle. "Are we to say to the world," President Kennedy had asked in 1962, "and more importantly to each other, that this is the land of the free, except for Negroes; that we have no second-class citizens, except for Negroes; that we have no class or caste system, no ghettos, no master race, except with respect to Negroes?" By the late 1960s, the inexorable logic of Kennedy's rhetoric extended itself to many groups; but women were the largest, with the loudest voice and the most to gain from agitation.

As a result, and partially because of the liberal political climate within the Washington beltway, these first years of the 1970s produced milestone after milestone: the passage of the Equal Rights Amendment by both houses of Congress in 1970; *Roe v. Wade* in 1973; desegregation of public places in New York and elsewhere; the official acceptance by the Government Printing Office of the new honorific "Ms."; and the endorsement of the ERA by the AFL-CIO.

The change wasn't wasted on the culture industry, which exploited it in nearly every medium. Low-grade action films such as *Switchblade Sisters, Get Christie Love!,* and *Coffy* featured emancipated heroines who, black and white, wreaked havoc on the men who would keep them down.[2] Women singer-songwriters such as Carole King, Joni Mitchell, and Carly Simon broke the male stranglehold on confessional/autobiographical rock music that had been in place since Bob Dylan invented the form. Occasionally, they even penned explicitly feminist anthems, the most famous of which, Helen Reddy's 1972 hit "I Am Woman," was one of the year's top singles.

> I am woman, hear me roar,
> In numbers too big to ignore
> And I know too much to lay down and pretend!
> 'Cause I've heard it all before,
> And I've been down there on the floor,
> No one's ever gonna keep me down again!
> Oh, yes!
> I am wise! But it's wisdom born of pain
> Yes, I've paid a price—
> But look how much I've gained
> I am strong! I am invincible!
> I am woman![3]

Of all the media that took up liberated women as the hot new thing, none did so more purposefully than did television, and the sitcom in particular. Women had always been the major target of television advertisers, since traditionally they made the buying decisions for the household, and this was particularly true of advertisers with the largest budgets, such as household goods. The discovery of demographics only accelerated this trend, and the emergence of a class of single working women only encouraged it further. CBS, in particular, rushed into the breach, offering prospective ad buyers a little demographic wheel entitled "Where the Girls Are," with which the indecisive sponsor could look up a product, such as "room vaporizer sprays" or "scouring powder," and find an "index of product usage by adult women" for each of five different age groups. "What can you learn from a woman's age?" asked the wheel rhetorically. "More today than you might suppose. Such as what she buys. What television shows she watches. And what a knowing advertiser can do about it. This wheel shows you what a woman's age means when she buys 91 different things. And the pages inside show how you can apply this handy information to Nielsen's new audience reports by age of lady viewer."[4]

For business purposes, then, the new woman was merely an empowered consumer, a kind of new and improved housewife—"Ms. Smart Shopper." Most women, the networks knew, may have been sympathetic to the movement but still had to buy household cleaners, perfumes, and deodorants, as well as an array of newly invented or improved versions of such. Rather than the perky blonde who makes dirt disappear effortlessly a la Samantha Stevens of *Bewitched,* the new commercial heroine was more like Mary Tyler Moore—harried but capable of coping good-humoredly.

Women were an attractive target for television's predatory energies for several reasons. First and most obvious was their immense consumer power. Second was the recent discovery of demographic wizardry that might be used to demonstrate, however speciously, the effective targeting advertisements might enjoy. But equally important in the creation of realistic women characters was a factor that did not directly involve "the bottom line" but was rather ephemeral, intangible, and rarely articulated: the desire of television producers, executives, and stars to produce meaningful work.

Of all the mass media, television enjoyed the least respect, often being spoken of as a "boob tube" or "idiot box" even by its defenders. Articles might occasionally appear in popular culture journals or *TV Guide* with titles like "There Need Be No Apology, No Lament," but it was taken for granted even by the stoutest of middlebrows that TV consisted largely of froth and sleek fraud. But now, with a newly fragmented audience and a business imperative to, as Ella Taylor puts it, "not . . . dismantle the mass audience but to fine-tune it, focusing on its most lucrative segments," producers were freed to create television shows in which they could invest their own tastes and sensibilities. In some cases, as with Lear, this was a New Deal ethnic liberalism; in others, as with MTM's James Brooks and Allen Burns, a baby-boom-formed sure-handedness unhindered by "boffo" punchlines and the lowest common denominator. In either case, the Lear/MTM standard became golden within the TV industry. The experience of one hapless would-be writer for the low-grade Bud Yorkin series *Carter Country* was typical: his rejection letter explained that, "It's only fair to tell you that as of last week, the company policy is that those few scripts that will not be written in-house will be assigned only to experienced 'All in the Family' and 'Mary Tyler

Moore' writers."[5] In TV, too, prestige means something and perhaps all the more so for the medium's low status in the culture. To achieve commercial success in the process became every producer's dream.

The way seemed clear. There was a model for sophisticated sitcoms, and that model was *The Mary Tyler Moore Show*. From the time of its debut in 1971 onward, sitcom heroes have usually been decent persons trying to make their way— "keeping your head above water," as *Good Times* had it. Although quirky or flawed, the sitcom hero is an audience representative who almost never takes strong religious or ethical stands that might alienate him or her from the vast audience. "Love is all around," this being America, and with a wisecrack and a little ingenuity, harmony can usually be restored despite episodic setbacks.

This was in keeping with the age: the 1960s had not been a good time for high principles, which now suffered from a terminal credibility gap. So the goofy goodwill of Mary Tyler Moore, Rhoda, Chico, Alice, Ann Romano of *One Day at a Time* (1975–1984), and others came to incarnate the assumptions of the 1970s. In the new sitcom consensus, those who would preach the hard line come off as hypocrites or bullies. The title character usually represents the sane center: she or he can usually be counted upon to steer a reasonable middle course, veering away from the Scylla and Charybdis of swingers and puritans, dropouts and martinets.

In many ways, the epitome of this trend was *The Bob Newhart Show,* a creation of MTM alumni that premiered in the fall of 1972. Newhart had been a successful comic in the early 1960s whose laconic low-key humor reverberated with hip Kennedy-era audiences. In his albums *The Button-Down Mind of Bob Newhart* and its sequels, Newhart seemed to mock the conformist WASP persona even as he impersonated it, an act of cool irony years ahead of his more frenetic peers, such as Mort Sahl or Lenny Bruce. Newhart had tapped into the detached mimicry that would be the hallmark of so much progressive 1960s comedy, from the improvisational turns of Mike Nichols and Elaine May to the measured sketch humor of the Second City.

Newhart's masterful stillness was perfect for television. "We're not trying to do Archie Bunker," his producers told him. "We're selling class and wit and charm."[6] In *The Bob Newhart Show,* he was cast as a Chicago psychologist—an ideal construction, given the psychologist's profession of listening with a straight face to other people's absurd notions. (A good part of Newhart's stand-up routine, in fact, consisted of his listening, and responding, to a telephone.) His character, Bob Hartley, was the embodiment of so many social givens of the 1970s— that is, givens of the educated middle class, its target demographic—as to be a kind of sociological primer.

Bob Hartley is the sane center of a constellation of eccentrics. There was the misanthropic Mr. Carlin and the Milquetoastish Mr. Peterson; Howard Borden, the Hartleys' childlike next-door neighbor who depended on Bob and his wife for guidance in every aspect of his life; his office neighbor, the swinging dentist Jerry Robinson; and various zany guest characters. The only people as sane as Bob are his receptionist, Carol, and more importantly, his wife Emily. The Hartleys had the ideal marriage of the 1970s: completely equal, completely secure in their jobs (Emily is a school teacher, later an assistant principal), affluent, enlightened, and childless. Every night, the two would sit up in a king-size bed, whose immaculately turned-down linens looked right out of the Spiegel catalog, and spar mordantly in wry, even tones.

Existing in perfect equilibrium to all those around him and dispensing commonsensical advice, Newhart on the show represented the 1970s version of the eighteenth-century man of sensibility—that is, a centered mind in whom the virtues of the age are embodied. Apolitical, urban, with no ethnic, sexual, religious, or racial grudges, Newhart was the passionless ideal of Christopher Lasch's America, a state in which "the minimal self" guarantees safety and enlightened self-interest ("I'm OK, you're OK") is the rule of the day.[7] *The Bob Newhart Show* was the culmination of the new liberal consensus as it was emerging on television in the early 1970s. With its fine writing, strong female characters, low-key humor, and appealing lead, the show was a critical and ratings success and took its place behind *The Mary Tyler Moore Show* on what is now considered the most dominant lineup in television history, shown in table 4.1.

Table 4.1
1973 Prime-Time Schedule, Saturday Night on CBS

	Program	Rating (overall rank)
8:00	*All in the Family*	31.2 (1)
8:30	*M*A*S*H*	25.7 (4)
9:00	*The Mary Tyler Moore Show*	23.1 (9)
9:30	*The Bob Newhart Show*	22.3 (12)
10:00	*The Carol Burnett Show*	20.2 (26)

The overall Nielsen ratings, even stripped of the demographics that supposedly rendered them irrelevant, reflected this change. Whether or not the audience had a hunger for shows with topical themes, those shows were the best made and most popular shows, the programs made with extra care, the programs that week in and week out had that capacity to surprise that only inspired talent can promise. And the model for this new genre of "quality TV," although superbly represented by *The Bob Newhart Show,* remained *The Mary Tyler Moore Show* itself.

The key to the show as a zeitgeist event was the women's movement. Women had long carried sitcom series, from *I Love Lucy* to *That Girl* in the late 1960s. But men were invariably the bosses in those shows, and rarely would a female sitcom lead choose anything but the (male) domestic ideal for her lot in life. A liberated female lead, on the other hand, might encounter all kinds of conflict in a man's world, conflict that, while it might be played for laughs on one level, could also serve to deepen viewer interest and develop character. In the first episode, when Lou Grant, Mary's new boss at WJM, drops by Mary's apartment, she (and we) expect some sort of sexual harassment, especially when Lou comments on her "caboose." As it turns out, he's a sentimental drunk and merely wants her to type a letter to his wife, Edie. But though Mary handles the situation well, there is a tension that isn't completely dissolved when she lets Lou know he's out of line. There's still much more to learn about both people. Mary's longtime boyfriend, incidentally, appears at the door on the tail end of this scene, but rather than saving the day, he is dismissed from Mary's life in a kind but decisive way. Mary will fend for herself. As the deathless theme song tells us, over external shots of Mary's daily life as a protoyuppie in the big city,

> How will you make it on your own?
> This world is awfully big, and this time girl you're on your own
> But it's time you started living,
> Time you let someone else do the giving!
>
> Love is all around, no need to waste it,
> Love is all around, why don't you take it?
> You're gonna make it after all!

It was the theme song of the Me Decade, even if they did change the first verse after the first season to the more sentimental "Who can turn the world on with her smile?" Even so, Mary Richards was out to build a life for herself. She would not be a man-hungry spinster like Our Miss Brooks, Sally of the old *Dick Van Dyke Show,* or her neighbor Rhoda. Nor would her occupation be secretary, bank teller, or maid—the big three of sitcom women. She was conceived as an independent, motivated woman at the most relevant career her creators could imagine: a TV producer. This situation created rich possibilities, and the MTM writing staff exploited them to the fullest. Television finally was recognizing itself onscreen, other than as a piece of furniture or a plot device to excite laughable hopes of fame and fortune. This germ of self-reflexiveness, so thoughtfully and moderately made use of on *The Mary Tyler Moore Show,* would grow to dominate television in the 1980s. Mary's workplace was a bastion of relevance, a kind of "media drama" different from the ones Norman Lear manufactured from the news.[8]

Mary's home life, too, was liberated. Instead of an uptight pill like Darrin Stevens of *Bewitched,* Major Nelson of *I Dream of Jeannie,* or a wet blanket like Ricky Ricardo, she could go out with a different man every week—again, rich possibilities, both for the writing and for the casting of the best young character actors. Between Mary's home and work life, the MTM writers had the opportunity to create what they liked to call "character comedy." Character comedy came to be known as the house style at MTM, and it defined all of their productions from *The Mary Tyler Moore Show* on. As Tom Carson has observed,

> In sitcoms, MTM's approach has always been quite specific, but its influence has also been so pervasive that it may be hard to remember what an innovation the style originally was. Before *The Mary Tyler Moore Show,* no one believed that a sitcom's foundation had to be in character ensembles, and humor wasn't even necessarily linked to motivation: on even the best pre-MTM sitcoms, with few exceptions, the personalities and interplay were machine-designed mostly to generate the maximum number of generic jokes. . . . After MTM made likeability the key, even the most mechanical sitcoms had to play lip service to the idea of the sitcom as a set of little epiphanies.[9]

Jane Feuer, in her definitive essay on MTM, embroiders upon this distinction by comparing the *Mary Tyler Moore Show* spin-off *Rhoda* with *Maude.* The two successful comedy series—each with a liberated woman lead, each spun off from the parent company's flagship show—typified the essential approaches of MTM and Lear. The Lear approach called, roughly speaking, for a big-mouthed, obnoxious woman who could and would dominate the men around her and in so doing serve as a sounding board for topical themes. Maude was essentially Archie Bunker's opposite, even more so than George Jefferson or Fred Sanford. "Maude," as Feuer observes, "is far more politically astute than Rhoda. She deals with controversial issues such as alcoholism and abortion; she is far more the 'liberated woman' than Rhoda aspires to be. Yet the show *Maude* is structurally simplistic: there is one important dilemma per week that is usually resolved at Maude's expense, the main comedy technique is the insult, and the characters are uni-dimensional and static."[10] *Rhoda,* on the other hand, like *Mary Tyler Moore* before it, internalizes the advances. Rather than an old-fashioned mechanical sitcom festooned with topical themes, insults, and catchphrases ("God will get you for that, Walter"), *Rhoda* offers a "rounder" character, a number of equally individuated supporting characters, and most importantly, a far more naturalistic style than the Punch-and-Judy show/editorial-page hybrid into which the Lear style often devolved.[11]

Such, in any case, was Jane Feuer's observation. Norman Lear probably would have disagreed. Nonetheless, the cold eye of history has seen thirty years of successful programming in the MTM mold, whereas the Lear style, although dominant in its era, is now seen as something of a self-contained phenomenon, an expression of early 1970s culture. Even the most politically conscious situation comedies of the 1990s, such as *Murphy Brown* or *Roseanne,* draw most of their humor from the interplay of a workplace character ensemble, or failing that, a home densely populated with individuated "round" characters, audience representatives of one sort or another. Occasionally, elements of farce intrude in the form of a "zany" character (*Family Matters'* Urkel, *Taxi's* Reverend Jim, *Laverne and Shirley's* Lenny and Squiggy) whose eccentricities can be the subject of "normal" characters' scorn or amusement. The whole arrangement has turned out to be a very dependable machine of its own, and even Lear saw the light early on: the later Lear programs, including *All in the Family's* later seasons, feature much more "character-driven" humor and much less overt politics than the didactic early years.

This gradual transformation of the sitcom in the 1970s, from a "relevant" comedy whose themes were borrowed from the front pages to a "quality" ensemble approach whose connections to the outside arise from naturalistic writing and acting echoes the general disengagement from the public sphere that marked the decade. The MTM style was first and foremost about private life. Even the trademark workplace settings were largely there to foster relationships, a "family" that the viewer came to know and care about.[12] The Lear shows, on the other hand, as Michael Arlen noted in 1974, "depend mainly neither on jokes nor on funny stories, nor even on family . . . but on the new contemporary consciousness of 'media.'"

> By this I mean that the base of the Lear programs is not so much the family and its problems as it is the commonality that seems to have been created largely by television itself, with its outpouring of casual worldliness and its ability to propel—as with some giant, invisible electric-utility feeder line—vast, undifferentiated quantities of topical information, problem discussions, psychiatric terminology, and surface political and social involvement through the national bloodstream.[13]

Nothing could be further from the atmosphere of the MTM shows. On *The Mary Tyler Moore Show,* for example, it is the people in front of the camera, the ones in the public sphere, anchorman Ted Baxter and "Happy Homemaker" Sue Ann Niven, who are the phonies, the cartoonish outsiders. The people Mary really relates to are her friends: producer Lou Grant, coworker Murray Slaughter, and neighbors Rhoda Morganstern and Phyllis Lindstrom. As portrayed by Ted Knight, Baxter is an unctuous fathead, whose fatuousness is always revealing it-

self from behind his anchorman's grave facade. Sue Ann is an even more significant figure, the show's one acknowledgment of TV's former artifice. WJM's
"Happy Homemaker," Sue Ann is a poison-pen caricature of the all-competent
suburban mom of Eisenhower-era sitcoms. (Early on in the first season, it is
mentioned that Sue Ann has been with WJM for thirteen years—dating her TV
presence to 1957.)[14] Sue Ann's primness, immobile hair, and impossibly unhip
TV image—typical show themes include "Salute to Fruit" and "What's All This
Fuss about Famine?"—highlight her identity as a send-up of pre-Mary television.
(Betty White, a prototypical 1950s matron, was selected to play a "sickening,
yucky, icky Betty White-type.")[15] Unlike the passive Ted, however, who is too
stupid to respond to the put-downs doled out to him by the newsroom staff, Sue
Ann reverses the stereotype: to highlight her incongruity in Mary's universe, the
MTM writers decided to make Sue Ann Niven offscreen venomously acerbic,
as well as making her a man-chaser with, in Ella Taylor's polite phrase, "a vora-
cious and undiscriminating sexual appetite."[16] Always getting the final word, Sue
Ann's fixed smile never changes as she dispenses insults that cut everyone around
her to the quick and that as often as not have a strong sexual venom to them: "I
know!" she says to Mary, presenting her with a food sculpture, "Why don't you
put it in your bedroom? I'm sure you must need something in there to relieve
the tedium."

Both Ted and Sue Ann are exceptions, "flat" characters in a "round" setting
put there to liven things up. But they were atypical. The MTM writers decided
early on that their shows "would never write in a gratuitous putdown just because it was funny. . . . The characters have a lot of affection for each other and
we don't want to destroy that."[17] Even the emasculated Murray, who puts down
Ted and is put down by Sue Ann, has a tenuous independent existence apart from
these encounters. And so also of all the other lead characters in MTM shows of
the early 1970s, most of which were spun off from *The Mary Tyler Moore Show*:
Rhoda (1974–1978), *Phyllis* (1975–1977), *The Betty White Show* (1977–1978), and,
eventually, *Lou Grant* (1977–1982).

The Lear shows, on the other hand, were unable to contain their derisive impulses. While *The Mary Tyler Moore Show* was able to sublimate it into secondary characters like Sue Ann, the rancor of all against all marked *All in the Family, Maude, The Jeffersons,* and *Sanford and Son.* As Michael Arlen noted in 1974,
"Anger as stage business runs through nearly all Norman Lear's comedies, but it
is a curious, modern, undifferentiated anger, which serves to provide the little
dramas with a kind of energizing dynamic—sometimes the only dynamic."[18]

Depending as they did on one-liners and sexually veiled put-downs, TV writers
were often forced to fill the gaping maw of weekly shows with what was coming
to be called "negative energy." Good vibrations may have been highly prized in

society, but they tend to not be very entertaining to watch. Punch and Judy is the essence of TV comedy, whether in a situation comedy, a muscular dystrophy telethon, or an elderly comedian's "goodwill tour" of a combat zone. The genius of the Mary concept was to contain it so well within the confines of ensemble and middle-class liberal consensus. Almost all the most successful TV comedies through the 1970s and 1980s—*Taxi* (1978–1983), *Mork and Mindy* (1978–1981), *Cheers* (1982–1993), *Family Ties* (1982–1989), and so on—copied it, and the sociology of these shows helps to define the late 1970s, in my view.[19] But the MTM model was hardly typical of TV in the first half of the decade. The process of remaking itself was violent, fragmentary, and essentially ad hoc; the early and middle 1970s are interesting because the streamlining of the new mass culture (of which *The Mary Tyler Moore Show, M*A*S*H,* and the other shows discussed above are such seminal examples) was still incomplete, accompanied by frequent breakdowns, lapses in taste, outbreaks of naked rancor. (In this, it happened to reflect the sitting president, who also suffered from public relations problems.)

More than coincidence allows the analogy. The political climate at the three networks (at least in their entertainment divisions) in the early 1970s was no longer what it had been in the late 1960s. Having been belatedly convinced of the centrality of their young, disaffected audience, the network programmers gave the go-ahead to programs that certainly would have been flagged by the standards and practices office in the earlier era. The release of TV from these artificial constraints was liberating, but with it inevitably came corrosive forces—sleazy energies that overran all of television during the next decade, corrupting every venue before finally being brought into line in the 1980s.

Consider *The Sonny and Cher Comedy Hour,* one of the definitive Nixon-era TV programs. As posthippie idealism had curdled under Nixon-Agnew, its dressings—long hair, outrageous fashions, idioms like *man* and *groovy*—flourished. This was in keeping with television's original courting of the young, which had depended so heavily on appearances. The spirit of Haight-Ashbury and "the movement" may have been extinguished, as so many radicals at the time claimed; but it was unlikely, given the fetish for youth and things antiestablishment, that television would mishandle the baby boom indefinitely. Hippies were to remain forever figures of fun, moving from tatterdemalion "flower children" to bedraggled anachronisms seemingly overnight; but the tendency of TV in the early to mid-1970s, however, was to domesticate their culture for home viewing.

The Sonny and Cher Show was the first and most sinister example of this, years before *Don Kirchner's Rock Concert, Saturday Night Live, WKRP in Cincinnati,* and other 1970s shows sympathetic to the former youth culture. In 1965, a husband and wife singing team called Sonny and Cher had enjoyed a top ten hit

Sonny and Cher as hippieish
pop stars in the 1960s . . .

. . . and in the 1970s, as the first
couple of TV

with "I Got You Babe," an us-against-the-world anthem about grown-ups mocking the couple's penniless love:

> Don't let them say your hair's too long
> 'Cause I don't care, with you I can't go wrong!
> Then put your little hand in mine
> There ain't no hill or mountain we can't climb . . .
> I got you babe!
> I got you babe![20]

By the late 1960s, Sonny and Cher were just another act on the road, playing small to midsize venues, long in the tooth for hippie lovebirds. Then Sonny had the idea of retooling the act. They would no longer be idealistic ragamuffins. Now they would become the Steve and Eydie of the hip set and would take their act to Vegas. "Cher, go out and buy a dress," he told his wife. "A long dress and spend a lot of money. It's time for you to start looking like a woman, and it's time for us to start appealing to adults. That's where the money is."[21] After new CBS programming head Fred Silverman saw the duo's nightclub act, he gave the couple a shot as a summer variety series in 1971, on Sunday night—family night. "They could be another George and Gracie," Silverman thought.[22] The show proved successful enough that the network brought it back as a second season replacement in December, running it at 10:00 on Monday night. The show was a hit, rising in the ratings to a peak of eight overall in 1973–1974 (with highly attractive demographics.)

The format of the show was rigid. Sonny and Cher would appear on a stage, Sonny usually wearing a velvet leisure suit or other postformal getup, and Cher, a revealing dress by designer Bob Mackie, whose signature style involved weirdly constructed, glittery nightclub gowns that torqued and twisted their way around Cher's slim, tanned torso. Sonny was short and homely, a contrast to the tall, glamorous Cher, and after an introductory musical number, the two would banter back and forth. Sonny would make a crack about Cher's big nose or low intelligence; and Cher, with a knowing eye on the camera, would come back with a wry riposte putting down Sonny's size, manhood, or ethnicity. "It was hip and kooky," Sonny Bono remembers, "but the best and most memorable part was the opening dialogue between Cher and me."[23]

The show was mildly licentious and filled with double entendres and showbiz hipness of the Vegas type. The entire production was suffused with a certain playful irony—"hey, we have our own show, let's have some fun with it." This was in stark contrast to their variety progenitors, like the Smothers Brothers, who for all their boyish irreverence were in dead earnest about producing a polished product. Sonny and Cher giggled at their own jokes, refused to take their skits seriously, refused to kowtow to "the great audience" the way more straitlaced entertainers did. They muffed their lines, ad-libbed often, and (the key to the show) really *related* to each other.

Thus did the informal atmosphere of the rock scene come to television by way of Las Vegas. As rock music began to be accepted by the Establishment as a fait accompli, television accommodated itself and rock did likewise. Professionalism went the way of live drama, and the proscenium separating audience from performer became only a matter of talent and/or good luck. Thus, the video archives of such buttoned-up interview programs as *The Mike Douglas Show, The Dick Cavett Show, The David Susskind Show,* and so on often feature mumbling, incoherent "celebrities" who looked high. Singers would forget the words to their songs. Comedians would "crack up" at their own jokes. This would have been scandalous or at least disastrous as late as the 1960s, but programs like *The Sonny and Cher Hour* eased the audience into the new culture, much as the Lear and MTM programs had eased them out of the old one.

The Sonny and Cher Comedy Hour was truer than most to the culture however, and it continued to be so as the Nixon nightmare wore on. The show was doing very well, but the marriage was not. Like another conspicuous TV marriage, that of the real-world Louds of PBS's *An American Family,* the Bonos' bond dissolved onscreen. The jokes came across less lightheartedly, Cher's deadpan put-downs ("if you've seen one naked goombah, you've seen them all") seeming more and more ill-spirited. When the couple separated in February 1974, the TV audience was treated to two, equally appalling solo efforts: *The Sonny Comedy Revue* on ABC, and CBS's *Cher.* Even more depressing, because even more expressive of the marital rancor, was CBS's effort at a professional reunion: *The Sonny and Cher Show,* which debuted in 1975. In the meantime, Cher had married Southern blues rocker Gregg Allman, a hard-living reprobate whose brawls and drug abuse reflected badly on Cher and even worse on Sonny, whose humiliating banter with Cher had always been predicated on the saving notion that the two really loved each other. There was nothing funny about it when both knew (as the audience did, too) that she was going home to another man—let alone Gregg Allman! This was an unconscionable lapse of taste, even by TV standards, which only network gold could have tempted the erstwhile pair into trying. Neither had their heart in the project, and Sonny could often be seen reading song lyrics off the TelePrompTer in a dispirited way. Cher remained professional, but it was a sad business all around and was mercifully canceled by CBS after a little over a year.

The forces of entropy apparent in the short life of the Sonny and Cher series were emblematic of larger forces informing American life. The women's movement, the fall of Nixon, and the overthrow of traditional attitudes regarding marriage, race, class, and deviance all combined with the largest and most acutely felt change of all—the collapse of the once-mighty American economy. The stylistic innovations of *All in the Family* and *The Mary Tyler Moore Show* were decisively engineered projects arising out of the network's perennial lust for ratings, "buzz," and advertising revenue. Now, shows for an unhappy culture began to come off the assembly line.

Naturally, this required some retooling, which finished off the Western for good. Only the antiquated *Gunsmoke,* kept alive by special order of William S. Paley, kept its head above water into mid-decade. The only Western to debut in the early 1970s was really an "Eastern": ABC's *Kung Fu* (1972–1975). But *Kung Fu* was a Nixon-era show through and through, as it had to be. (Its syndication ads portentously announced "a new direction in human values," adding "and audience values" in smaller bold type underneath.) It followed a half-Chinese monk, Kwai Chang Caine, as he trekked across the old West in search of his brother. Invariably, whiskey-swilling louts, hardhats in Stetsons, hector him with racial epithets and try to gang up on him. However, Caine, portrayed with sleepy-eyed calm by David Carradine, is a master of martial arts and disposes of them with slow-motion ease. When the backward Westerners present him with more difficult problems, the meditative Caine remembers the lessons of his Buddhist masters, who called him "Grasshopper" and taught him the paradoxical wisdom of the natural world. Caine solves everybody's problems, much as all wandering Western heroes do, but he is clearly too good for the land he is in. These are the kind of people that would set fire to huts, and do. *Kung Fu* summed up in one gratifying package American self-loathing, the 1960s' infatuation with the Orient, and the characteristically American desire to have the best of both worlds: Caine is a pacifist as pure as Gandhi or Daniel Berrigan, but he can kick anybody's ass, and does.[24] It was a fitting epitaph to the Western genre after Vietnam.

The variety show, too, once the show business embodiment of the "vital center," was now a dead item, despite periodic attempts to revive it. It, too, was a casualty of the 1960s. The entropy of the period was pervasive and enveloped all genres. *The Sonny and Cher Hour,* with its exposed viscera, is edifying as a kind of Visible Man doll, of the sort used in health classes. But the "great undoing" is better and more subtly shown by the plethora of police shows that flooded the airwaves in the 1973–1974 season and by *their* powerful ambiguities. Situation comedies would continue to dominate the Nielsen top twenty-five, rounded out by a handful of dramas and adventure shows. But the police drama was ubiquitous during the 1970s and as a single genre dominated programming more than any other form. Unlike the Western from which it descended, the police drama betrayed a culture that had lost its moorings.

The fall of 1973 saw ten new police dramas, a record high. Police shows had become, in recent years, a bread-and-butter standby of network programming.

Although seldom attracting the vast, loyal audiences of the situation comedies that dominated the Nielsens year in and year out, they could be depended upon to draw respectable ratings. By the 1973 season, however, the police format was growing in numbers and ratings strength even as Westerns, variety shows, war comedies, and other old genres were becoming extinct. In 1965, only two shows that could vaguely be classified as police shows were on prime time, out of a total of ninety-eight series; ten years later, police shows accounted for almost *one third* of all network series: nineteen out of a total of fifty-eight shows.

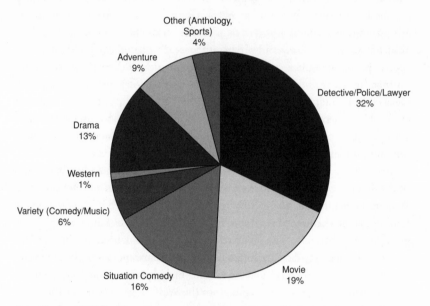

Distribution of Prime-Time Programming for 1975. Police dramas take over the airwaves in the mid-1970s.

What was responsible for this crime-show boom? Ed Papazian, in *Medium Rare,* points to public unrest: "the public's receptivity to contemporary law-and-order themes," he writes, "revived in the mid-1960s as the nation was rocked by urban ghetto unrest, radical protests, and rising crime rates. Responding to the concerns aroused by such disturbances, the networks encouraged the studios to develop new law enforcer entries."[25]

Such programming was no departure, ideologically, from the crime shows of the 1950s. In the intervening years, however, the form of the crime drama had changed significantly. The genre had passed from radio to television in the latter medium's early years more or less unchanged: such programs as *Gangbusters* (1952) or *Man Against Crime* (1949–1956) were distillates of the conventions of cheap fiction and B-movies, in which tough-guy heroes bulled their way to jus-tice through rudimentary police work, fights, and shoot-outs, amid much gaudy patter. Although not so brutal as Mickey Spillane's spectacularly sadistic Mike Hammer, their heroes were cut from similar cloth and offered the audience crude and predictable action.

Jack Webb's *Dragnet* (1952–1959) changed that. As creator, producer, writer, and star, Webb brought a distinct vision to bear on the detective hero, remaking the genre into a conservative ode to bureaucratic process, where before there had been urban anarchy and the law of the jungle.[26] *Dragnet*'s Sergeant Joe Friday was neither a violent man nor an emotional one. A dedicated civil servant, he had no desire to exchange blows or gunshots with criminals, nor did he take their misdeeds personally. Law and order incarnate, Friday existed to enforce "the book," having little interest in anything other than the orderly process of police work, scientifically understood and executed with single-minded devotion. Poker-faced and methodical, he considered himself a cog in the vast and inexorable machine of justice operated by the City of Los Angeles: "My name is Friday. I carry a badge," he would typically say in voice-over as the show began; it seemed to sum up his existence.

Friday was not an inhumane or indifferent person, in the sense of not "car-ing." On the contrary, he was a martyr to his vision, an underpaid ascetic with no visible personal life and no interest in anybody else's. He lived to serve the law. The citizens he encountered were either lawbreakers or could be of some service in tracking lawbreakers: "just the facts, ma'am," he would interrupt, when frivo-lous citizens threatened to communicate with him on a personal level.

Dragnet was a sophisticated show. Its dour hero was an unlikely competition for the he-men of competing shows, but *Dragnet* became TV's first great police show success in 1951. The distance between the character of Friday and the auteur Webb was not so far, the latter informing the show with all the loving detail of police work the former could hope for. The method, jargon, and bureaucratic channels of a modern police station were the show's true subject. Such phrases as "can you give me an M.O.?" or "book him on a 358" entered public conscious-ness for the first time, as Friday's narration offered the viewer a guided tour of police duty, complete with precise, log-style entries: "it was 3:55. We were work-ing the day watch out of Homicide."[27]

And yet, there was more to *Dragnet* that mere documentary-style veracity. It was an act of ingenious artistry that a moralism as utopian as Mike Hammer's came disguised as a glamourless dispatch from the real world. An elaborate mecha-nism furthered this illusion: each episode began with the announcement "the story you are about to hear is true. Only the names have been changed to pro-tect the innocent." But there could be little doubt that the innocence referred to was by no means legal innocence. It was innocence in some absolute sense. Those who were innocent were set on Friday's right, and those who were not, on his left. The signature martial music followed, DUM de DUM DUM, and Friday's voice-over would then begin. Friday, every bit as much as Mike Hammer, was the work of a gifted fabulist.

That this was not apparent to everybody was a measure of the times. In any case, *Dragnet* was easily imitable and set the tone for police shows throughout the 1950s and early 1960s. Other, less successful shows such as *M-Squad* featured dedicated, humorless professionals, even if they eschewed *Dragnet's* no-action format. By 1965, however, the genre was in decline, and only one representative survived on network TV: the Webb-inspired *The F.B.I.*, another "true to life" series, in which stern operatives under the paranoid direction of "the Chief" stalked down malfeasance with emotionless rigor. *The F.B.I.* never caught on until the 1967–1968 season, when it became a favorite of alarmed silent majoritarians. By that time, however, it had to compete with a revamped *Dragnet,* which was given a second life in color, as Sergeant Friday faced crazed hippies and drug gurus, along with the usual misguided felons. *Dragnet '67* was, as David Marc and others have attempted to argue, successful with a broad audience largely *because* it was so absurdly militant and old-fashioned.[28] Far less entertaining was Webb's attempt to "go young" with *Adam-12* (1968–1975), a series about two dutiful, young patrolmen. *Adam-12* enjoyed the loyalty of older viewers, but it attempted to rehabilitate youth by offering them unlikely young role models in the straighter-than-straight officers Reed and Malloy.[29] Meanwhile, ABC's *The Mod Squad* was monopolizing the attention of young viewers with its antiestablishment rhetoric and alienated heroes.

Throughout the late 1960s and early 1970s, a new genre came into being that tended to synthesize both approaches. A series of detective and police shows were emerging that portrayed police officers as dedicated professionals and in many cases as the agents of morality. However, in these new programs, such as *Ironside* (1967–1975), *Cannon* (1971–1976), and *Columbo* (1971–1977), the heroes tended to be outsiders, individuals with special claims on the viewer's sympathy. In one way or another, all of these men were a concession to the viewing public's disenchantment with straight arrows, as the failure of two 1971 Webb series, *The D.A.* and *O'Hara,* demonstrated.

Ironside was, of the three, the strangest combination of old and new. The victim of an assassination attempt, the crippled "police genius" Robert Ironside sat, wheelchair-bound, directing three young operatives in the battle against crime: one black, one white, and one blonde. Played by Raymond Burr, fresh from eight years of uninterrupted triumph as the brilliant attorney Perry Mason, Ironside operated as a kind of prime mover around which youthful idealism might safely orbit. So prone to youthful error were his three charges that the omniscient Ironside had to constantly correct them, dispensing investigative insights and moral wisdom *ex cathedra* from his wheelchair. That the authority-figure Ironside should be immobile and unmanned, while at the same time maintaining his power and superiority, was a paradox that seemed to please both sides of the generation gap. In any case, the show's success in 1967 and 1968 provoked a rash of flawed or unconventional loner detectives. A number of these debuted in 1971, the year of Robert Wood's television reformation.

Cannon was fat, old, and friendless. With neither coworkers, a love interest, a longstanding nemesis, nor even a friend on the force, the show's hero was unique in detective annals. Cannon solved cases only for princely sums, which he squandered on such solo and unwholesome pleasures as elaborate meals and fine wines. Unable to threaten anyone physically, the corpulent sleuth drove around in an immense Lincoln Continental, getting his man with the aid of able-bodied policemen. *Columbo* was rumpled and eccentric, a slovenly man who drove around in a beat-up Peugeot and rambled on during police interviews about his home life. Invariably, the murderer, an accomplished person of some sort—a surgeon, matador, famous chef, conductor, or admiral—underestimated Columbo, who was for all his eccentricities an even more brilliant "police genius" than Ironside. This superbly written show, which was refined down to an unvarying structure early in the series' history, would then consist of a cat-and-mouse game with Columbo pestering the criminals, tricking them into verbal slips, irritating them, playing to their arrogance, and then at the end of the ninety-minute program, arresting them for their crime and (more importantly) punishing them for hubris. *Longstreet* (1971–1972) was blind. *Sarge* (1971–1972) was an activist priest. *Barnaby Jones* (1971–1977) was old, featuring a refurbished Buddy Ebsen, former patriarch of the Beverly Hillbillies.

By 1973, the outsider cop show was beginning to coalesce as an expression of mass ambivalences. What had begun as a programming gimmick was beginning to acquire real ideological weight. For one thing, the detective was beginning to assume an ethnic identity, which brought with it much more of a positive valence than the mannerisms and handicaps that had previously individuated TV cops. Moreover, the TV cop was beginning to chafe much more dramatically against "the system" that employed him. Although private eyes had traditionally operated in a vaguely adversarial relationship with the police, generally intrapolice conflicts had been matters of a bad apple or martinet, corrected by the end of the episode.

"The Marcus-Nelson Murders" was different. The two-hour pilot for what would become the *Kojak* series (1973–1978) introduced viewers to Theo Kojak, a bald, Greek NYPD detective who sucked lollipops and battled the police establishment.[30] Appalled by the railroading of a black youth, Kojak after a lengthy trial and much legwork proves the boy to be innocent of the double murder he was accused of; determining to salvage "law and order" prestige from the case, however, the police and prosecutors dig up another baseless charge, this time sending the boy away for rape. The end. Kojak had been defeated in his maiden voyage, but a virile, contrarian place inside "the system" would be his for years to come.[31]

The detective hero of the mid-1970s followed Kojak's lead. Working against the system as well as against the criminals, he was doubly oppositional, doubly angst-ridden, doubly full of ire. Just as anger was becoming the dominant theme music to the Lear comedies, rancorous police officers were fulminating on the other channels. They were mad as hell, and they weren't going to take it anymore.

Kojak was Greek. *Toma,* another 1973 debut, was a foul-mouthed Italian cop who terrorized pimps and street criminals in Newark, New Jersey, site of race riots a few years earlier. *Toma* was too brutal to last, but the real-life character it was based on inspired another Italian cop show, *Baretta* (1975–1978), which was an enormous hit. *Delvecchio* (1976–1977) was even more ethnic, covering two bases as an Italian played by a Jew, Judd Hirsch. *Nakia* (1974), an ABC entry airing after *Kung Fu,* was Native American and walked the line between his tribal loyalties and his duties as a New Mexico policeman. The black cop/private eye had obvious reasons for bucking the system, so NBC's *Shaft* (1973–1974) and ABC's *Get Christie Love!* (1974–1975) featured black protagonists borrowed from stylish, ultraviolent "blaxpoitation" films that did well with young and urban viewers. (NBC, in an attempt to buck the trend, offered the Milquetoastish *Tenafly* (1973–1974), a devoted, utterly deracinated detective and family man. *Tenafly* was shown once a month for a season, then dropped.)

All these series tended to follow the basic conventions of police shows, but the new atmosphere, along with a commitment to on-location filming in gritty urban environments—particularly New York—led to a changed role for the TV police show. The Webb-inspired series had been essentially reassuring and consensual; the loners had been a reaction to that. The ethnic heroes went a step further, adopting an antiestablishment posture that appealed to a large section of the populace. The Establishment took quite a beating in the early 1970s. Spiro Agnew's conviction on graft charges, the endless war in Vietnam and its unsatisfactory conclusion, and, of course, Watergate all helped to midwife a cop for whom authority rested only in his own integrity. The settings of police shows represented this disillusion with authority: the station house was no longer an immaculate planning center but an overburdened, overage environment in which police detectives stood around wearing rolled up shirtsleeves and shoulder harnesses, their jackets draped limply on swivel chairs.

The cop on the beat received the richest literary characterization in the work of Joseph Wambaugh. Wambaugh was a former cop whose brilliantly realized novels of police life had been well received and widely read. In 1973, Wambaugh brought his warts-and-all style to two different TV projects. *Police Story* was an anthology that focused each week on a different character. The freedom of having a hero who didn't have to be back on the job each week allowed Wambaugh to experiment with different themes, darker outcomes, and most importantly, to bypass the cat-and-mouse inevitability of capture that trivialized all cop shows.

Wambaugh's heroes tended to be lower-level working-class men and women who did their job for all its faults and all theirs. And this was the theme of his other project in 1973, a miniseries called *The Blue Knight*. Centering on an aging beat cop, it starred William Holden as Bumper Morgan, a patrolman on the verge of retirement. Over its four-night run, *The Blue Knight* followed its weathered hero through a case that was ostensibly about the murder of a prostitute, but whose real theme was a man's attempts to fend off age, and (again) the need for a man to find his way in a world of moral twilight. Returning in full-fledged series format, Morgan wearily carried on, working to keep order in his inner-city environment. There, he was a kind of community figure, protecting his ghetto charges even when they were technically breaking the law.

The Blue Knight's combination of mission and cynicism was typical of the hybrid vigor of early 1970s programming. Again and again on television in this transitional period, with the social and political scene outside it in unprecedented flux, one sees strange tensions, contradictions, accommodations. Police shows are vastly popular, but the police tend to be loners, ethnics, and/or cripples, with "the system" taking almost as much abuse as the criminals. The egalitarian rhetoric of feminism and minority rights moves to the center of sitcom life but leads to a bumper crop of racial epithets, licentiousness, and regressive phenomena like the Jimmie Walker fad. The "hip" youth/drug/rock music culture begins to be mainstreamed via television, at the cost of its own identity and, eventually, a terminal encounter with mass acceptance and formless, omnivorous showbiz. The period gave birth to strange crossbreedings, creative and fluid responses. *Barney Miller* (1975–1981) was an ensemble sitcom made up of ethnic cops; *Rhoda* (1974–1979), about Mary Richard's spinster neighbor, enjoyed a successful run of its own but lost much of its audience when Rhoda found a happy marriage. (It alienated the remnant when the producers crassly divorced her in a last-ditch attempt to recover lost viewers.) Even the Richard Nixon show was taking new forms, as audiences were pummelled with interminable Watergate hearings and the terminus of the war that, as much as anything, defined the era now coming to a vexed, ambivalent, and thoroughly conflicted close.

With the culture and conflicts of the 1960s attenuated and politics having discredited itself for years to come, it would fall to television, by default, to pick up the pieces.

5
"Sunday, Monday, Happy Days . . . Tuesday, Wednesday, Happy Days": Return to Normalcy, 1975–1977

"Our long national nightmare is over," President Ford told the nation on 9 August 1974. He may have been speaking prematurely; recent historiography suggests that Ford's decision to pardon Nixon on 8 September and so spare the country an endless impeachment trial may have done more harm than good in the long run.[1] But there was little doubt that Nixon's exile to private life, though leaving numerous toxins in the body politic, provided longed-for closure. By the summer of 1974, and throughout Ford's remaining term, having an unimaginative party functionary as chief executive helped to dampen the passions of Watergate. Ford was himself conscious of his role. "I do not want a honeymoon," the incoming president told a joint session of Congress. "I want a good marriage."[2]

Declaring himself "a Ford, not a Lincoln," the staid new president oversaw a burnt-out America in which private concerns utterly overwhelmed public ones, at terrible cost to both. Lowered expectations about politics combined, very unhappily, with sky-high expectations of personal fulfillment. The 1960s were clearly and unmistakably a closed book: their two great causes, the Vietnam War and the civil rights struggle, had found their end points in the fall of Saigon and the Boston busing war. The image of South Vietnamese refugees hanging from the last helicopter to leave the U.S. embassy was brought to the nation by the same TV cameras that had chronicled the war since its inception; images of angry Bostonians protesting forced integration in what had traditionally been America's most liberal and progressive city likewise carried great symbolic weight. "We're seeing a national backlash against the movement toward economic and racial equality," said Vernon Jordan of the National Urban League.[3] No one disagreed with him.

Many observers went even further. Social critic Philip Slater, in his influential book *The Pursuit of Loneliness,* wrote, "Our society is much divided. There are fewer and fewer things that people agree about. The furor of the sixties has died down, but the conflicts that caused it persist. The bitterness has merely been diluted by despair."[4] If Slater had any doubt about the consequences of this, Christopher Lasch didn't. His 1978 book *The Culture of Narcissism* was a tour de force jeremiad, built of equal parts history, social psychology, and hard-edged social criticism. "After the political turmoil of the sixties," writes Lasch, "Americans have retreated to purely personal preoccupations." This expressed itself in new "lifestyles," such as

> getting in touch with their feelings, eating health food, taking lessons in ballet or belly-dancing, immersing themselves in the wisdom of the East, jogging, learning how to "relate," overcoming the "fear of pleasure." Harmless in themselves, these pursuits, elevated to a program and wrapped in the rhetoric of authenticity and awareness, signify a retreat from politics and a repudiation of the recent past.
>
> Indeed Americans seem to wish to forget not only the sixties, the riots, the new left, the disruptions on college campuses, Vietnam, Watergate, and the Nixon presidency, but their entire collective past.[5]

You didn't need an eminent historian to tell you what the mood was. It was expressed explicitly everywhere.

> I don't want to be a candidate
> For Vietnam or Watergate
> All I wanna do is
> Bicycle! Bicycle!
> I want to ride my bicycle[6]

sang the rock group Queen in their 1977 hit "Bicycle Races."

Radical sentiments of the Nixon era seemed in full retreat on almost every front. Draft protesters were returning home, although few took advantage of President Ford's ungenerous offer of conditional amnesty. An Ohio jury ruled against the Kent State survivors' suit against the National Guard in 1975. Jane Albert, the second most famous of the radical fugitives still in hiding (hostage-turned-guerrilla heiress Patty Hearst was the first) turned herself in. Albert's imprisoned lover was dead, Albert insisted, "and so was the movement." Hearst surrendered a few weeks later and was tried and convicted for bank robbery.

"The Sixties," "the Movement," "Consciousness III," "the Vietnam era," "the age of Aquarius": endlessly labeled, the twelve-year period coming to a close in 1975 was the most singular since the Depression, with the assassination of John

Kennedy marking its generally agreed-upon beginning and with a number of candidates for its end, none later than the fall of Saigon. By 1975, most of what had made the period so remarkable—the counterculture, minority rights, drugs, sex, rock and roll, and so on—had been thoroughly assimilated. Veterans of the counterculture disagreed on what this meant. Was this the "repressive tolerance" that Herbert Marcuse had written of, a pleasure-granting gambit by which the status quo would be preserved for the elite? Or had the 1960s, with its rhetoric of love and liberation, actually made headway in partially liberating a puritan America from its narrowness and repression? Certainly, the tokens of hippie life were now squarely in the American mainstream: married couples in small towns were carrying on like nineteenth-century libertines. Marijuana use was a given among the young. Drugged-out celebrities often appeared on TV talk shows, heavy-lidded and rambling or hyperkinetic and giggly. Sammy Davis Jr. appeared in public with a tiny gold cocaine spoon around his neck. Such venerable institutions as the presidency, anticommunism, and the economy were now laughingstocks. Higher education was in political and intellectual purgatory: it would spend the next thirty years trying to acclimate itself to the 1960s and its armies of sanctimonious students, many of whom would become faculty and administration. Certainly, the economic and political support of the cold war was gone, and the "ivory tower" of gentleman-scholars was no longer acceptable even as an ideal.

No less a personage than the president himself would sum up the impact of the 1960s in one of his most memorable addresses. "We were sure ours was a nation of the ballot, not the bullet," Jimmy Carter told the nation in 1979,

> until the murders of John Kennedy and Robert Kennedy and Martin Luther King, Jr. We were taught that our armies were always invincible and our causes were always just, only to suffer the agony of Vietnam. We respected the Presidency as a place of honor until the shock of Watergate. We remember when the phrase "sound as a dollar" was an expression of absolute dependability, until 10 years of inflation began to shrink our dollar and our savings. . . .
>
> These wounds are still very deep. They have never been healed.

This from the president himself! But the 1970s was the period in which these shocks were, if not healed, than at least absorbed, stabilized. That was the least America could do. If anything, things were getting worse. The nation's newfound impotence was highlighted by the OPEC boycott, in which a handful of tiny, backward, plutocratic nations enforced their will on the United States without fear of retribution. Such was to become the norm in the post–Vietnam War world, but it was upon the already frazzled consciousness of the 1970s that OPEC impacted.

The year 1976 was supposed to be one of national affirmation and pride. Instead, as Norman Lear would say, in his appearance before a Congressional subcommittee: "I feel, maybe because of this bicentennial celebration, but I feel that this country is searching around for new purposes and new meaning, and we have gone through a terrible trauma; Vietnam and Watergate and a complete loss of respect for those who are to be our leaders—as individuals and as models."[7]

Nothing "our leaders" could do was likely to change that. The Norman Lear programs, the MTM studios ensemble programs, even the postauthoritarian "loner cop" shows of the early 1970s had done their part in both exploiting and reflecting contemporary unease. At the very least, disaffection with old models had been taken for granted by programmers made. But then that changed. After 1974, there was a broad retreat from controversy and "relevant" programming; the Ford years enveloped television like cascading billows of cotton. Television's second coming ended with Nixon's; its Watergate was the controversy over NBC's *Born Innocent* in September 1974.

Born Innocent was a typical TV movie of the era. In an increasingly competitive atmosphere, all three networks had come to rely upon specials and movies to goose ratings, as well as to counterprogram against popular series. Given the cultural pressures on series evolution, the pressure on TV movies to be controversial and titillating was that much stronger. TV movies have no built-in loyal audience and often go up against series that do. So the TV movie, the bawdy celebrity "roast," the Las Vegas spectacular, and other unwholesome productions tend to represent the fringe of respectability. Such was not the case, as it happened, with *Born Innocent,* which was produced by Richard Rosenberg and Robert Christiansen, who earlier that year had been behind the highly lauded *Autobiography of Miss Jane Pittman.* The story, which featured a post-*Exorcist* Linda Blair as a fourteen-year-old inmate of a juvenile facility for girls, was handled in a mature, restrained way for the most part. Only the climactic final scene, in which a gang of girls rapes Blair with a plunger handle, crying "Now you're one of us!" seemed over the line. A few days later, however, a teenage girl was raped in a similar way in California, and her parents sued NBC for having inspired the crime. Years later, NBC would win the case, but the publicity at the time was disastrous and all the more so for inspiring yet another wave of protest against "sex and violence" on the airwaves.

Glad to have something to distract from Watergate, the House and Senate committees in charge of the FCC's budget responded to the vigorous lobbying efforts of citizen's groups and ordered the FCC to take some sort of action. The FCC responded in January 1975 with Access III, a complicated set of guidelines that were to take place in the fall. Though filled with loopholes, the measure in effect handed an hour of prime time a week—Sunday from 7 to 8—back to the networks on the condition that they program some sort of children's or educational fare there.

Such directives turned out to be unnecessary, however, because the networks had chosen to mollify protests voluntarily. President Arthur Taylor of CBS a few weeks earlier had, in an act of madness that would come back to haunt him, proposed that all three networks institute a "family hour" each night between 8 and 9 P.M., during which "programming inappropriate for a general audience" would not be aired. The other networks were privately outraged but were forced to go along with this draconian plan, which was far more difficult to follow than the FCC decree they rightly assumed was approaching.

The National Association of Broadcasters (NAB) adopted the "Family Hour" as official policy in January, even revising its ancient code of practices to incorporate the new rule. The problem for the networks was immediate and insoluble. They now had to program fifteen hours a week of innocuous entertainments and submit them to a de facto censorship board of millions. Moreover, few networks had the resources to do it well; the FCC, in making its Access III ruling, cited NBC's *The Wonderful World of Disney* as an example of the kind of programming it had in mind. This proved less than useful, however, since few other producers happened to own a forty-year archive of family entertainments, along with thousands of hours of the best animation ever made. Most producers were not so lucky, and as a result, the rest of the 1970s saw the schedules filled with the sort of banal, escapist fare that had been thought banished by *All in the Family* and *The Mary Tyler Moore Show* just a few years earlier. Or not quite the same sort; because even escapism had to adapt to changing times. And adapt it did.

The Family Hour was instrumental in remaking television politically. The most talked about and prestigious shows of the first part of the decade had been progressive and/or controversial, and behind this vanguard, even less ambitious programming, such as *Kung Fu* or *The Streets of San Francisco* (1972–1977), had absorbed something of the new spirit. Urban "grit," realistic language, topicality, and a raised expectation of the audience were all now standard. Television was, everyone agreed, the lowest common denominator in American society, and so its elevation was no small thing in the life of the country.

The Family Hour undid all this. The protests that brought it about were localized and disproportionate, the result of canny lobbying by well-organized moralists in the Bible Belt and elsewhere, such as the Rev. Donald Wildmon's National Federation for Decency. Still, that they were able to change the face of television was a tribute not to their typewriters and homilies but rather to the political climate of the times. Television's power to reflect that climate was once again a result of specific actions and consequences with the polity and within the networks: a complex relationship but not a mysterious one. TV's mid-decade turnaround may well have been symptomatic of a Ford-era "return to normalcy," but no semimystical zeitgeist machinery was required to transfer moods from the real world to the TV one. Just as in the 1950s, when television had been directly influenced by HUAC and Senator McCarthy, the tendons were all too visible, and in the 1970s, television responded to political pressures as best it could. But "family television," as its proponents thought of it, was gone forever; a few prestigious shows such as the nostalgic *The Waltons* (1972–1979) or the frontier pastoral *Little House on the Prairie* (1974–1980) would be held up as examples, but even these would have to address real-world issues to some degree and in any case would be less appealing to the most significant sections of the audience (from the networks' point of view). William Tankersly's dream of "a universal television that plays to everyone and offends no one" had gone the way of "ask not what your country can do for you."

The immediate implications of the Family Hour, in the meantime, were depressingly obvious to the networks. They were going to have to fill the plum period of every weeknight, the primest of prime time, with programming denuded of violence, titillation, or controversial themes. CBS, the network behind the Family Hour's advent, suffered the most from its grandstanding gesture. Its year in, year out success was built on the popularity of sophisticated shows: in 1974, the "Tiffany network," as it was called for its prestigious programming, occupied nine of the top ten Nielsen spots. Of these, *All in the Family* was number one, and five other shows—*M*A*S*H, Maude, Kojak, The Sonny and Cher Show,* and *The Mary Tyler Moore Show*—all depended on varying degrees of sophistication. In retrospect, all seem harmless enough twenty years later, but at the time, all were deemed unsuitable for eight o'clock, which hurt their ratings potential enormously. Norman Lear, rather than tone *All in the Family* down, chose instead to have it moved to Thursday night at nine, thus robbing all the CBS shows of their invaluable lead-in. Without it, not one of the Saturday night shows made the top ten, including *The Mary Tyler Moore Show,* and *The Bob Newhart Show* fell out of the top twenty-five completely. Lear, more sensitive than anyone in television to network conservatism and its stultifying effects, formed a group of top producers and proceeded to successfully sue the NAB for violating their First Amendment rights. But by the time of their victory in 1977, the damage had been done, and television had remade itself for the second time in five years.

No single indicator of the shift could be more telling than the supplanting of *All in the Family* in the top Neilsen spot by the pointedly named *Happy Days* (1974–1984). *All in the Family* had occupied it for the previous five years—the longest such run in network history. It would never be on top again. The transition was one of those few, perfectly apt, utterly illustrative moments for which cultural historians usually hunt in vain.

As Robert Sklar remarked in 1979,

> *All in the Family* and similar productions were in their way responses
> to the contemporary realities that surrounded prime time television
> on the 7:00 and 11:00 PM news. *Happy Days* and its associated shows
> were in another way responses to the fatigue with and retreat from
> years of turmoil—but with the critical proviso that they did not reject
> the changes those turbulent years wrought, [and] they were able to
> incorporate at least some of them into genre forms.[8]

The entire point of the cultural revolution of the 1960s and early 1970s, it will
be remembered, was to escape from the 1950s; but contempt had softened into
indulgence as the youth culture of the 1950s moved into early middle age. The
youth culture of the 1960s rediscovered the 1950s not as the HUAC era nor the
Eisenhower equilibrium but rather as a series of attractive images: greasers, hot-
rods, Elvis, teen wonderland.[9] *American Graffiti* (1973) had much to do with this.
The film depicted the time as an idyll in which teens cruise through a mytholo-
gized city, stopping at Mel's Drive-In and knowing little of sin, death, or Vietnam. The film was the first great success for director George Lucas, who would
reinvent American movies a few years later with *Star Wars*. Hollywood apocry-
pha has it that Lucas was inspired to cast Ron Howard, the former child-star of
The Andy Griffith Show, by an episode of the ABC series *Love American Style*.
Entitled "Love and the Happy Day," it featured Howard as an all-American teen-
ager in the 1950s; actress Marion Ross played his Donna Reedesque mother.[10]

Thus, in the wake of *American Graffiti*'s success, ABC turned to *Love American Style* producer Garry Marshall for a series starring Howard. The series, which
was to be called *Happy Days*, would ride the new wave of 1950s nostalgia. Howard
would play Richie Cunningham, an all-American teen who faces conventional
teen-sitcom problems (Betty versus Veronica, etc.) with his slightly brasher but
equally innocent friend Potsie. To balance out the Wonder Bread blandness of
this insipid pair, a supporting character was added into the mix: a vaguely James
Deanish hoodlum named Arthur Fonzarelli, or "the Fonz." The Fonz was to be
shown wearing a leather jacket and surrounded by adoring girls.[11] Richie's parents would be vaguely based on 1950s sitcom characters, just as Richie himself
was a kind of Ricky Nelson/Dobie Gillis figure. This was hardly a stretch for
Howard, himself a product of the era's television.

Ironically, as Harry Castleman and Walter Podzarik note, *Happy Days* debuted
just as the two greatest relics of the 1950s still persisting into the 1970s finally
passed into history. Richard Nixon, the man who after Dwight Eisenhower and
Joe McCarthy best symbolized the era's politics, finally left the public eye; and
Lucille Ball, the undisputed queen of 1950s television, finally left the networks

as *Here's Lucy* was canceled in the fall of 1974. Such disappearances coincided with the discovery of the 1950s as a lost era, a *belle epoque* that might be profitably mined for nostalgia. *Happy Days* was in the vanguard of this in more ways than one. Not only was it one of the first idealizations of what had been seen by many as a wretched time; more significantly, it was among the first to identify a period strictly from its television.

Happy Days, that is to say, was not properly about the 1950s. It was about 1950s television, from whose conventions it drew all its ideas for setting, characters, idioms, plots, and essence. And 1950s sitcoms, it will be remembered, were an artificial construct even by TV standards, a narrow and evasive vision of the postwar suburban ideal only occasionally illuminated by flashes of Lucille Ball's or Jackie Gleason's brilliance; otherwise, the 1950s sitcom was almost surreal in its cloistered airlessness. This may have been part of the appeal of *Happy Days*, which was protected from reality in a way that few series had been in years. "I wanted to be the Norman Rockwell of television," Garry Marshall remembers, "by creating warm, humorous entertainment that the whole family could watch together in the same room."[12]

By this point, such sentiments were deeply out-of-date. By 1974, not a single series on network TV, with the possible exception of *Gunsmoke* (in its penultimate season), was without some concession to relevancy. Even explicitly family-oriented dramas set in the past, such as *The Waltons* (1972–1981) and *Little House on the Prairie* (1974–1983), were realistic and thoughtful and consistently grappled with real-world problems that TV families had been spared for many years. And of course, the fullness of the sea change had brought ripe decadence to the schedule as well: *The Sonny Comedy Hour* (1974), *Bob & Carol & Ted & Alice* (a 1974 sitcom based on the spouse-swapping movie of the same name), *Planet of the Apes* (1974), and the like. *Happy Days* was progressive in its embrace of pure television, unencumbered by the outside world; its reactionary quality actually put it ahead of the curve.

Happy Days, like all transcendent hits, came along at exactly the right time. No network was helped more by the Family Hour than ABC, the perennial number three network, which had specialized in youth programming. Any blow to grown-up programming was automatically a help to it. Moreover, ABC now had the invaluable advantage of having the most sought-after programmer in television working for them in Fred Silverman.

Silverman had been Mike Dann's replacement as programming chief at CBS in 1970; it was he who helped to implement President Wood's changes. Prior to that, he had been wildly successful as the head of daytime programming, an acknowledged master of soap opera and children's programming.[13] Silverman left CBS in 1974, just in time to help ABC capitalize on President Taylor's colossal blunder. (In retrospect, letting Silverman go may have been an even greater one.) Although he was not involved directly in *Happy Days'* development, Silverman was the man responsible for retooling the show for its third season in 1976. "[Marshall] did *Happy Days* to Silverman's guidelines," remembers Paul Klein of NBC.[14] Silverman recognized that Fonzie was the main draw and decided that *Happy Days* ought to be riding Fonzie's popularity for all it was worth—a lot, as it turned out.

Silverman was not the only new leader at ABC. President Fred Pierce had recently taken over and immediately launched a shake-up meant to pull the network out of third place. *Happy Days* was the flagship effort of his administration, much as *All in the Family* had been for Wood. And like *All in the Family, Happy Days* was a hit for a number of reasons. Nineteen fifties nostalgia on its own had a limited appeal. In the same season as *Happy Days'* debut, another series set in the 1950s and focused on teenagers also debuted. *Sons and Daughters* (1974) is forgotten now, a two-month wonder too obscure even to qualify as a trivia question, whereas *Happy Days* has placed its props in the Smithsonian's National Museum of American History, alongside Archie Bunker's chair and other certified pieces of Americana. *Happy Days* received poor reviews, which were as usual irrelevant to its success or failure. But neither was the show a ratings smash in the early going. Slotted against CBS's *Good Times* (hip, ethnic, with a dynamic young star) and NBC's *Adam-12,* the series produced only a twenty share—that is, it was watched by only one fifth of households measured by the Nielsen survey. This was a shabby enough rating, which on its own might have made the series a candidate for cancellation. However, demographics again saved the day.

Happy Days was "skewed" in the right direction, demographically speaking. It was watched most by children, who were utterly oblivious to the show's setting or to 1950s nostalgia. For kids, *Happy Days* was funny and appealing, especially the character of Fonzie, for whom they went crazy, sending in fan letters by the thousands.[15] "The Fonz" was a James Dean for the grade school set: tough, irresistible to women, and most of all ultra-cool. The ambiguities and tensions of the vulnerable-hood type, which had been played at various times by Dean, Brando, and many lesser lights, were smoothed over, and Fonzie made a kind of semidivine figure. He was particularly attractive compared to the nerdy Richie and Potsie, who were reduced to audience surrogates in looking up to Fonzie as a god. This was borne out over the first two seasons, as ABC began to receive an avalanche of fan mail from children. Silverman knew a good thing when he saw it.

And he knew how to make it better. With the start of the third season, the "hoodlum" became domesticated. Fonzie's outsider image was shed, as the leather-jacketed icon was invited to move upstairs to the Cunningham's garage apartment. The housebreaking of Fonzie, along with his new place in the middle of nearly every episode, had its desired effect: *Happy Days* finished the season eleventh overall, reaching a quarter of the nation's homes each episode.[16] The following season it was number one, reaching a third of the nation's homes and 41 percent of all American children between the ages of six and eleven. Its teen rating was predictably spectacular, although not so high as its rating among kids, who were fixated by the show and flooded the nation's schools with Fonzie lunch boxes and iron-on T-shirts. The affluent watched as often as the poor, and the show's appeal was geographically uniform, enjoying the same success in the cities as in the "C and D counties" in rural areas.[17] Eureka! Silverman had struck the mother lode: a show, in Marshall's words, "which the whole family could watch together in the same room." William Tankersly could turn back over in his grave.

The domesticated Fonzie *(center)* with his adopted parents

ABC was ecstatic. The third-place network was overjoyed to have found its way to the ratings summit at last. Paley's counterpart at ABC, Leonard Goldenson, later went on to actually publish a book about this feat entitled *Beating the Odds*. Moreover, as the revenues began to pour in for ABC's other "kid-vid" shows, it became apparent that the network had found the formula for success.

Marshall was encouraged to spin off series, which he did with amazing success. As a midseason replacement in 1975, Marshall created *Laverne and Shirley* (1976–1983), a blue-collar show about two working women who, like Mary Tyler Moore, wanted to "make our dreams come true—doing it our way!" The show, looser and more comical than the hero-worshipping *Happy Days,* was immediately a hit, joining the latter show in the top ten. The next year, *Happy Days* and *Laverne and Shirley* were first and second in the Nielsens, respectively, after which they switched positions, and *Laverne and Shirley* enjoyed a two-year run as number one. In the 1978–79 season, another *Happy Days* spin-off, *Mork and Mindy,* about a childish space alien and his pretty, chaste girlfriend, became the surprise hit of the season. Marshall was king of the ratings; and by that time, series aimed at kids and teenagers had become the norm. A show such as *Laverne and Shirley* was almost twice as popular as the average-rated situation comedy with teenagers but also had a huge spike (85 percent above average) for women 18–34, or so its producers boasted in *Broadcast Magazine.* (Kids, of course, had the biggest spike of all, over 257 percent compared to the average prime-time program.) Shows aimed at the young were now the prime audience gatherers on television. The children were leading.

And ABC, king of kid-vid, was the beneficiary. Sitcoms were an important part of their schedule, because sitcoms remained the mainstay of all programming, but ABC found special success in action and adventure shows, often featuring comic book style superheroes. The first of these was *The Six Million Dollar Man,* (1974–1983) a show ABC premiered in early 1974, right alongside *Happy Days.* Unlike that show, however, *The Six Million Dollar Man* got right down to business in the matter of manufacturing a teen idol. Astronaut Steve Austin, the memorable credit sequence told us, had been "a man more dead than alive," the victim of a terrible rocket accident. Empowered by the Office of Scientific Information, however, a team of scientists decided to rebuild the maimed astronaut with robot limbs and a telescopic eye—"better, stronger, faster" than any ordinary man. Thus refurbished, Austin served the agency as a superagent, traveling around in leisure suits, annihilating evildoers, and reporting to his controller at the OSI. Before *Happy Days* hit it big, *The Six Million Dollar Man* was ABC's top rated show.

And unlike *Batman* and *The Mod Squad,* ABC's last two action hits, the show made no pretension toward pleasing grown-ups, whether through irony or relevancy. So immune was ABC to adult criticism, in fact, that they manufactured a mate for Steve Austin, *The Bionic Woman* (1976–78). The two shows then ran in tandem, the lead characters often appearing on each other's program and the programs occasionally even switching time slots. Eventually, a bionic child was introduced and even a bionic dog, as the concept entered its terminal stages in the late 1970s.

In the wake of the *Six Million Dollar Man*'s success, ABC and NBC flooded the airwaves with superheroes: *The Incredible Hulk* (1978–1982), *The New Adventures of Wonder Woman* (1976–1979), *The Amazing Spider-Man* (1978–1979), *Matt Helm* (1975–1976, secret agent), *The Invisible Man* (1975–1976, ditto), *Baa Baa Black Sheep* (1975–1976, WWII fighter pilots), *The Man from Atlantis* (1977–1978, merman). All aimed for the gold mine of millions of attentive children, fixated on the screen. CBS decided to take the high road, assuming that viewers would tire of juvenilia and return to their old standbys. In this, it was mistaken; demographics were once again against them. The ground continued to shift under TV's feet.

By 1975, a working father, a housekeeping mom, and two children—still the standard used by the Department of Labor to define a typical household—accounted for only 7 percent of all American families.[18] Between 1970 and 1979, the number of people living alone increased 60 percent, amounting to a whopping 23 percent of all 1980 households.[19] Books such as George and Nena O'Neill's *Open Marriage* (1973) and Mel Kranzler's *Creative Divorce* (1974) were considered timely and enlightened, along with free-love novels such as Erica Jong's *Fear of Flying* (which celebrated the commitment-free "zipless fuck"). Marriages were happening later in life and less often and were producing fewer children, as newspaper and magazine articles constantly noted. CBS still was banking on truisms about American behavior to save their bacon—a mistake, as Detroit was finding out. The kids often had the run of the TV dial now, even in double-parent families. The "Family Hour" was a mirage.

The successful new shows aimed at the child of the 1970s, a worldly being who had received baby-boom values as givens. Thus, the superhero shows were now tempered with liberal-pacifist moralism, psychobabble, untrustworthy politicians, military madmen, environmental crises, and—with the exception of Steve Austin, "more dead than alive" even after his operation—heroes who belonged to the culture of the 1970s. The days of Superman standing up for truth, justice, and the American way were gone; when an old-time superhero was the star of a series, as with *The New Adventures of Wonder Woman,* a sugarcoating of camp was laid heavily on. But this was the exception. The 1970s superhero was young, laid-back, frisky, and tended to eschew violence—another aftereffect of the Family Hour. *The Incredible Hulk,* for example, was a sensitive, thoughtful scientist wandering from town to town and helping people help themselves—until they got in too tight a spot for self-esteem to rescue them; then he would turn into a green-skinned monster, also sensitive, who would throw his opponents harmlessly into barrels or stacked cans of soup. (Even this tepid catharsis was carefully figured to avoid inflaming conservative critics: the Incredible Hulk was only allowed to have two fights a week.) Even Steve Austin neither worked for law-enforcement nor with it; he was yet another outsider cop and was often called upon to mediate emotional disputes as well.

If any one program of the mid-1970s proved that the pendulum had swung away from adult themes on TV, it was, paradoxically, one aimed far above the heads of children. *Soap* (1977–1981) was a creation of Lear alumna Susan Harris. Harris had been one of Lear's most successful proteges and was the woman responsible for writing the courageous but highly inflammatory two-part episode, "Maude's Dilemma," in which the character had an abortion.[20]

Harris had already had one major run-in with the network hierarchy. In 1975, she created a serious sitcom called *Fay*, which was to star blacklist veteran Lee Grant as a middle-aged divorcée trying to make it on her own. Whatever the chances for *Fay*'s success (and they seemed slim enough), the show was devastated by the Family Hour, which caused it to be radically redone as an innocuous sitcom in *The Doris Day Show* mold—an impossibility, given the people involved, and a move that would lead to the program's prompt cancellation.

The *Fay* debacle should have alerted the creative community, if the Family Hour had not, to a shift in the political climate. The liberations of the 1960s and early 1970s had been permanent, as advertised; but as America settled down to digest its newly weakened, rudderless state, the liberation theology of the 1960s was of little comfort. Programming predicated on it was, too. *Soap* was the Waterloo of Lear-era progressive television.

Harris created the show as an ironic take-off on the sexual cauldron of daytime soap operas. The show was to have over-the-top plot concepts and wacky characters. Bereft of their ironic tint, however—that is, their claim to mean something different than what they seemed to mean—the plots, as summaries, seemed merely prurient. One example that drew much attention was a plotline in which a priest would be seduced in church. Conservative and religious viewers were predictably outraged. Roughly contemporaneous with Anita Bryant's antigay campaign in Miami, Phyllis Schlafly's agitation against the Equal Rights Amendment, and other backlash movements, the furor over *Soap* was far more intense than anyone, including veterans of Norman Lear controversies, had come to expect. Protestant religious groups were enraged; the U.S. Catholic Conference pronounced the show "morally reprehensible." The network was besieged by protests and petitions.

One of the biggest activists in this small but vocal minority was the Rev. Donald Wildmon, one of the pioneers of religious lobbying. Wildmon and other media-saavy church leaders were wielding increased political clout in the late 1970s, a fact that would contribute in no small measure to the election of Ronald Reagan in 1980. In the meantime, Wildmon was making his name with *Soap*. The show was a success anyway, even generating a spin-off, as the urbane black butler Benson, a kind of Fonzie for adult liberals, was given his own show as adviser to a bumbling white governor.

Nonetheless, the lesson of *Soap* was not lost on the networks. *Welcome Back, Kotter*, for example, had a premise that seems lifted from the early "relevancy" shows: a graduate of an inner-city high school returns as a young adult to teach a racially mixed group of underachievers. Moreover, the show was free to discuss heretofore taboo or controversial issues as Wood's shows had not been. But, in fact, *Welcome Back, Kotter* (1975–1979) was a broad comedy, played for laughs. Its students were all stereotypes: a jive-talking Jimmie Walker-style black, Boom-Boom Washington; Juan Epstein, half Jewish, half Puerto Rican ("half of my brothers were out stealing pants—the other half were altering them"); Arnold Horshack, nerd; and Vinnie Barbarino, a dumb but handsome Italian kid played by a young John Travolta, in a dress run for his iconic role in *Saturday Night Fever*. Stand-up comic Gabe Kaplan was the teacher, Gabe Kotter, and his lectures were mostly joke-filled monologues, in which he asked the kids straight-man questions on the level of "who discovered America?"

Welcome Back, Kotter was, of course, a huge hit, another win for ABC. Early on, however, its subject matter—which would have earned it kudos a few years earlier—made it controversial, though never as much so as *Soap*. Even submerged as it was in cartoonish mirth, the once-popular relevancy theme was now seen as dangerous. The show was banned in Boston, which was then in the grip of the busing struggle. The National Education Association, on the defensive over falling test scores and the busing crisis, was in no mood to see urban teachers made a laughing-stock and petitioned the network to let them place an "adviser" on the show, "in order to protect the image of schoolteachers."[21]

It was easier to avoid trouble, then as ever. *Kotter* was, in any case, in no danger of becoming a flash point for political struggle. Even so, the show eventually was capsized by a power struggle that emerged between its star, Kaplan, who wanted a more realistic approach, and producer James Komack, who didn't. Komack eventually fired all of Kaplan's writers and allies and installed in their place veterans of *The Carol Burnett Show*. Still more gags were piled on. The ratings were unhurt. Only when Kaplan and Travolta both left the show did it really begin to suffer, and even then it soldiered on for another full season before being put down in 1979.

The telling point about *Welcome Back, Kotter* was that even as it recoiled from controversy, it still enjoyed the forms and freedoms of the "relevant" show. Nearly every other show did likewise, if they knew what was good for them. Controversial issues were touched upon in a harmless way in an occasional bid for prestige. There were plenty of ethnics. Liberal attitudes toward poverty, education, and authority were taken for granted.[22] But of all the newfound post-Lear freedoms, the new sexual frankness was the most aggressively exploited and the most thoroughly trivialized.

For Paul Klein, as astute an observer as there was inside television, the defining programming trend of the time was sex, particularly in the form of "jiggle television." Klein defined jiggle TV as, starkly stated, "when you have a young, attractive television personality running at top speed wearing a limited amount of underwear."[23] In the "jiggle" shows, women whose bust size ranged from medium to large moved around a lot without wearing a bra. A simple formula for success, but an effective one: the breakout show of 1976 was *Charlie's Angels* (1976–1981), a transparently exploitative show about three hot women detectives in skimpy outfits. The appeal of *Charlie's Angels* was timeless, and it drew large audiences from the start. It was the fifth-rated show overall in both 1976–1977 and 1977–1978, beaten in the former year only by the fearsome *Happy Days* and *Laverne and Shirley* combo, *The ABC Monday Night Movie* (which doesn't count), and *M*A*S*H*, by this time a television institution on the most appallingly self-congratulatory, Red Skelton-esque scale.

The following season, *Charlie's Angels* was still resting in its eminent niche at number five, but there had been two changes in the top five. The Marshall shows still retained their sovereignty, and CBS's venerable news magazin⌐ *60 Minutes*, had a fine year, displacing *M*A*S*H* at number four. But another ɪ iggle show had shot to number three, having debuted at the end of the prᴇ ᴏus season. *Three's Company* remains the epitome of mindless, titillating programming from the mid 1970s, the *Texaco Star Theater* of jiggle TV.

From its bubbly theme song ("Come and knock on our door/Try a place that is new!/Where the kisses are *hers* and *hers* and *his*/Three's company too!") to the one-liners, mistaken-identity plots, jiggling, and most of all, the endless, labored double entendres ("Jack, shouldn't we be cooking?" "That's what *I* say!"), *Three's Company* was strictly a bottom-denominator feeder. Its plot, however, played on contemporary mores in typically pious fashion. Jack, a swinging young playboy, wakes up one morning after a party in the apartment of two attractive young women—pert Janet and buxom "dumb blonde" Chrissy. He has slept in the bathtub, and nothing unwholesome has happened, and the two girls need a roommate. So does Jack. Everything would be fine for the uninhibited trio, except for one problem: the girls' prurient old landlord, Mr. Roper, is incapable of believing that a young man could live with two pretty girls platonically. Therefore, Jack pretends to be gay, and hijinx ensue.

Sociologically speaking, Mr. and Mrs. Roper are the most interesting characters on television during this period. For one thing, the Ropers are meant to stand for all of the worst characteristics of pre-1960s, unliberated America. Mr. Roper is a dirty-minded prude. Predictably, he is impotent, a fact that accounts for nearly all of Mrs. Roper's lines ("You're not in a rising market." "Neither are *you*."). Mrs. Roper is more sympathetic; she knows Jack's secret, and although unable to enjoy the salvation of Charles Reich's America, with its new freedom and honesty, she is not so benighted as to begrudge it to the younger generation. Such role-modeling was barely commented upon in the America that made *Three's Company* the number three show in the land—an eminence that, it ought to be remembered, is unattainable without large audiences in every demographic sector.

The enlightened, fresh-scrubbed stars of *Three's Company* and their abject elders, Mr. and Mrs. Roper

Three's Company was a throwback show, a bare-bones production recalling the 1950s in many ways. Its set was theatrical, a small living room with entrances left and right. The other locales featured on the show—the kitchen, the Roper's bed, the local singles bar—accounted only for a small fraction of airtime. Although there was endless talk about sex, none ever happened—a neurotic fact that Castleman and Podzarik liken to the chaste but suggestive Doris Day/Rock Hudson movie cycle of the 1950s.[24] And, for all its liberated posturing, the show was sexist to the core. Chrissy was plainly in direct line of descent from such Eisenhower-era blonde bombshells as Marilyn Monroe, Jayne Mansfield, and Mamie Van Doren. (Jiggle mogul Aaron Spelling habitually referred to such women on TV as "eye candy.") And Jack, although sensitive, was an old-fashioned wolf who lusted after and "dated" a different woman every week, while both Janet and Chrissy stayed relatively pure.

Such strange combinations of "silent generation" and baby-boom mores were a kind of leitmotiv of Ford-era television. Thus, in the police drama, the outsider cop now worked apart from the system less and less, reforming the system "from the inside," just as Joe Friday would have wanted. *Starsky and Hutch* (1975–79), the most popular cop show of the time, thus featured two young policemen, counterparts to *Adam-12*'s Reed and Malloy, who unlike them enjoyed a swinging lifestyle on the job. Rather than staidly patrolling in a black and white, the pair cruised around in a sporty Ford Torino, getting mixed up with wild women and colorful street criminals. As David Marc noted, "*Starsky and Hutch* . . . seems to be suggesting that it is downright uncool not to be a cop."[25] The pair lacked the rebelliousness of the Mod Squad, who had been turned to the side of the law only in order to help the downtrodden. Interestingly, the same producer, Aaron Spelling, produced both shows and *Charlie's Angels* as well. (Spelling, the industry's all-time master at keeping up with the times, was the hidden hero of 1970s television.) In *Starsky and Hutch,* Spelling took pains to keep the multiracial aspect of the *Mod Squad* (Hutch was a blonde WASP, Starsky a curly-haired Jewish type; both reported to a black sergeant) and also the squad's youth and friskiness. But Starsky and Hutch weren't out to change the world; and although capable of an earnest hatred now and again, most of their energy was spent racing through the streets and trading wisecracks with their buffoonish black street informant, Huggy Bear.

Yet another Spelling show, *S.W.A.T.* (1975–1976), dispensed with outsiders entirely. As crime had become more and more of an issue in the public mind, particularly in the large cities, the ever-attuned Spelling brought the war on crime to its logical conclusion. Premiering during the close of the war in early 1975, the show featured a special team of paramilitary police officers who waged full-scale warfare against criminals. The dark-uniformed *S.W.A.T.* team, Vietnam veterans all, would typically burst from an armored personnel carrier and open fire with dozens of automatic weapons. The series was loosely based on the riot teams that had been formed in the late 1960s, and this was law and order at its most potent. The show touched a nerve, flaring briefly into the top ten before extinguishing itself early in its second season. The show's violence was too much of a good thing: America was not yet ready to embrace the fascist glory of *S. W.A. T.,* preferring easygoing heroes such as Jim Rockford of *The Rockford Files* and Dan Tanna of *Vega$,* who muddled through.

Although by the early 1980s a recrudescent conservatism would generate a flurry of right-leaning shows, the mid-to-late 1970s were preeminently a time of retreat, not affirmation. *Happy Days, Laverne and Shirley, Three's Company, Welcome Back, Kotter:* all were inoffensive entertainments built in the same spirit, and to nearly the same specifications, as the hit shows of the 1950s and 1960s. The only difference was that they partook selectively of the culture, ideology, and lifestyles of the baby boom. Like many American institutions, television was adapting itself to the cultural current that had swept through the 1960s and become the mainstream a decade later.

Radicals maintain to this day that the counterculture was absorbed, neutralized, defused by an absorbent capitalism and its "repressive tolerance," as Herbert Marcuse called it. Possibly. This much can certainly be said without much dispute: a few key elements of 1960s culture emerged on TV in the early 1970s, programming polarized around them for several years, and by mid-decade, these elements were absent, except as plot devices, such as Jack Tripper's living arrangements in *Three's Company* or *Charlie's Angels'* skimpy outfits.[26] When Garry Marshall set out to be "Norman Rockwell for the seventies," he realized that three things were needed: "creativity, time slot, and time in history."[27] The first two were readily at hand for Marshall; and the third, as the ratings proved again and again, was to be found in the enervated years after Watergate and Vietnam.

6
"It Takes Different Strokes":
TV and America, 1978

The paradox of Wood's and Lear's "relevancy" boom in the early 1970s—and in this it resembled the counterculture more than anyone knew—was that all the upheaval only served to further consolidate and conserve the existing status quo. CBS had always been number one, and the scrambling army of bigots, ethnics, and independent-minded women who overran the Nielsens in the early 1970s only served to keep "the Tiffany network" in first place.

The Silverman and Marshall counterreformation, on the other hand, was paradoxical for precisely opposite reasons. The shows were reverting to old norms—banality, mindless "jiggling," and other kid stuff. Few of the advances of Norman Lear and Mary Tyler Moore were visible: TV remained a "vast wasteland" of irrelevance and "appealing to the lowest common denominator," as critics called it.[1] But if programming seemed more conservative and less adventurous, this facade masked a period of wild intranetwork warfare and desperate power struggles. CBS's stranglehold on the ratings had been forever broken, and with it, the stability of the industry. This was the wildcat period of network television, conducted in the shadow of cable and fiber optics, and an end to the period of the networks' absolute monopoly. "It's Die Gotterdammerung," one expert noted in May 1978. "The twilight of the gods."[2]

At the center of it all was Fred Silverman. Silverman had been Mike Dann's lieutenant at CBS, and afterwards, the man behind ABC's improbable ascent to the top of the ratings heap. All three networks were making record profits, but the indignity of being displaced by the weak sister network sent both CBS and NBC into a frenzy of counterprogramming and pitched competition. The wild success of ABC's *Roots,* a miniseries about the generations of an African American family, seemed to break all the rules.[3] The series had been a smash in early 1977, as Silverman scheduled it on eight consecutive nights, as opposed to the weekly format used by earlier miniseries, such as the highly successful *Rich Man,*

Poor Man. This seemed at first like a formula for disaster, but ABC was by then in the lead with its mighty series and so could afford to take a chance. Critically, opinion was mixed. But the concluding night was the highest rated entertainment show in TV history, snaring 71 percent of the audience. "ABC, *Roots* Storm Neilsens for Historic Ratings Victory" announced the *Hollywood Reporter*.[4]

Roots was indeed a historical precedent and not just for ABC. It demonstrated that the predictable herd mentality of the viewing audience, which programmers had counted upon for decades, was now yet another discredited doctrine, like America's military invincibility and the soundness of the dollar. Rather than demonstrating the need for innovative, original programming like *Roots,* however, the networks had learned nothing and forgotten nothing from the early 1970s. Now, it seemed to them that, as *TV Guide* remarked, "audiences would bust out of old viewing habits for something new, shiny, and different."[5] It was as simple as that. "Is Kunte Kinte the Next Fonzie?" asked one magazine.[6] Clearly the hunt was on. And one man was leading it.

Silverman was the figure associated with *Roots,* as he had been associated with ABC's other hits. The other programmers and executives took to their weapons, and the 1977–1978 season went down in network history as (*TV Guide* again) "the most tumultuous and bitterly contested in the medium's thirty year history."[7] Series were whisked from night to night in the schedule like assignations in a cad's date book. Miniseries, special events, movies of the week, sports spectaculars, celebrity roasts—every week was filled with short-term gambits for a few extra ratings points. New series were short-ordered for five or six episodes, since no programmer felt secure even committing to a thirteen-week run. Now that overnight Nielsens were de rigueur for every executive's desk, each quarter, each week, each *night* was something a bureaucrat might get fired over. "How in hell do we stop this network mania?" asked Aaron Spelling. Norman Lear called the ratings competition "the most destructive force in television today."[8] And then, on 20 January 1978, NBC hired Fred Silverman and made him president of the network.

Silverman was now TV incarnate. He had shaped CBS to some extent; he had redefined ABC's programming; and now he was to take charge at NBC. Noted *Esquire,* "Hundreds of years ago, it would have been almost as if one man controlled most of the printing presses most of the time."[9] The result was a renewed fury among TV executives to compete on purely egotistical grounds. As always, all three networks were raking in money: even NBC, bringing up the rear, was deeply in the black. The business had always been prone to personalization because of the size and proximity of the players, as Mike Dann's and Paul Klein's ratings duels of the late 1960s and early 1970s had shown. But now, whatever financial reality had checked these shenanigans was gone. The "ratings mania" that had for several years been growing found its supreme expression in Fred Silverman's rise and fall.

The Silverman era will be remembered as a particularly garish one in TV history, a gilded age if ever there was one. Barry Diller, the head of Paramount at the time and Silverman's predecessor at ABC, said that the new rules of the era became apparent to him several years earlier when engaged in a bidding war for the rights to the hit disaster film *The Poseidon Adventure:*

> The bidding passed two million dollars, and it was getting past the point where any of us could make a profit. But it kept going up— it was a nightmare. It became a test of corporate pride. It wasn't business and it wasn't entertainment: it was a loss of everything but ego! We didn't care. We finally bought it for three million. I knew we had lost our sanity, but we just kept going because we didn't want to lose, ' we weren't going to let anyone beat us. Ego, it was just ego. Ten, twelve, fifteen men in an ego contest—that's what television has come down to.[10]

Silverman had slipped away from CBS because President Arthur Taylor was unwilling to grant the wunderkind some ego-stroking perks—a new title, more money, a limousine. When ABC came calling with these and more, Silverman jumped ship. ABC's subsequent rise therefore seemed a matter of personal vindication for Silverman and established him as a figure in the public mind, television's first such star. It was a dramatic departure. Previously, network television had been a supremely low-key enterprise, in which decisions were made by bland, anonymous men behind the scenes. A WASPish gentility was expected of network executives, and even the most successful knew better than to make public spectacles of themselves, after the fashion of movie tycoons.[11] Silverman was the first network bigwig to become famous in his own right. His name came to represent the industry; *Time Magazine* even put "TV's Master Showman" on its cover, publishing an awe-struck feature on "the man with the golden gut."[12]

The elevation of Fred Silverman to national figure marked a turning point in television history. From the longest perspective, it marked the culmination of a trend that had been noticeable since the early 1950s: television's consciousness of itself—not its stars, not any particular show, but the medium and industry— as a central, if not the central, fact of American life. This had long been axiomatic for pessimistic intellectuals, but it was now beginning to dawn on television itself. "I've been pleasantly surprised," wrote Kevin Phillips in *TV Guide's* "Newswatch" column in 1977, "at the growing network realization that TV power has become so awesome that it, too, must be grist for the mill of television news and dramatization. *Television is finally beginning to cover television.*"[13] Throughout the

1960s, defenders of the industry, when confronted with accusations that TV was—to take one example—weakening the war effort, consistently claimed that TV was merely reporting the news. Television, according to this view, was nothing more than a conduit for information; and in prime time, a harmless diversion whose content was mandated by egalitarian viewer response. By the mid-1970s, that claim could no longer be sustained. The presidency had waged war with the media and lost: television, it was commonly offered, was now the most important, meaningful institution in America. In Paddy Chayefsky's *Network* (1976), a highly acclaimed satire of the television industry, anchorman Howard Beale tells his nationwide audience, "the only truth you know is what you get over this tube. . . . There is a whole generation that never knew anything that did not come out of this tube. This tube is the gospel, the ultimate revelation. This tube can make or break popes, presidents and prime ministers. This tube is the most awesome god-damned power in the whole godless world! . . . We're all you know!" Beale is dismissed as a Jeremiah, the "mad prophet of the airwaves," but this point is the moral of the movie, and one that struck home to many.

Consider: the churches had long lost their authority. The family, as observers like Christopher Lasch and so many others had noted, was no longer a "haven in a heartless world," controlled from within. The new president, Jimmy Carter, was elected as the anti-Washington candidate: as Lewis Lapham wrote at the time of his nomination, "he assumed, correctly, that the vast majority of the American people . . . wanted to forget about politics. They were sick to death of politicians, tired of issues they didn't understand and which didn't admit of easy answers, disappointed by the chronicle of failure that seemed to delight the Eastern press."[14] As president, Carter turned to moralizing in an attempt to renew faith in government. He tried micromanagement of Washington affairs, such as insisting that cabinet officers drive themselves to work and carry their own luggage, and moral philosophizing, as with his infamous "malaise" speech. Nothing worked, and his presidency disappeared under a suffocating blanket of minor scandals, ongoing crises (energy, terrorism, inflation), cynicism, and general disaffection. Congress fared little better, a Gallup poll in 1979 finding public approval of Congress at 19 percent.[15] So much for government. Academe was on the run from protests and economic pressures; and what little authority traditional mores, conventions, and standards had exerted were long gone, largely swept away by the upheavals of the 1960s. Meanwhile, the percentage of American homes with television sets jumped in 1975 to 97.1, an all-time high. The following year, gross broadcast revenues jumped from $4.86 billion to $6.19 billion, another record increase.[16] Television, more than any other institution, had inherited the wind.

By the mid-1970s, the centrality of television was being tacitly affirmed by most media. "The most popular art" having been taken up by traumatized academe, television was no longer dismissed as "mass culture"; its ascendancy was by now a fait accompli, and many intellectuals had followed the example of Marshall McLuhan in riding the trend rather than bucking it. The Smithsonian put Archie Bunker's chair and Fonzie's leather jacket in its National Museum of American History. *Network,* written and directed by veterans of the industry, brought the politics and policies of TV infighting to the big screen as an epic satire.[17] The only significant debate about television as a presence by now was how much sex and/or violence might be allowed on it, and even this was an ongoing negotiation.

It was thus almost inevitable that TV would begin to eat its own tail. The industry became engaged in an arms race, the limits of which were only those of TV itself: that is to say, almost none. "Television was never a business seeking greatness," Barry Diller pointed out. "But there were boundaries. Now those boundaries have been shattered."[18] In the strange new world of the ratings frenzy, broadcasting wisdom seemed to go for naught. The intuitive wunderkind Silverman threw garbage at viewers, who seemed to eat it up. More and more, statisticians and business experts were making the decisions.[19] The ratings and research data was voluble, sophisticated, and baffling to nonexperts. Even the Nielsens were by 1978 so segmented that they featured no less than eight categories: the original, golden 18–35 was now supplemented by 3–11, 12–17, 18–49, 25–49, 35–49, 50–64, and 65+. William Paley himself, the very personification of the old network establishment, stepped down in 1977 as CEO of CBS, handing the reins over to John Backe—a businessman with no broadcasting experience.

As television attempted blindly to generate ratings any which way—"on automatic pilot," as one prominent executive put it—the patterns that emerged provided an even better Rorschach image of American life than ever before. In an America without a center and without traditional corporate mores, the television industry threw programs helter-skelter at the viewers, whom they hoped desperately to attract, even for a few weeks. What they came up with demonstrates better than any census how broken up America really had become.

In the fall of 1977, for example, ABC debuted a new series, *The Love Boat.* The premise was simple, expressly designed to attract the most diverse possible audience. Youth would be served but so would the elderly, minorities, and every viewer bloc worth having. An ocean liner would be the setting each week for three different romantic stories. They would be tendentiously cross-sectional in their appeal, with, for example, one featuring Jimmie Walker and Shirley Hemphill as black honeymooners, another with Ethel Merman and Forrest Tucker as separated sweethearts, and a third featuring a pretty guest, Jill St. John or Barbi Benton, falling for the ship's Milquetoastish doctor (Bernie Koppel). Girls in bikinis would wander around for no reason in the background, and stars with high Q-ratings from ABC and other networks would insure scientifically tested levels of likability. Significantly, the three stories never intersected. Why should they? "The Love Boat," its theme song boasted, "promises something for every one!"

For a newly balkanized nation, such an innovation served the networks well, and another successful series, *Fantasy Island,* soon followed.[20] The show's conception was so perfectly emblematic of ratings mania that even Paddy Chayefsky couldn't have dreamed it up. Having had a number of TV movie ideas rejected, Aaron Spelling remembers at one meeting finally losing his temper:

> Finally, I kind of went crazy. I said, "you guys don't want a show. You don't want something with characters or a plot or story. You just want to have some sort of an island, where you can go and act out all your dumb fantasies. You want a show about some guy on an island to make all your sexual and other fantasies come true." And that was when they started jumping up and down and shouting, "do it, do it."[21]

On *Fantasy Island,* guests came to make their dreams come true and were accommodated by the mysterious Mr. Roarke and his midget assistant Tattoo. Mr. Roarke could do anything, and did—but invariably the guests found that their dreams were less than what they had bargained for and only served to teach them useful truths about themselves with which to go back and face the world. Though dismal in its moral, *Fantasy Island* enjoyed wide appeal, and both shows finished in the top 20 in 1978.

Upon his ascension to NBC's presidency, Silverman announced that his strategy for the third-place network would be opposite to the shameless tactics he had used at ABC. NBC would not only be a ratings leader, he announced, but "would also be the most respected network."[22] The ABC formula of jiggling and like childishness was wearing out its welcome, Silverman intuited. The path for the future lay in "quality TV." As it happened, Silverman was not the one to lead NBC to the promised land. That was left to Brandon Tartikoff in the 1980s, and when it did happen, it came through the CBS/MTM formula of making ensemble shows with bomber crews of bankable stars at their center. In the late 1970s, Silverman flailed about wildly, trying to regain the center. Lacking a zeitgeist curve to ride, however, he was left, like President Carter, with micromanagement—jerking shows around from night to night, switching time slots, premiering spectacularly dumb new series and miniseries such as the *Love Boat*-modeled *Supertrain,* a remake of *Columbo* without Columbo *(Mrs. Columbo),* and a TV adaptation of the hopelessly R-rated hit *Animal House (Delta House),* all in 1979.

All failed, naturally. Nor was there the same success to be found in kid-vid. Television in the late 1970s rebuilt its audience piece by piece, and everybody had to do their part. A youthful demographic was still highly sought after, but programmers had ceased to make a fetish of it. As Robert Wood would remark a few years later, "I never felt it was safe to be represented very strongly in one category at the expense of all other age categories. The idea is, if you can, to distribute your audience in equal incremental parts. You know, the young, the thirties, the forties, the fifties, the sixties. If you can spread it like peanut butter, even, across the bread, that's terrific."[23] Clearly, Wood was speaking in idealized terms. No programmer wanted a show that counted the same number of retirees as the prized "young marrieds"; but the industry began to move away from overtargeting and attempted, like the rest of the country, to reestablish connections. One way to start was through ensemble sitcoms.

Since the introduction of *The Mary Tyler Moore Show* and its many spin-offs in the early part of the decade, a blueprint for success had been the ensemble structure. This format, as perfected by such hits as *The Bob Newhart Show, Barney Miller, M*A*S*H,* and others involved a large and diverse cast of characters, generally held together by a workplace setting.[24] There would, of course, be a proven star at its center, someone who, like Moore or Alan Alda, could be counted on to appeal to wide audiences of both men and women; but the lesser characters would target the various different sectors of the audience. The fact was, as the networks were belatedly realizing, America was now a complex, heterogeneous society for whom single titans like Lucille Ball or Jackie Gleason no longer sufficed.[25]

In their place would be an assortment of cultural types, as Stephen Stark has described them: "the liberal, the member of the upper crust, the religious figure, the feminist woman, and the dissenter—all serving together in a collage that could reassure the anxious audience that melting-pot America still worked."[26] The network sales departments, with their highly sophisticated demographic research, had told them as much many times—as had audiences themselves, ever more exhaustively researched by nightly national Nielsen ratings, Simmons studies, special network testing facilities in New York and Los Angeles, and half a dozen other redundant methods.

With an ensemble show, the thorniest of topical problems could be dealt with in amusing ways. One character encounters bigotry, say, or gets a girlfriend pregnant—the others are there to help him deal with it. The comic load is spread around. An assortment of social types play to the demographic mosaic the audience had become. And finally, such a show tends to take place in workplace settings, permanent sets that no one character claimed and that would allow a constant stream of visitors and guest stars, both "relevant" and otherwise, from the outside world. A remarkable *four* shows debuting in the 1978 season, all of which would have long and successful runs, demonstrated what workhorses ensemble shows could be.

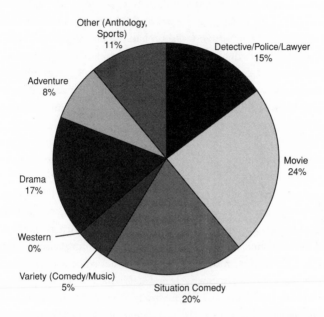

Distribution of Prime-Time Programming for 1978. The sitcom ascendant.

The first, CBS's *Lou Grant,* was technically a spin-off from the original ensemble show, Mary Tyler Moore's. Actor Ed Asner played Mary's gruff boss, newsroom chief Lou Grant. On the original show, Grant was a crusty-but-benevolent father figure whose main function was to advise Mary about her personal life, and only as an afterthought to manage the workplace. Only infrequently was he shown making news decisions.

On the new show, *Lou Grant,* this was not to be the case. The show would be a drama, and Grant would be the city editor of a big-city newspaper, the *Los Angeles Tribune.* Grant would now be shown filling the duties of a real city editor, such as making assignments, deciding what the *Tribune* would run and at what risk, and overseeing a large staff. The show would center on topical issues in which Grant would be supported by a large ensemble: a spunky woman reporter, Billie Newman; an irascible, snowy-haired editor in chief, Charlie Hume; an ethnic, Carl Bernstein–style reporter, Joe Rossi; a WASPy, handsome assistant city editor in his forties, Art Donovan; and a long-haired Vietnam veteran, photographer Dennis "Animal" Price.

Lou Grant's first season was disappointing, and the show was renewed for a second only because of the dependable appeal of Asner's character. But in the second season, the show's focus shifted away from the "hard news," expose-oriented themes of the previous year and more to character studies, plots involving the news staff's personal lives, and news stories lacking bold-faced "relevance." The *Lou Grant* cast and writing staff soon had the show working as a well-oiled machine, turning out "quality" episodes every week and appealing to a fairly broad spectrum of the audience. By the summer of 1978, it was finishing in the Nielsen top ten consistently. It was a prestige show, the sort of flagship series that "the Tiffany network" had prided itself on in past days, and a ratings winner as well. Everyone was pleased, and the ensemble format was further entrenched into television.

What MTM had done successfully with one drama show, they felt they could do with another. The studio was asked in 1977 to develop *The White Shadow* (1978–1981), an hour-long drama series about a retired white pro basketball star who takes a coaching job at an all-black inner-city high school. Using their perfected ensemble system, MTM produced another hit. Topical themes were softly sold, and the characters were relatively authentic and multifaceted (four blacks, a Jew, an Italian, and an unidentified white ethnic, led by a blonde WASP.) Although not as accomplished creatively as *Lou Grant, The White Shadow* received critical and ratings success. It was "quality television," with a wide appeal and none of the noxious, mindless antics that characterized the hits of the Silverman years—jiggling, superpowers, prurient miniseries. And MTM wasn't finished yet.

The studio managed a hat trick by introducing one of the most successful comedy series of the 1978 season in *WKRP in Cincinnati* (1978–1982). Comedy was, after all, MTM's forte, and *WKRP* was the workplace sitcom that finally provided the network with a worthy successor to the original *Mary Tyler Moore Show. WKRP* was updated, as an MTM show needed to be. The women's movement having diminished as a social issue, the level-headed Midwestern star of the series was made a handsome young male ingénue, Gary Sandy. Sandy would play Andy Travis, a young program director for a Midwestern radio station in a moderate-sized city (like WJM of Minneapolis). The cast would include a funky black DJ, Venus Flytrap; a long-haired ex-hippie DJ, Dr. Johnny Fever (played by ex–Second City and Committee regular Howard Hesseman); a straitlaced nerd at the news desk, Les Nessman; a buxom and highly intelligent receptionist, Jennifer Marlowe; a loudly dressed, glad-handing sales manager, Herb Tarlek; and a bumbling but benevolent station manager, the vaguely patrician Arthur Carlsen.

WKRP, like *The Mary Tyler Moore Show* before it, overcame a rocky start to become one of the most popular programs of the late 1970s and early 1980s. And as with its predecessor, much of the credit was due to the balanced dynamics of the ensemble. Politically, a cross-section of society spun around the white-bread axis of the Andy Travis character. Few viewers took Travis to heart, though, and by the end of the show's first season, it was clear that Sandy's character was far down on the list of characters favored by the audience. But neither was there a Fonzie to dwarf the rest into insignificance. On one side, marginal types such as Fever and Flytrap were entertainingly outrageous and carried besides a counter-cultural panache smuggled in from their 1960s pasts (Fever's drug use was frequently alluded to; Flytrap used a borrowed name to avoid detection as a draft dodger). On the other side, characters such as Nessman and Tarlek were squares of flawless pedigree, Nessman a bow-tied nerd, and Tarlek a Babbit in the loud sports jacket of the stage bumpkin. Between these two extremes, Marlowe, with her centerfold looks and superior mind, was a perfect expression of *Cosmopolitan*-style feminism, and Carlsen, the ever-popular, discredited authority figure, a bumbling non-boss much like Commander Henry Blake of *M*A*S*H*. By summer, *WKRP* was a top five performer, outdistancing even *M*A*S*H* in the ratings.

Rounding out this quartet of ensembles was yet another MTM production—even if it did not technically emerge from MTM studios. In this season of ensembles, the most long-lived and influential was probably *Taxi*, a creation of four veteran MTM producers, including Mary Tyler Moore's cocreator, Jim Brooks, and the earlier show's coproducers, Ed Weinberg and Stan Daniels.

Taxi was conceived as an ensemble show, but it broke the mold in one important way: it was conceived as a New York show, and every employee of the Sunshine Taxi Company, the show's workplace setting, reflected it. The Sane Center, Alex Rieger, was played by Judd Hirsch, one of the most identifiably Jewish actors to ever star in a network series. This might have qualified him in another ensemble as the sharp-tongued outsider, like Morey Amsterdam's Buddy from the old *Dick Van Dyke Show*; but *Taxi*'s cast was so ethnic and urban that Rieger seemed like a Jewish Ozzie Nelson by comparison. Latka, the immigrant mechanic, was portrayed by Andy Kaufman, one of the great eccentric talents in the medium's history. Kaufman, with his bizarre accents and bewildered, innocent manner, made Latka one of the most unforgettably realized characters ever seen on TV. Louie DiPalma, the squat and hostile dispatcher, was Italian, as was Tony Banta, a punchy but sweet ex-boxer. Other drivers besides Banta included lion-maned actor Bobby Wheeler, single mom Elaine Nardo, and eventually, burned-out 1960s refugee "Reverend" Jim Ignatowski.

Taxi demonstrates the ease with which ensembles could make consensus models out of anything. Consensus on the older sitcoms and detective shows usually came at a heavy price: some authority figure alternatively called Joe Friday or Jim Anderson or Marcus Welby would lay down the law, and the offending characters would either learn the folly of their way (the haircut solution) or reap the wages of sin (prison, loss of spouse, etc.). The Lear shows had the offenders as antiheroes, put down by family and neighbors, constantly making fools of themselves.[27] Ensembles let the burden of being wrong settle on a different character every episode, without anyone having to carry the weight of always being right or always being wrong. Anyone might go astray in any given episode but would be reeled back by affection and the demands of the workplace, whether it was a newsroom, a cab company, or even a mobile army surgical hospital. Even a show like *Taxi,* which was so urban, with some of the most far-out plots on the airwaves (the ones involving Latka became especially surreal), could appeal to the sensibilities of both big cities and "the C and D counties" and among many age groups.

Inevitably, part of finding a working consensus meant dealing with the 1960s. Hippies and other countercultural types had been sinister buffoons in the 1960s, then sensitive (if misguided) young idealists in the early 1970s. By the late 1970s, as the four shows described above suggest, few ensembles could be complete without a resident "space cadet" or "burnout." *Taxi's* Reverend Jim was the paragon of this type. A shambling, denim-clad mess, Reverend Jim was hopelessly out of it, a basket case who occasionally uttered words of wisdom. Like *Lou Grant's* Animal, or *WKRP's* Dr. Johnny Fever, he could be counted on to voice noble, utopian sentiments from time to time—sentiments that more level-headed members of the cast (e.g., the Sane Center) could sympathize with. But invariably, the burnout would then be reeled back to reality for his own good.

The ideology of the 1960s was troubling to the consciences of late 1970s sitcom characters. They feared even the appearance of bigotry; they worried, like Andy Travis, about the morality of compromise, when it came to free expression, or making a living, like Alex Rieger. The role of the "space cadet" was to help them align themselves in the strange new moral compass of the 1970s. Just what that moral compass was, is a subject for a deeper study than this one; but there can be little doubt that it was essentially different from the sureties of the civil rights era, the antiwar movement, and the Reich/Roszak platitudes.

It was television's task in these years to rebuild mass audiences in the wake of those great moral movements, and ensemble series were one way to do this on a structural level, without seeming to pander to politics. But even on the bread-and-butter level of plot and character developments, TV displayed breathtaking adaptive powers. Having at first counterfeited the new values *(The Storefront Lawyers),* then exploited them for comic effect *(All in the Family),* and finally run from them at breakneck speed *(Happy Days),* television accommodated their gradual passing through an even more adroit and subtle maneuver in the late 1970s: it simply absorbed their remains into itself.

In a certain sense, the culture at large was already at work performing the same work. Examples were gleefully noted in the press daily. Black Panther leader

Eldridge Cleaver, a fugitive from the law for years, returned to stand trial as a born-again Christian. Given community service and a judge's blessing, Cleaver started a new life as a manufacturer of expensive codpiece trousers.[28] "New Right" and "neoconservative" movements sprung up through the country, particularly after the stunning success of Howard Jarvis's tax-cutting Proposition 13 in 1978. Even Theodore Roszak, the prophet of the counterculture, spoke up for "creative social disintegration" and "conviviality" as solutions to the times.[29]

Television, having never adopted the values of the 1960s, had no need to justify turning away from them. What could be easier than to simply adjust the behavior and attitudes of its characters for the changing times? Thus, Archie Bunker, the epitome of the hardhat, by 1977 found himself longing to enter the bourgeoisie. "I wanna raise myself up. I want my name on somethin' more than just a lunchpail," the lovable bigot told his wife. Even the Meathead understood: "He resented me because he never had a chance to better himself. Well, now he's got that chance. In Archie's mind it's a chance for him to be somebody. I don't think you can take that away from him."[30] Thus, in the fall of 1978, Archie Bunker became the proprietor of a neighborhood bar, Archie's Place. By this time, Bunker had become a shadow of his former self, at least insofar as his hostility and wrongheadedness were concerned. Although still a champion malapropist, Archie by this time had commenced his metamorphosis into a crusty-but-benevolent figure of the kind so common on the airwaves at the time. Supplied with a Jewish partner, a Jewish stepdaughter, Hispanic employees, an Irish cook (the pretense was still being maintained that Archie was not Irish), and eventually, a spunky, liberal teenage boarder and even a black live-in maid, Archie became only superficially bigoted. He was really a big teddy bear, once you got beyond his ignorance. After a few token slurs, he could be counted upon to defend the rights of minorities and adjust to middle-class mores as best he could. *Archie Bunker's Place* (1979–1983), the sequel to *All in the Family,* thus used Archie as the centerpiece of a middle-class ensemble, a would-be burgher who keeps stepping on the toes of his peeved but understanding comrades. Edith having been killed off in the 1978 season, the show featured an unmoored and unmanned Archie, a character who had lost all connection to the outside world or his own past. The show expired unmourned in 1983.

Archie Bunker's evolution (or devolution) from archetypal bigot/white ethnic to sitcom revenant was echoed throughout the schedule. Wherever possible, series' leads became less threatening and more a part of the great, new enlightened middle class. *Happy Days*' Fonzie, who had found stardom as a quasirebellious hood in a leather jacket, had by 1978 become so much a role model among America's young that his creators could not forbear from making him into a mouthpiece for grown-up pieties—all delivered with "the Fonz's" trademark swagger. Fonzie advised kids to stay in school, to avoid fights, not to drink or smoke, even to get library cards—a directive that resulted in the American Library Association's issuance of thousands of new cards across the country. Explained producer Marshall, "*Leave It to Beaver, Father Knows Best* were about nice men saying, 'be nice.' Can't do that anymore; nobody listens. Now I got a guy with a leather jacket and black boots who says, 'I can beat you up. I can ride a bike better than you, I do a lot of things better than you, and I get girls, and I'm kind of a rebel, but, also, be nice.' It's the same message, only it's coming from a more modern voice."[31] By the end of the series' run, Fonzie had accepted a post as dean of boys at the local prep school.[32]

Marginal characters were moving to the dead center of society, at least on television. Fonzie was written out just before Marshall got around to sewing patches on the elbows of his leather jacket, but the direction was certainly clear enough. And Marshall's last great hit, 1978's *Mork and Mindy,* continued the absorption of outsider characters into the mainstream. Mork was a space alien who had visited the *Happy Days* crew on one of those "special episodes" with which already-popular series goose ratings from time to time. Mork appeared human enough, but as portrayed by improv comic Robin Williams, he was closer to television incarnate than to a flesh-and-blood person, or even a *Happy Days* character. Marshall had the good sense to let Williams improvise on camera, and the result was electric: Mork was a blur of impressions, funny voices, weird physical comedy, and in-humor. With his baggy pants, rainbow suspenders, long hair, and manic, irreverent style, Mork was an emigrant from the nightclub/improv circuit, not another planet.

There was, of course, nothing new about a stand-up comic on sitcoms. A hundred comics, from Don Rickles to Bob Newhart, had found an occasional home on TV, whether on series, talk shows, or specials like the celebrity "roasts." But these comics had bona fides, had made their bones in Vegas or New York, or (if older) on the borscht belt of the Catskill Mountains, or even in vaudeville. Performers such as Williams (and *Taxi*'s Kaufman, and *WKRP*'s Hesseman) were from outside the show-business establishment, or at least had been. They had trained in a cafe culture, a subterranean comedy establishment appreciated only by hip elites in a few cities. And now, they were enjoying mainstream success on an unthinkable scale. By 1978, Robin Williams was the most popular comedian in America.

Mork and Mindy was an innocuous show. Mork was essentially a child, albeit a savant, and his roommate, the wholesome and beautiful Mindy, more of a surrogate mom or big sister than a girlfriend or wife. Mork's eccentric brothers on other sitcoms were cared for in the same way. Hesseman's Johnny Fever was watched over by the Mindy-like Bailey Quarters; Kaufman's Latka was married to Sipka (Carol Kane), a zany character herself, but relatively stable compared to Latka. The Reverend Jim was protected by the whole Sunshine Garage Company, especially the sober and responsible Alex. And thus it went, throughout the period: emissaries from the margins of the Nixon era spiced up prime time and were themselves contained by stable environments. The two streetwise and cynical black urchins of *Different Strokes* nestled comfortably in the penthouse bosom of a wealthy white patrician and his all-American daughter; Andy Warhol appeared as a guest star on an episode of *The Love Boat.*

That television was having no trouble digesting the cultural legacy of the 1960s was apparent; what was less noted at the time was the extent to which that legacy accommodated television. In the 1960s, it had been taken more or less for granted by the intelligentsia that enlightened culture and television didn't mix: that was almost the only point left and right met on in those divided years. But a new generation of college students and intellectuals was coming into society unformed by Kent State and the war, and with a markedly less hostile attitude toward television. This was no longer the medium, after all, of Jack Webb and Paul Henning, of "square" programming and Agnew-style cultural polemics. It had been years since Norman Lear and MTM had brought at least the appearance of relevance or realism to the small screen. Now those innovations were the rule; so it was hardly to be expected that young people would continue to see TV as "the window on the Establishment . . . the meretricious huckster of the plastic world they were rebelling against," as Les Brown had noted in 1970.[33] And as young people found an image of themselves on the small screen, so did nearly every other part of American society.

Consider the program lineup for our randomly selected night of 18 February, this time of 1978. A thousand flowers bloom: 8:00 P.M. brings us *The Bionic Woman* on NBC, harboring a princess from the other side of the galaxy; on CBS, a droll episode of *The Bob Newhart Show* dealing with Bob advising a would-be TV star who stammered (a bit of self-reflexiveness there, Newhart being often chided for his stammer); on ABC, *What's Happening!!*, the funky sitcom about three black teenagers and their adventures. CBS, in an effort to capture the interests of the urban/sophisticated bloc, lays in a one-hour claim at 8:30 with *The Tony Randall Show,* which features the urbane star as a Philadelphia judge. At 9:00 on NBC, a "supernatural mystery," *The Ghost of Flight 401,* occupies the rest of the evening. On ABC, *The Love Boat,* taking another cross-generational cruise; on CBS's *The Jeffersons,* in *TV Guide's* description, "George must endure the sass of his visiting nephew, a streetwise 8-year-old," played by guest star Gary Coleman, soon to star in *Different Strokes.* At 9:30, CBS reels women viewers in further with a new *Maude,* in which "Viviane's college reunion revives old dreams of heady independence, and she resolves to leave Arthur," followed by *Kojak* at 10:00.

A short history of the counterculture on prime time. From outright detestation *(Dragnet '67, top)* to dogged tolerance *(Star Trek, bottom)* . . .

. . . to inclusion, and finally absorption, by ensemble and consensus *(Taxi's* Reverend Jim, *top; WKRP in Cincinnati's* Dr. Johnny Fever, *bottom).*

Meanwhile, back at ABC, the wide net of *The Love Boat* is kept open, in the hope that precisely the same vast and heterogeneous audience will disembark on Mr. Roarke's *Fantasy Island.*[34] Something for everyone, but not the same something; not anymore.

What all of these shows conspicuously lacked, though, was the electric quality of "hipness," the thing that supposedly separated cultural elites from the hoi polloi and had been behind the most visceral objections to TV by the young a decade earlier. Even having conquered the 1960s, it was not enough for the new television to be merely a "mass medium," a default position with no claim upon its audience's self-respect. To purge the bad old feelings of the old days, television became both the butt and medium for a new humor at its own expense. It was mocked, but through imitation and parody, not direct burlesque; a kind of formal self-deprecation became more and more common. And why not? Now immune to all criticism, having absorbed its most heavy-handed critics, and mopped up every demographic taste group that might have held out against its new, variegated attack, television by 1978 was perfectly suited to pioneer a self-reflexive humor, a humor directed harmlessly against itself.

The watershed in this process was the debut, in 1975, of *Saturday Night Live* (1975–present) on NBC. The network hired former *Laugh-In* writer Lorne Michaels to produce a late-night variety program targeted at the elusive 18–35 viewer. NBC had had some success a few seasons earlier with a late-night rock music program, *The Midnight Special;* it was thought that the young adults would go out for the evening but return home in the wee hours to tune in to their favorite acts. Michaels was given a creative green light, therefore, to make a show that would appeal to his generation. It was on late enough at night that there would be little risk of offending a mainstream audience and little to lose, given the paucity of viewers at that hour. (*The Midnight Special* was the latest-scheduled network show in history at that time.)

Much to the surprise and delight of NBC, Michaels's show was an immediate cult hit. Michaels had set out to make the show "cutting edge," to give it the underground cachet of the *National Lampoon,* the Second City, and the Committee. Michaels had, in fact, recruited writers and players from all of the above, most notably Michael O'Donahue and Anne Beatts from the *National Lampoon,* at that time the most accomplished and uncompromising satirical organ going. Among the cast were a number of alumni from *National Lampoon*'s off-Broadway production *Lemmings,* including John Belushi and Chevy Chase, and a number of other actors associated with *National Lampoon* and Second City. The material would be irreverent and zany. In form, the show was meant to be a throwback to the immediacy and riskiness of early television, performed "live, from New York," as opposed to filmed, from Hollywood, the capital city of plastic, processed material, and canned laughter. *Saturday Night Live,* not to put too fine a point on it, was tailored to the cultural specifications of the baby boomers, whom Lorne Michaels regarded as neglected. He would be their Ed Sullivan; he would finally create the hip TV show.[35]

Saturday Night Live was this. It captured the young audience it was designed for, and it captured them in far greater numbers than anyone had hoped, especially after the show caught on as a cult item. Better still, it gave last-place NBC a much-needed injection of prestige and publicity "buzz." Although tame by the standards of *National Lampoon* and the Committee, the show was unlike anything seen on television since the early days of *Your Show of Shows.* There was an undeniable electricity; the "Not Ready for Prime Time Players" (as they were pointedly called) *were* strikingly original and talented, with a minimum of show-business streamlining; and the subject matter *was* daring, the language and humor licentious and unpredictable. On numerous occasions (and this is a feat dear to the hearts of baby-boomer chroniclers of the show), the *SNL* writing staff went over the line and had to be restrained, even at that late hour, by the network's standards and practices department. (A racially charged monologue by Richard Pryor stayed; a commercial for "Placenta Helper" meal extender didn't.)

What *Saturday Night Live* did not attempt, however, was to cause trouble with its politics. It had none. When it spoofed Presidents Ford and Carter, it was never their policies as much as their personal mannerisms that bore the brunt of the assault. The show was brilliant, and the satire dead-on. But the show was also consciously distancing itself from the committed earnestness of the *Smothers Brothers* and the "message humor" of the previous decade: remembered Michaels some years later, "suddenly things I once felt so strongly about, I didn't feel strongly about at all. It was hard for me to believe I actually once grew my hair long to stop the war. We had to learn to laugh at ourselves—at our follies."[36] As a *Laugh-In* alumni, there was no reason for Michaels to get worked up; the politics of his humor had never gone more than gag deep.

Thus, *SNL*'s cutting edge cut only into space: for the most part, the subject of its humor was television itself. From its trademark Weekend Update news parody ("Hello, I'm Chevy Chase, and you're not") to its fake commercials ("Its a floor wax *and* a dessert topping!") and blackout sketches, the show referred largely to contemporary American TV culture and its foibles—along with a number of character-driven sketches that turned out to be the most memorable work *SNL* produced. The *Washington Post* caught on to *SNL*'s orientation quite early, hailing the very first show as a "live, lovely, raucously disdainful view of a world that television largely shaped."[37]

That world was not all television largely shaped; the same could be said for *SNL*'s audience. The latter end of the baby boom, those kids born in the mid-

to-late 1950s, were teenagers and college students in 1975. Having grown up taking rock music, reflexive antiauthoritarianism, and "sick" humor for granted, the
show spoke to their sensibilities far more than it did those of the older boomer
humorists—many of whom, such as George Carlin (b. 1934), Lenny Bruce (b.
1925), or Mort Sahl (b. 1927), were actually products of the Depression. For these
kids, jokes about Watergate or Southern bigots were about as meaningful as jokes
about cheap Scotchmen or women drivers. Jokes about media culture resonated,
however, as Michael Arlen had noted in his 1975 essay on Norman Lear. Of *SNL*,
Arlen wrote, "It is an attempt, finally, to provide entertainment on television that
tries to deal with the morass of media-induced show-business culture that increasingly pervades American life."[38]

What Arlen mistook for a way out, however, was in reality a dead end. Mastery of the television environment was second nature to *SNL* and its many imitators since; what was difficult for them was to transcend that environment. The
rancor that made the Lear shows so unappetizing, and that eventually resulted
in their extinction in favor of innocuous kid-vid, was paradoxically the only thing
that prevented them from disappearing into the numbing snowscape of least
objectionable programming. *SNL* easily mocked that rancor, along with Captain Kirk's resolve, Ricky Nelson's naïveté, and all other states of mind that lacked
the ultrasophisticated distance, the straight-faced ironic attitude, that the show
and its personality-free cast displayed; because the Not Ready for Prime Time
Players, with the notable exceptions of Belushi and Bill Murray, were ciphers,
disappearing completely into their roles and carrying little with them from one
to the next. It might have been these very men and women of whom Christopher Lasch wrote in *The Minimal Self: Psychic Survival in Troubled Times* three
years later. Almost to a person, their movie careers were washouts when not re-
prising *SNL* roles.

Of all the cast of *SNL,* one in particular stood out as TV culture incarnate,
irony's master and slave. This was Murray, a writer who joined the show's cast
after Chevy Chase left for Hollywood. Like Chase, Murray was a master at the
poker-faced, knowing expression—the guy who never really meant what he said
and around whose every utterance invisible quotation marks hovered. Murray
took this part even farther than Chase had and in the process created a comic
style that has yet to be eradicated from our culture. Whenever a David Letterman
pointedly mouths a trite, empty phrase ("from the home office in Scottsdale,
Arizona"); whenever some sitcom rebel in dark sunglasses assures a traffic court
judge or detention monitor that "I truly regret what I've done"; whenever two
people in conversation fall into what author Douglas Coupland called "telethonese"—unctuous phrases like "you're beautiful," "I love this guy," "what a
nut," etc.—Bill Murray's wings beat overhead.

Irony was what Murray made so glamorous. It had been a technique, used by shows such as *Batman* to amuse older viewers as well as kids, or *M*A*S*H* to elevate pedestrian gag writing; in the mid-1970s, it became a full-blown lifestyle decision. Alongside the ensemble show in mid-decade developed a trickier, but equally effective and much flashier formula for success. Make television that seemed to be better than television, television whose self-consciousness made it seem somehow transcendent when, in fact, it was just getting smaller and more narcissistic (to use another Laschism). As critic Robert Sklar noted in 1978, "*Saturday Night Live* is a program for people who both love television and disdain it; it allows viewers to express both feelings at once. They can enjoy the show and also take pleasure in the fact that it parodies and puts down conventional television."[39]

Saturday Night Live pointed the way toward this and was soon exceeded by the compulsively parodic *SCTV* (1977–1984), a syndicated series patterned after *SNL*. *SCTV* was obsessed with combining and parodying the most minute features of television from the framework of an imaginary television network, SCTV of Melonville. *SCTV* was even more the brainchild of Canadians than *SNL* had been, and it took the outsider's obsessive mania to an even greater degree. Third-rate stars such as Merlin Olson, Gavin McLeod, and Jamie Farr were given faithful impersonations. Made-up stars such as Sammy Maudlin, Bobby Bittman, and Johnny LaRue were featured in their own continuing TV series. In one episode, Hank Bain, the real-life brother of *Different Strokes'* star Conrad Bain, guest-starred as himself, as an alien agent set to infiltrate the network; in another, the network was preempted by its Soviet counterpart, CCCP-1 and its lineup of sitcoms *(Hey, Gyorgi!)* and game shows *(Uboscrabblenik)*. The show was far too baroque to ever become a big hit, but it remains a cult favorite today.[40]

This was indeed another way in which, to borrow Johnson's definition of *irony,* "the meaning is contrary to the words." It was hardly a new invention, even on popular entertainments: the old *George Burns Show* had featured a self-conscious device whereby Burns, the host/comedian, stepped outside of Burns the sitcom character to comment on the action directly to the audience. The Crosby/Hope movies were filled with asides and allusions to the movie the two were supposedly characters in. Jack Benny seemed to be playing himself in life as well as on radio and TV.

But now, the ironic device seemed to be more. *SNL* helped to point the direction for far less sophisticated entertainments. In the new vein, one could makes jokes that seemed to point beyond themselves, to some knowingness on the part of both producer and audience. The titans of the industry all tried, in one way or another, to embrace the new style. Lear was the first, premiering *Mary Hartman, Mary Hartman* in 1975. Since the show would be highly controversial, Lear went directly to local affiliates themselves, offering them direct deals.[41] *Mary Hartman,*

Mary Hartman was a comic soap opera, much like *Soap* on ABC. Unlike that show, however, its wellsprings were not risqué topics and broad humor but an acute parody of the televised life. Mary worried about "waxy yellow buildup" on her floors and was eventually admitted to a mental asylum whose television room was counted as a Nielsen household. Another character had an accident at work and was forced to have plastic surgery that resulted in his looking like Tab Hunter—and Tab Hunter took over the role. The line between TV reality and Mary's reality was not so much blurred as nonexistent; and soon became even more so. So popular did *Mary Hartman, Mary Hartman* become that it soon produced a spin-off, a talk-show parody entitled *Fernwood 2-Night,* later *America 2-Night*. *Fernwood 2-Night* was hosted by Barth Gimbel, a Bill Murray/Sammy Maudlin-style meta-TV star, and the show in fact resembled nothing so much as a long continuing *SNL* skit. And if the new style attracted Lear, it was hardly surprising that the other great TV pioneer of the early 1970s would follow suit.

In 1978, Mary Tyler Moore premiered her long-awaited successor to *The Mary Tyler Moore Show*. On 28 September, *Mary* debuted. Moore had faced a problem common to all stars of long-running, popular series. How would she address the audience's identification of her with her previous character? Picking up on the new fashion for self-referentiality, Moore and her husband, producer Grant Tinker, decided to simply anticipate the problem and turn it against the audience. *Mary* referred to *The Mary Tyler Moore Show* at every turn, grossly flattering the audience with an inclusive, "hip" self-awareness. The first episode featured the Ed Asner Dancers, a chorus of middle-aged bald men; a skit in which cast members of the new show audition by imitating Mary's lines from old episodes of the MTM show; and at the end, a "historic moments from the first twenty-five minutes of *Mary*" skit. The fun-house mirrors and false bottoms of *Mary* could not have been more oppressive. The show starts out referring to its star's last TV show (the Asner Dancers), then refers to its referral (the auditions), and then finally refers to itself referring to itself, all while counterfeiting false humility. It was no wonder the thing lasted only three weeks.

Undeterred, Tinker premiered a replacement a few months later: *The Mary Tyler Moore Hour*. Having decided to be less Escheresque in conception, Tinker remained committed to the concept of self-reflexive TV—a testament to the trend, given Tinker's standing in the industry and his acknowledged taste and intelligence. *The Mary Tyler Moore Hour* was a show-within-a-show modeled after the old *George Burns* program. Mary Tyler Moore would play Mary McKinnon, the host of a musical variety show not unlike the late *Mary*. Each episode would deal with backstage show-business problems, which would give the audience their meta-TV fix and would allow Moore to eat her cake, too, by singing and dancing as well as playing a character. But this show, too, became mired down in self-indulgent allusions: when Dick Van Dyke guest hosted, a producer was made to ask him, "don't you think that Mary looks like the girl who played Laura Petrie?" pausing for a too pregnant beat.

The Mary Tyler Moore Hour was canceled also, but MTM committed itself to ironic/self-reflexive tropes in all their shows. On *Taxi,* the Reverend Jim becomes an adviser to a programming executive, or dates Marcia Wallace, the actress who played Bob Newhart's secretary, believing her to be her character Carol. On *The White Shadow,* Coolidge is recruited to play a streetwise black kid on a *White Shadow*-type show called "Downtown High." *The Betty White Show,* another failure, featured White as the star of a TV show, and it was, as Jane Feuer points out, "the only recorded instance of a TV pilot within a TV pilot."[42] One MTM program, *The Lorenzo Music Show,* would feature canned-laughter virtuoso Carroll Pratt operating his laugh machine on camera. And so on.

Its excesses aside, self-allusive television came into its own as a mainstream style. It had to. Ensemble series were a good way to appeal to the new audience, but they were hard to produce, requiring great care, expense, and risk. And the networks had to learn other ways of cheaply producing shows that would appeal, if not to "America" then at least to this or that demographic niche. Politics would not henceforth be a problem. It was easier by far to produce shows that simply acknowledged the changed reality of America, a country that had made its peace with both the Establishment and the medium that defined it. Television that did so either explicitly (as with *SNL* or *SCTV*) or implicitly (in such with-it shows as *Mork and Mindy, Soap,* and *WKRP*) was able to find a center to play to after all. The one thing people still had in common in America, when all was said and done, was that they all watched TV. The politics of the 1960s were purged, just as the cultural standards of the 1950s had been, and the networks took what was left and presented it, for ratings' sake, to America. What was left was mostly TV itself, complex, apolitical, cynical, neurotic: a mirror of its audiences, relevant after all.

Epilogue

If the 1970s represented television's fiercest *Kulturkampf,* the 1980s were the years of conquest and consolidation. The long struggle was over; network prime-time TV largely *was* American culture, and while there would always be unyielding elements in American society, they could no longer speak for the center. More importantly, they could no longer speak as one.

Not many groups could. America had been disunited for so long that many now doubted if indeed there ever had been a center. Nonetheless, it had been possible, even as late as 1968, to speak as if there were one: as if the profound cultural disruptions of the time were the product of the war, or foolish federal policies, or the gullibility of youth. Over the course of a decade, it became obvious they were not, and any hope of a "silent majority" finding its voice was abandoned. In 1980, Republican voters rejoiced at their deliverance from liberalism by Ronald Reagan, as did many struggling workers, white ethnics, and other fed-up citizens. Conservatives now held the whip at last, and they scourged the left, who for the most part went into hiding and stayed there, except where the academy offered shelter or in a few coastal strongholds. Neither group pretended to speak for America as a whole and dismissed their counterparts as brainwashed, gullible, self-righteous boors.

Interestingly, over the next twenty years, both groups would likewise pillory "the media" for propagating each other's faults. The media was probusiness and antibusiness, conservative mind control and liberal propaganda, the tool of a prying, expansive government and the pawn of a do-nothing plutocracy. Both sides agreed it should be different. Neither side made much headway. The academy, itself lusting for "relevance," began to embrace the theoretical study of media, advancing ideas about how TV functioned as an instrument of hegemonic power and how it could be reordered at will by empowered intellects. Nobody paid any attention. Likewise, there would continue to be a certain amount of lobbying for TV to trim its excesses of sex and violence; and occasionally, TV would comply.

What kept any of these factions from connecting, either with the American people as a whole, or for that matter, with each other, was television's ongoing reinvention by, and for, baby boomers. Putting it so baldly inevitably overstates what is a complex and subtle shift, but there can be little doubt that the culture of television had been unmistakably boomerized by the early 1980s. The events of the 1970s were a necessary prologue, and being piecemeal, are more revealing for historical purposes. But baby boomers took over television with a series of successive innovations in the early 1980s, the most dramatic being the advent of David Letterman as television's dominant persona.

Letterman was a protégé of Johnny Carson, whose supremely laid-back, self-contained style had made him the quintessential TV personality. But while Carson's impeccable cool assured that his vast nightly audiences would never tire of him (what was there, really, to tire of?), the comic portions of his program were embarrassingly corny. Busty blondes, turbaned psychics, oily mustachioed pitchmen—it was least objectionable humor, meant to neither offend nor inspire.

Letterman's humor, on the other hand, could hardly have been hipper. Either you got it, or you didn't. And if you did, you were rewarded with a sense of enlightenment. *Late Night with David Letterman,* its host seemed to be saying, wasn't a polished network production as much as an in-joke, a guerrilla production thrown together by someone much like yourself—assuming you went to college and thought television was really stupid. *Late Night* seemed to imply that it existed by accident and would no doubt be canceled sometime very soon. Letterman never tired of demonstrating that he was no better than his audience, whom he went out of his way to make part of the spectacle. *The Tonight Show* had had a clear and prominent proscenium: Johnny was boss, and the audience an adulatory mass. Letterman's aggressively self-deprecating humor and refusal to act as a traditional "host," on the other hand, brought audiences onto the set, behind the scenes, and encouraged them to share his Olympian disdain for TV and everything about it, including himself. "Both Carson and Letterman possess the same effortless wit, but David seems closer to his audience," said *Newsweek* in 1980, when Letterman was first getting his feet wet with an NBC morning show. Singled out for special praise by Harry Waters, *Newsweek*'s critic, was Letterman's winning awareness of TV's paltriness: "To assure home viewers that there was nothing better going on down the dial, [Letterman] hauled out a portable TV and reported: 'There's an "Alice" rerun on Channel 2. . . . I think they found something in Mel's stew. . . . The Lone Ranger's on 5. . . . Uh oh, here's Dinah cooking an omelet.'"[1]

This basic trope, which Letterman has battered audiences with for more than twenty years, has to rank as one of the most successful inventions in the history of American comedy. Besides being inexhaustible, it was irresistible to viewers, including critics, who thought of themselves as smart, with it, hip. And by 1982,

thanks to a decade of boomer culture, this was a sizable portion of the population. *Late Night with David Letterman* became the standard-bearer of the new
irony, the metatelevisual self-awareness that put down TV even as it represented
the best TV had to offer. Letterman became televisual irony incarnate, surpass-
ing even Bill Murray as its greatest avatar.[2] As Richard Corliss wrote in *Time*,
"[Letterman] seems to have been created for and by television, working within
a narrow band of emotions, charming viewers with his unflappable attitude rather
than with quick reactions, political satire and confrontation comedy."[3] Just so.
And his brilliant writing staff produced sketches and parodies so accurate and
original that they easily relieved Letterman's phlegmatic personality.

Late Night with David Letterman premiered in 1982; a year earlier, almost
unnoticed, a fledgling cable network called MTV began broadcasting. As influential as the Letterman show was, MTV may have been even more so. Its formal
effects alone, in accelerating the transition from a linear, narrative-based visual
medium patterned on movies to a hyperkinetic, semihypnotic, free-form one
based on everything and nothing, deserve a full-length study. But for here, it's
sufficient to note how much a rock-television marriage meant.

Boomers had long observed that rock music and television had never really
mixed—to the great credit (or at least credibility) of rock and roll. Live network
TV appearances by the Grateful Dead, Elvis Costello, and other nonmainstream
artists were one reason why *Saturday Night Live* had seemed revolutionary. Like
Don Kirchner's Rock Concert before it, however, *SNL* was perceived as an exception, an oasis of rock music in an easy-listening medium. MTV changed all that.
Created, produced, staffed, and watched by young people (its founder, Bob
Pittman, was twenty-seven at the time), it very quickly accomplished the once
unthinkable feat of making television necessary for rock's success.

The importance of this can hardly be exaggerated. It changed television; it
changed rock music; it changed youth culture; it changed America. But for the
purpose of this essay, it's sufficient to note that rock music, supposedly one of
the greatest oppositional energies in the culture, went overnight from being on
the periphery of TV to becoming a pillar of it.

Beyond late night and cable, however, the change could be seen most promi-
nently in that epicenter of American mass culture that is prime-time network
television. As a result of accelerated evolution in the 1970s, prime time in the
1980s seemed to get better: more sophisticated, better written, more knowing.
There was still plenty of terrible, old-fashioned, least objectionable programming
on the air, shows such as *The Dukes of Hazard* or *B.J. and the Bear*. But the future, particularly as it was shaping up under Brandon Tartikoff, Fred Silverman's
young replacement at NBC, belonged to the MTM model of "quality" ensemble
series. *Cosby, Cheers, Hill Street Blues, Family Ties, St. Elsewhere,* and even the

MTV-inspired *Miami Vice:* these would be the standard-bearers for TV culture in the early to mid-1980s and would make the medium look pretty good.

Key to accomplishing this was the presence, at nearly every level of production, of baby boomers. No doubt, older or younger writers and producers could, and often did, produce programming of which any network could be proud. But the essential note in so many of the successful shows was a baby-boom sense of world order and an internalized sense of hip identity that suffused every scene. "In Bruce Willis, and/or in David Letterman, and/or in Mariette Hartley, or in any of a hundred other aging wise guys," one saw "the generation that once laughed off TV . . . trying still to laugh it off while disappearing into it," observed Mark Crispin Miller in 1988.[4] As usual, only a few programs were true baby-boomer productions: for every *Family Ties* or *L.A. Law,* there were two or three *Matlock*s and *Webster*s. But the boomer shows suffused their style throughout the schedule. Each year as the 1980s progressed brought fewer LOP-type shows and more programming within the tent of boomer tastes and folkways. The ratings supremacy of urbane shows such as *Seinfeld* and *Frazier* in the 1990s, unimaginable ten years earlier, was made possible by this accelerated change.

The changes on the screen in the 1980s were unmistakable. But as in previous decades, they told only half the story. The structure of television had changed as well. No longer was TV, as it had always been, a monopoly shared by three, nearly indistinguishable corporations. Now, cable television brought several more networks into the picture. By 1980, according the A. C. Nielsen Company, 17,671,490 American homes had cable; the following year, it was 23,219,200; by 1982, 29,340,570.[5] As more and more Americans received cable service, television meant dozens of channels rather than three. The networks, as the primary purveyors of original programming, still were the dominant presence on television; but the structure of the marketplace fragmented, just as programming strategies had a few years earlier and as the audience had a few years before that. In television, as in the rest of America, centrifugal force trumped inertia every time.

Still, though television had changed, in no way had these changes made it any more legible as a presence in society. If anything, as it grew more channels, brighter spectacles, more interesting sitcoms, and more self-referential tropes, paradoxically, the more invisible TV grew. Particular programs were much discussed, as were certain controversial figures, such as Madonna or Ronald Reagan; but television had finally outgrown America's field of vision and could seldom be viewed but in parts; or, as here, from a distance.

The strange career of *The Brady Bunch* helps put some of the changes of the past thirty years of television culture in perspective. The original show, which premiered in 1969, typified the "escapist" sitcom at its surreal best. It sprang from the ultimate escapist pedigree—its creator was none other than Sherwood Schwartz, the auteur behind *Gilligan's Island*. Schwartz, a typical Californian, had noticed that there were many families like his own, in which both partners had brought the children of an earlier marriage with them. How they cobbled those families together might be the stuff of a good sitcom, he reasoned. The success of the 1968 film *Yours, Mine and Ours* convinced ABC to take a chance. The series wouldn't be progressive in any way except for its founding conceit, however; the novelty of its premise freed the show to transport the reality-free suburban idylls of 1950s sitcoms intact to the Norman Lear/MTM era. Heroically irrelevant, the last of a once mighty race, *The Brady Bunch* enjoyed a successful five-year run on ABC and expired peacefully in 1974. Few expected the series to do much syndication business; but in the atmosphere of the squalid 1970s, the pristine Brady world became increasingly attractive. Schwartz was nothing if not a good businessman, and the second act of the Brady saga is characterized by the vicissitudes of the Silverman years.

In those times, it will be remembered, the networks flailed helplessly at each other, each one grasping desperately at new gimmicks and formulas in a frantic attempt to rebuild disintegrating audience blocs. What a time! And it served the Bradys well. The second Brady incarnation came through the enterprising minds of Sid and Marty Krofft, two brothers who had carved out a kid-vid empire for themselves based on groovy, underproduced shows such as *H.R. Pufnstuf* and *Sigmund and the Sea Monsters*. The Kroffts, who were obviously born TV producers, came up with the most 1970s idea ever conceived: they would create a *variety show* hosted by the Brady Bunch. It was the best of all possible worlds! It would have something for everybody! Such was the thinking for twenty years among the networks, who refused to believe that the variety show could really be dead. So the Bradys appeared in big production numbers wearing spangled, bell-bottomed jumpsuits of the sort favored by Elvis Presley and Evel Kneivel. The show became a treasure for kitsch connoisseurs within days; but it got poor ratings. In addition, the Kroffts in their enthusiasm had forgotten to mention *The Brady Bunch Variety Hour* to Sherwood Schwartz or Paramount Studios, who owned the franchise. Eight shows were aired before the program disappeared back into the vacuum.

But the Brady clan was not so easily disposed of. As a stable and predictable commodity, they remained a valuable franchise, and NBC was happy to debut, in 1981, a series called *The Brady Brides*. In this one, Jan and Marcia had both married; one husband, Wally Covington, was happy-go-lucky, and the other, Philip Covington III, a buttoned-up snob. The whole family was on hand to mediate, and even the original theme song was refurbished with a synthesizer beat. The show, to the dismay of its buyers, did not tap into the nation's love for all things Brady, as demonstrated through rerun ratings. How could it? The whole value of the original was in its timelessness, its antimodernity. Who wanted to see menopausal parents, and seedy-looking Brady boys? Marcia was as beautiful as ever, but the rest of the clan was decaying before America's eyes. NBC pulled the plug after ten episodes—a successful run by the standards of 1981, one of the last years of NBC's decline before Brandon Tartikoff's magic began to work.

Certainly by the late 1980s, one would have thought that the Brady saga would have run its course. The characters had been good for three separate TV series, not to mention a Saturday morning cartoon series. It continued to do well in syndication. And TV had finally changed somewhat, as the "quality" TV of the Tartikoff administration had diffused itself across other networks. But no. In 1988, the same self-evident truth struck CBS that had impressed itself upon Sid and Marty Krofft: the Bradys, even in their attenuated state, were still more valuable than an original, untested pilot. And as with the Kroffts' effort, the show in which the Bradys reemerged was a pure distillate of the times.

A Very Brady Christmas, a made-for-TV movie, featured a motley Brady clan in which everyone suffered from significant but solvable life problems. This was no suburban dreamscape, such as they had inhabited in the early 1970s. No, these Bradys would outdo even the cast of *thirtysomething* in personal strife. Marcia's husband has been fired. Jan's husband is moving out. Peter is having girlfriend troubles because he can't commit. Bobby has dropped out of graduate school. Even Alice is suffering after being left by Sam the butcher! The dialogue is consciously more worldly and cynical than it had been when last manufactured, for *The Brady Brides.* By the end of the movie, of course, all problems had been solved—this being the Bradys, after all—and so delighted were audiences with them that *A Very Brady Christmas* was the top-rated TV movie of 1988. This really was having your cake and eating it too, or so it seemed, and the special's success inspired an entire "mature Brady" series, *The Bradys,* in 1990.

The show began with a more soulful-sounding theme song, set to the same tune, but proclaiming the show's advances:

> When our kids were small their problems all were smaller
> When they changed, so did their point of view
> The world has taken on a larger meaning,
> Since the family grew!
> The Bradys . . . oh, the Bradys . . .

The show was not a success, however, and was soon canceled. Schwartz blamed the time slot, claiming that 8 P.M. was too early for the "mature" themes the show dealt with. Such may have been the case; but more likely, the Bradys had just outstayed their welcome. People continued to love the original series, and in the TV-suffused culture of the 1990s, it was common for people in their twenties to identify each other by Brady shibboleths—"pork chops and applesauce," the voodoo tiki, and so on—from dimly remembered episodes. But the whole point of *The Brady Bunch* was that it was self-contained, stylized, a fertile ground for nostalgia and escapism—none of which were delivered by its squalid sequels.

Still, somehow, all was not yet lost for the Bradys. There was still the irony wave to ride, then as ever the last refuge of the bad. By the 1990s, televisual irony, pioneered by Bill Murray and David Letterman, had finally come into its majority. Nowhere on TV was TV not derided for laughs: "you prove your superiority to TV's garbage," wrote Miller in 1988, "not by criticizing it or refusing it, but by feeding on it, taking in its oblique assurances that you're too smart to swallow any of it." Miller was one of the first critics of television to really understand the value of the ironic posture to cheap entertainment: "And as it permeates TV, so does this prophylactic irony now suffuse TV's culture, whose main attractions, however gross, seem admirable, as long as—like Hulk Hogan, 'Sledge Hammer,' Joe Isuzu—they play their grossness 'tongue in cheek.'"[6]

The best thing about ironic TV, though, was that you got to enjoy not only the slick derision and reassurance but also the homely pleasures nestled inside, like the center of a Tootsie-Roll Pop. Thus, the emergence of the Bradys in ironic form was inevitable. *The Real Live Brady Bunch* featured actors performing *Brady Bunch* episodes before audiences of hipsters in major U.S. cities. Recently identified in the media as "Generation X," these aging youths lacked anything else around which to form a generational identity, and so, as with so much else in recent history, TV filled the vacuum. "Audience members sing along to the theme song, shout out lines and generally act as if they were gathered in their living rooms, eyes glued to the old Quasar," wrote reviewer John Kelly in the *Washington Post*. What could be better? The show featured actors who attempted to minutely re-create the set, pace, intonations, and even the physical appearance of the original Brady actors; and it goes without saying that every episode was performed line for line, underscoring Johnson's definition of irony as "a mode of speech in which the meaning is contrary to the words."

Given the self-replicating, self-referential, and utterly enclosed orb that TV culture had become by the 1990s, it was inevitable that *The Real Live Brady Bunch* would not only prosper but multiply. *The Brady Bunch Movie*, in 1995, set the family, outfits, and folkways intact into the present day, there to be mocked and identified with; a sequel appeared two years later. When Greg Williamson, the actor who played Peter Brady, wrote a memoir titled *Growing Up Brady*, the book was an immediate success; predictably, it inspired its own TV movie, with its own cast of Brady simulacra.

The *Brady Bunch* phenomenon was now growing exponentially; and as of this writing, it still shows no sign of becoming extinct. The small, gemlike fire at its heart is the virgin earnestness of the original show, so comforting in its very cluelessness. Unhappily for the adults who remember it warmly from childhood, however, that innocence can be neither counterfeited nor reproduced. Like the culture that created it, it exists now only as memory.

Notes
Selected Bibliography
Index

Notes

1. "Green Acres Is the Place to Be": America and TV, 1968

1. David Halberstam, *The Powers That Be* (New York: McGraw-Hill, 1979), 511–14.

2. Each rating point represents a percentage of the whole viewing audience, as measured by Nielsen. Needless to say, these ratings are highly generalized and, at this time, were quite crude. Nonetheless, they provided the major source of information by which all network decisions were made. It should be noted that these shows, although rated through April, represent the programming through the following summer, albeit in reruns. The following year's programs debut in fall.

3. Throughout this work, I use the word *television* as shorthand to describe the culture of prime-time network entertainment programming, which of course is only one small part of television, taken as a medium or an industry. Culturally, however, it had an impact and centrality that far transcended its place on either the schedule or the broadcast spectrum.

4. Eric Barnouw, *Tube of Plenty: The Evolution of American Television* (New York: Oxford University Press, 1975), 355–56.

5. Muriel Cantor, *The Hollywood TV Producer* (New York: Transaction Publishing, 1970), 219–28. For an interesting articulation of the attitude of even some media executives toward the code's hypocrisy, see Donald H. McGannon, "Is the TV Code a Fraud?" in *Television Today: A Close-Up View*, ed. Barry Cole (New York: Oxford University Press, 1981), 318. McGannon was at the time of writing the chairman of Westinghouse Broadcasting Company, a major power in the media business.

6. For a good treatment of the stormy relationship between Minow and the broadcast industry, see Mary Ann Watson, *The Expanding Vista* (New York: Oxford University Press, 1990), 18–40. Watson's study describes the Kennedy years as a breakthrough period for television, which it indeed was in many ways; however, as Watson points out repeatedly, despite the protests of the FCC, the NAACP, and other groups, entertainment programming changed very little as the networks chafed against "coercion."

7. The practice of dispatching silver-haired titans to Washington for symposia or committees, or even informal communing with government leaders, is a recurring one; witness President Bill Clinton's "summit meeting" over sex and violence in the spring of 1996.

8. Harry Castleman and Walter Podzarik, *Watching TV: Four Decades of American Television* (New York: McGraw-Hill, 1981), 206.

9. Michael Dann, Oral History Interview, 2 November 1998, Academy of Television Arts and Sciences Archive of American Television, Los Angeles (archive cited hereafter as ATAS).

10. Tankersly quoted in Richard Adler, *All in the Family: A Critical Appraisal* (Aspen: Praeger, 1979), xxiii. The standards and practices division head is the de facto chief censor for the network.

11. Paul Klein, "Programming," in *Inside the TV Business,* ed. Steve Morgenstern (New York: Sterling, 1979), 16–17; see also Paul Klein, "Why You Watch, What You Watch, When You Watch," *TV Guide,* 24 July 1971, 6–10. All *TV Guide* citations are taken from the Wilkes-Barre, Pennsylvania, edition, the magazine's edition of record.

12. Wizbar quoted in Castleman and Podzarik, *Watching TV,* 78.

13. Gilbert Seldes, *The Great Audience* (New York: Viking, 1950), 252–64.

14. For a larger historical context, see Lawrence Levine, *Highbrow/Lowbrow: The Emergence of Cultural Hierarchy in America* (Cambridge: Harvard University Press, 1988); cf. Dwight Macdonald's seminal essay, "A Theory of Mass Culture," in *Mass Culture: The Popular Arts in America,* ed. Bernard Rosenberg and David Manning White (New York: Free Press, 1957).

15. Stanton and Sarnoff quoted in William L. O'Neill, *American High: The Years of Confidence, 1945–1960* (New York: Free Press, 1986), 82.

16. The fullest exploration of this theme, Richard Hofstatder's *Anti-Intellectualism in American Life* (New York: Knopf, 1963) was partially inspired by the anti-"egghead" mood of his times. For a more detached perspective, see Richard H. Pells, *The Liberal Mind in a Conservative Age: American Intellectuals in the 1940s and 1950s* (New York: Harper and Row, 1985).

17. Les Brown, *Television: The Business Behind the Box* (New York: Harcourt, Brace, Jovanovich, 1971), 77.

18. Treyz quoted in J. Fred Macdonald, *One Nation under Television* (Chicago: Nelson-Hall, 1994), 124–25. Paley quoted in Todd Gitlin, *Inside Prime Time* (New York: Pantheon, 1984), 64. See also Brown, *Television,* 111–12. "You can hate someone in a movie and enjoy it," producer Paul Henning once said, "but you don't want to see him again—or ever. In television, you need characters you'll like and want to see every week for years" (quoted in David Marc, *Demographic Vistas* [Philadelphia: University of Pennsylvania Press, 1984], 44).

19. Gitlin, *Inside Prime Time,* 63; Paul Klein, interview by author, New York City, 1 October 1996.

20. Ray Bradbury, "A Writers' Symposium," in *Television: The Creative Experience* (New York: Hastings House, 1967), 65.

21. M. Cantor, *Hollywood TV Producer,* 167–69.

22. Sally Bedell, *Up the Tube: Prime Time in the Silverman Years* (New York: Viking, 1981), 64; see also Grant Tinker, *Tinker in Television: From General Sarnoff to General Electric* (New York: Simon and Schuster, 1994), 90–91.

23. For an interesting discussion of *The Dick Van Dyke Show* as an expression of the Kennedy era, see David Marc, "The Making of the Sitcom, 1961," in *Comic Visions* (Malden: Blackwell, 1997); see also Watson, *The Expanding Vista.*

24. Ed Papazian, *Medium Rare: The Evolution, Workings, and Impact of Commercial Television* (New York: Media Dynamics, 1991), 187.

25. Dick Van Dyke, Oral History Interview, 8 January 1998, ATAS.

26. Papazian, *Medium Rare,* 188.

27. The best single discussion of *The Beverly Hillbillies* is David Marc's "The Situation Comedy of Paul Henning: Modernity and the American Folk Myth in the *Beverly Hillbillies,*" in *Demographic Vistas,* 39–64.

28. Quoted in Andrew Edelstein, *The Pop Sixties: A Personal and Irreverent Guide* (New York: World Almanac Publications, 1985), 61.

29. John Steinbeck, "Have We Gone Soft?" *New Republic,* 15 February 1960, 11–15.

30. Henning quoted in David Marc and Robert J. Thompson, *Prime Time Prime Movers: From I Love Lucy to L.A. Law—America's Greatest TV Shows and the People Who Created Them* (Syracuse: Syracuse University Press, 1992), 33.

31. Marc and Thompson, *Prime Time Prime Movers,* 30.

32. Leonard quoted in *Television Quarterly,* summer 1962, 11–12.

33. Barnouw, *Tube of Plenty,* 403. It is entirely possible that shows which drew on, rather than studiously avoided, the outside world might have been a success. Some relatively "realistic" shows were successful. *Mission: Impossible* (1966–1972), for example, was a commercial for the CIA and its clandestine missions in third world countries, in much the same way as *The F.B.I.* was for that agency's no-holds-barred war on domestic subversion. *Mission: Impossible* was straightforward and attentive to method, with a believably worldly amoralism. At the start of each episode, a hidden recording would tell the show's hero, a silver-haired bureaucrat who did no dirty work himself, that "as usual, should you or any member of your I.M. force be captured or killed, the Secretary will disavow any knowledge of your existence." The tape recorder would then self-destruct.

34. Aubrey's career at CBS testifies mightily to the old adage that nobody ever went broke underestimating the American public. Many executives at "the Tif-

fany network" were embarrassed by Aubrey's programs, particularly when it was revealed during congressional hearings on juvenile delinquency that Aubrey's dictum was "broads, bosoms, and fun." Aubrey called the quote a "Hollywood paraphrase" but otherwise didn't deny the directive. See Watson, *The Expanding Vista*, 50.

35. Castleman and Podzarik, *Watching TV,* 171.

36. Papazian, *Medium Rare,* 46.

37. Castleman and Podzarik, *Watching TV,* 171.

38. That these declining revenues were largely a result of TV had been a major stumbling block; the collapse of the old studio system, however, with its vertical integration of production, distribution, and exhibition, made the move inevitable. The transition to filmed broadcasting is usefully summed up in J. Macdonald, *One Nation under Television,* 118–22. For a fuller treatment, see Frank Sturcken, *Live Television* (Jefferson: McFarland, 1990); and for greater detail still, see William Boddy, *Fifties Television* (Urbana: University of Illinois Press, 1990).

39. Previously, catchphrases were fallbacks developed ad lib in live situations. "This is a radical departure from the usual procedure," wrote *TV Guide* in 1965, "for trying to anticipate what will break people up is as unpredictable as the vagaries of female behavior." The article went on to point up the contrast between the practice and its precedents in burlesque and vaudeville, such as Frank "Wanna Wrestle?" Lavan and Jack "Vas ya dere, Charlie?" Pearl. *TV Guide,* 22 November 1965, 12.

40. Quoted in Dick Hobson, "Help! I'm a Prisoner in a Laff Box!" *TV Guide,* 9 July 1966, 22.

41. Paul Krassner, editorial, *Realist,* spring 1990, 44.

42. Coogan quoted in Hobson, "Help!" 21.

43. Castleman and Podzarik, *Watching TV,* 171.

44. The stereotyping of the characters was visibly deliberate, as Schwartz has acknowledged: "The . . . characters were meant to be a social microcosm. . . . Rich is Rich. Stupid is Stupid. Beautiful is Beautiful" (quoted in Edelstein, *Pop Sixties,* 67).

45. Dubrow quoted in Marc and Thompson, *Prime Time Prime Movers,* 40.

46. A more recent school of thought holds that *Gilligan's Island,* escapist or no, has its own, highly political valences. In *Gilligan Unbound: Pop Culture in an Age of Globalization,* Paul Cantor sees the castaways as avatars of cold-war optimism. "When one thinks about it," he writes,

> the premise of the show was really quite remarkable and revealing. A representative group of Americans could be dropped anywhere on the planet—even in the middle of the Pacific Ocean—and they would still feel at home—indeed they would *rule.* With a minimum

of resources at their disposal, they could re-create the American way of life in a new wilderness, from its democratic organization to the panoply of labor-saving devices that at the time were making the United States consumer the envy of the world. Nothing about the remote and exotic locale of the island unsettles the castaways. They are never led to question their assumptions and beliefs. If anything, their displacement strengthens their attachment to America and its way of life. . . . they stay fixated on home and the single goal of returning to the United States, and in the meantime do whatever they can to fashion a replica of America in the middle of the Pacific. (23)

47. Susan J. Douglas, *Where the Girls Are: Growing Up Female with the Mass Media* (New York: Times Books, 1995), 134.

48. For an interesting perspective on the "magical sitcoms," see Lynn Spigal, "From Domestic Space to Outer Space: The 6os Fantastic Family Sitcom," in *Close Encounters: Film, Feminism, and Science Fiction,* ed. Constance Penley (Minneapolis: University of Minnesota Press, 1991).

49. The theme of repressed animosity between the sexes on television has been one of the most frequently, if not ubiquitously, discussed themes of contemporary media studies. See Lynn Spigal, *Make Room for TV: Television and the Family Ideal in Postwar America* (New York: Routledge, 1987); also see Andrea Lea Press, *Women Watching Television: Gender, Class, and Generation in the American TV Experience* (Philadelphia: University of Pennsylvania Press, 1991), and Nina C. Leibman, *Living Room Lectures: Fifties Family in Film and Television* (Austin: University of Texas Press, 1995).

50. Eric Barnouw, *The Image Empire: A History of Broadcasting in the United States from 1953* (New York: Oxford University Press, 1970), 308.

51. By making Darrin Stevens an advertising executive, the writers of *Bewitched* marked him like banished Cain in terms of the culture of the day. An advertising executive, whose livelihood depends on the creation of jingles and slogans, represented in this period the epitome of vocational emptiness in the new America. In the 1950s, Sloan Wilson had made *The Man in the Gray Flannel Suit* a publicist, Vance Packard had published *The Hidden Persuaders,* and the phrase "Madison Avenue" had come to connote everything that was phony, trivial, and manipulative in American culture. No more perfect containment of the limitless power and freedom Samantha's magic represented could be found than to marry her to a sycophantic Organization Man.

52. *TV Guide,* 14 February 1965, A30.

53. Among the better-remembered of *Playhouse 90*'s "heavy" productions were *The Days of Wine and Roses,* about alcoholism, *Judgment at Nuremberg,* about the war crimes trials, Rod Serling's tragic *Requiem for a Heavyweight,* and other seri-

ous themes. Plays like *Charley's Aunt* were common on *Playhouse 90* too, but this provides only more argument for its essential unpredictability and hence its incongruity beside standard TV programming. See Sturcken, *Live Television;* and for greater detail still, see Boddy, *Fifties Television.*

54. J. Macdonald, *One Nation under Television,* 125.

55. Brown, *Television,* 237–41. In Klein's case, his intelligence and obstreperousness had much to do with his downfall, but the ratings war with Dann was considered an embarrassment by many low-profile executives.

56. Mills quoted in Gitlin, *Inside Prime Time,* 48.

57. Arthur C. Nielsen Jr. and Theodore Berland, "Nielsen Defends His Ratings," in *Television Today: A Close-Up View,* ed. Barry Cole (New York: Oxford University Press, 1981).

58. David Potter, *People of Plenty: Economic Abundance and the American Character* (Chicago: University of Chicago Press, 1954). For a brief but informative overview of changing perspectives on ethnicity and culture, see J. Philip Gleason, "American Identity and Americanization," in *Harvard Encyclopedia of American Ethnic Groups* (Cambridge: Harvard University Press, 1975), 31–58.

59. The other six rules were similarly disdainful of intrinsic merit, e.g., "Remember, the position a program is assigned is far more important than the content of the program itself." *TV Guide,* 17 September 1977, 8.

60. "By 1968 . . . a majority of people believed [Johnson] regularly lied to them" (Doris Kearns, *Lyndon Johnson and the American Dream* [New York: Signet, 1976], 351–53). See also Paul Conkin, *Big Daddy from the Pedernales: Lyndon Baines Johnson* (Boston: Twayne, 1986), 268–69.

61. An excellent summary of this, upon which I have drawn extensively, is William Leuchetenburg's *A Troubled Feast: American Society since 1945* (Boston: Little, Brown, 1973), 69–83. For a penetrating, if highly subjective, view of the same phenomena, see O'Neill, *American High,* 23–28.

62. Mumford quoted in Kenneth Jackson, *The Crabgrass Frontier: The Suburbanization of the United States* (New York: Oxford University Press, 1985), 244.

63. D. Macdonald, "Theory of Mass Culture," 62.

2. The Demographic Imperative: Culture and Counterculture, 1968–1970

1. Theodore Roszak, *The Making of a Counter Culture* (Garden City: Doubleday, 1969), 121; Charles Reich, *The Greening of America* (New York: Random House, 1968).

2. Even at the time, some campus radicals were willing to admit this. Todd Gitlin, the second president of Students for a Democratic Society (SDS), writes in his memoir, *The Sixties: Years of Hope, Days of Rage* (New York: Bantam Books, 1987): "The movement, whatever it says, has no serious intention of ruling; we

are once and for all a youth movement, aiming to reform our elders, and if they will not reform, there is no alternative but to throw ourselves down on the floor and scream—to act, in fact, like children" (338).

3. Landon Y. Jones, *Great Expectations: American and the Baby Boom Generation* (New York: Ballantine Books, 1980), 90.

4. Jones, *Great Expectations,* 91–92.

5. Chuck Berry, *Chuck Berry: His Best,* vol. 1, MCA, ASIN: B00000SKQ1, 1997.

6. Greil Marcus, "Who Put the Bomp in the Bomp De Bomp?" in *Mass Culture Revisited,* ed. Bernard Rosenberg and David Manning White (New York: Van Nostrand Reinhold, 1971), 446.

7. Bernstein and Lennon quoted in Gitlin, *The Sixties,* 38.

8. Philips quoted in David Halberstam, *The Fifties* (New York: Villard, 1994), 457.

9. Paul Klein, interview by author, New York City, 1 October 1996.

10. Gilbert quoted in Jones, *Great Expectations,* 49.

11. Buffalo Bob quoted in Tom Engelhardt, "The Shortcake Strategy," in *Watching Television,* ed. Todd Gitlin (New York: Pantheon, 1986), 71.

12. J. Fred Macdonald, *One Nation under Television* (Chicago: Nelson-Hall, 1994), 170.

13. Jones, *Great Expectations,* 85.

14. Ed Papazian, telephone conversation with author, 2 October 1996.

15. Jerry Dominus, telephone conversation with author, 4 October, 1996.

16. Melnick quoted in Leonard H. Goldenson and Marvin J. Wolf, *Beating the Odds: The Untold Story Behind the Rise of ABC: The Stars, Struggles, and Egos That Transformed Network Television* (New York: Scribner's, 1991), 151.

17. Goldenson and Wolf, *Beating the Odds,* 149.

18. Goldenson and Wolf, *Beating the Odds,* 246.

19. "It looks alright when you're reading it," the title character tells his new sweetheart in Charles Portis's novel *Norwood* (New York: Simon and Schuster, 1966). "I didn't believe none of it on television." "You're not supposed to believe it," she replies. Answers Norwood, "You're supposed to believe it a little bit. I didn't believe none of it" (147–48).

20. Susan Sontag, *Against Interpretation* (New York: Farrar, Straus and Giroux, 1964), 283.

21. Sontag, *Against Interpretation,* 288.

22. Sherick quoted in Goldenson, *Beating the Odds,* 246.

23. Dozier quoted in George Gent, "They Love to Be Mean to Batman," *New York Times,* 1 May 1966, C8.

24. Tom Frank, *The Conquest of Cool: Business Culture, Counterculture, and the Rise of Hip Consumerism* (Chicago: University of Chicago Press, 1997), 118.

25. Frank, *Conquest of Cool,* 118.

26. Harry Castleman and Walter Podzarik, *Watching TV: Four Decades of American Television* (New York: McGraw-Hill, 1981), 192.

27. Tony Hendra, *Going Too Far: The Rise and Demise of Sick, Gross, Black, Sophomoric, Weirdo, Pinko, Anarchist, Underground, Anti-Establishment Humor* (New York: Doubleday, 1987), 203. Much of the material that follows dealing with the *Smothers Brothers* draws heavily on pp. 202–26.

28. Mike Dann, interview by author, New York City, 17 October 1996.

29. The Friar's Club is a New York fraternity of "made" comedians, agents, and TV executives; it functions as the Valhalla of the comedy establishment.

30. Les Brown, "Teens Dictate 'Adult' Culture," *Variety,* 2 June 1965, 48.

31. Generally, this says much more about the era a show was produced in, I believe, than does the explicitly "relevant" content of a topical show; the distinction is worth bearing in mind.

32. Tom Smothers quoted in Hendra, *Going Too Far,* 208.

33. Aniko Bodroghkozy, "*The Smothers Brothers Comedy Hour* and the Youth Rebellion," in *The Revolution Wasn't Televised: 60s TV and Social Conflict,* ed. Lynn Spigal and Michael Curtin (New York: Routledge, 1997), 203–4.

34. Hendra quoted in Bodroghkozy, "*Smothers Brothers,*" 205.

35. Castleman and Podzarik, *Watching TV,* 208. Although outside the compass of this study, the counterculture had a far more extensive exposure on television, and a much earlier one, on the news than on prime time. Interested readers should see Todd Gitlin, *The Whole World Is Watching: Mass Media in the Making and Unmaking of the New Left* (Berkeley: University of California Press, 1984); and see also memoirs and histories of the hippies, particularly Charles Perry, *The Haight-Ashbury: A History* (New York: Random House, 1984).

36. "The Way to Eden," originally broadcast 21 February 1969, shelf no. FDA 2911, Motion Picture, Broadcasting, and Recorded Sound Division, Library of Congress (archive cited hereafter as LOC). Where extended discussions of particular episodes of television series are presented, the reader is directed to this archive in the Library of Congress's collection—the most comprehensive, as well as researcher-friendly, repository of these primary sources. Episodes are given with date of airing, as well as LOC shelf number. For an overview of the video collection, see *Three Decades of Television: A Catalog of Television Programs Acquired by the Library of Congress 1949–1979,* comp. Sarah Rouse and Katherine Loughney (Washington, DC: Library of Congress, 1989). The Museum of TV and Radio, in New York City, does not use call numbers per se, and for programs not in the Library of Congress's collection, the reader is referred to the MTV&R's considerable archive.

37. Ellison quoted in Bodroghkozy, "*Smothers Brothers,*" 213.

38. Hendra notes, "throughout the fall of 1967—the period of the show's greatest climb in the ratings—a subtle atmosphere of secrecy characterized the relationship between the performers and the audience. The laughter of the audience was increasingly knowing. They and the brothers knew what was being accomplished even if everyone else involved in the show didn't" (*Going Too Far*, 209).

39. David Marc, *Demographic Vistas* (Philadelphia: University of Pennsylvania Press, 1984), 78–79.

40. Jack Gould, "The Offbeat Smothers Brothers," *New York Times*, 16 October 1967, 91.

41. Dann, interview.

42. Perry Lafferty, Oral History Interview, 4 December 1997, ATAS.

43. Quoted in Bodroghkozy, "*Smothers Brothers*," 214.

44. Lafferty quoted in Bert Spector, "A Clash of Cultures: The Smothers Brothers vs. CBS Television," in *American History/American Television: Interpreting the Video Past*, ed. John E. O'Connor (New York: Frederick Ungar Publishing, 1983), 178.

45. See Robert E. Dallos, "Pete Seeger Gets New Chance on TV," *New York Times*, 25 August 1967, C1.

46. Pete Seeger, *Pete Seeger's Greatest Hits*, Sony, ASIN: B000063WD4, 2002, CD.

47. Jack Gould, "C.B.S. to Drop Smothers Hour; Cites Failure to Get Previews," *New York Times*, 15 April 1969, 1.

48. Hendra, *Going Too Far*, 211.

49. *New York Times*, 23 January 1968, 91.

50. Hendra, *Going Too Far*, 212.

51. Kovacs's genius was not limited to blackout humor. He produced a series of continuing characters—sissy poet Percy Dovetonsils, German DJ Wolfgang Sauerbraten, horror-movie hostess Auntie Gruesome—of exactly the sort that were to become the franchise of sketch comedy in the late 1970s. Unlike Gleason's Poor Soul and Ralph Kramden, or Skelton's Mean Widdle Kid, Willie Lump-Lump, and Clem Kadiddlehopper, none of these characters were the sympathetic heroes of sketches nor could they be affectionately identified with their portrayer, so bizarre and numerous were they. See Diana Rico, *Kovacsland: A Biography of Ernie Kovacs* (San Diego: HBJ, 1990).

52. Castleman and Podzarik, *Watching TV*, 198.

53. Promotional brochure, "Selling the American Youth Market" (N.p.: AMR International, n.d.), quoted in Abbie Hoffman, *Woodstock Nation* (New York: Vintage Books, 1969), 95. I give this quote because it clearly made an impact on a leading countercultural figure such as Hoffman, but dozens of other examples are quoted in Frank, *Conquest of Cool*, esp. pp. 105–30.

54. One of the most significant aspects of baby-boom culture is its discontinuity with previous generations. John Lennon's remark that "before Elvis there was nothing" and Abbie Hoffman's claim, under oath, that he was born "psychologically, in 1960" and that the only state he belonged to was "the Woodstock nation" were typical expressions of this atemporality. For further discussion of baby-boom discontinuities, see Christopher Lasch, "The Waning of Historical Time," in *The Culture of Narcissism* (New York: W. W. Norton, 1978). Also see Tom Wolfe, "The Me Generation and the Third Great Awakening," in *Mauve Gloves and Madmen, Clutter and Vine* (New York: Farrar, Straus and Giroux, 1976).

55. The Grass Roots, *Anthology: 1965–1975,* Rhino Records, ASIN: B000003ZMQ, 1991.

56. Mark Crispin Miller, "The Hipness unto Death," in *Boxed In: The Culture of Television* (Evanston: Northwestern University Press, 1988), 8.

57. Harlan Ellison, *The Glass Teat* (Los Angeles: Free Press, 1968), 13. Or consider Frank Zappa's "I'm the Slime" (*The Real Frank Zappa Book* [New York: Hyperion Press, 1987], 89; released on Frank Zappa, *Overnite Sensation,* Warner's, ASIN: B00000095G, 1973):

> I am gross and perverted
> I am obsessed and deranged
> I have existed for years
> But very little has changed
> I'm the tool of the Government, and Industry too
> For I am destined to rule and regulate you
> I might be vile and pernicious
> But you can't look away
> I make you think I'm delicious
> With the stuff that I say
> I'm the best you can get
> Have you guessed me yet?
> I'm the slime oozing out from your TV set!
> . . . .
> Your mind is totally controlled
> It is stuffed into my mold
> And you will do what you are told
> Until the rights to you are sold!
> I am the slime from your video . . .

58. *Statistical Abstract of the United States,* 1980, 597, table 1016, "Advertising—Estimated Expenditures: 1950–1979."

59. Les Brown, *Television: The Business Behind the Box* (New York: Harcourt, Brace, Jovanovich, 1971), 263. This attitude was particularly worrisome to advertisers. Herb Fisher, the executive vice president of a leading New York agency, Wells, Rich, Green, wrote of the new consumer, "He is a very hip, aware character. . . . Exposure to [media] stimuli produces skepticism. Today's consumer . . . has developed sophistication about, an imperviousness to, the 'big sell.'" Quoted in Frank, *Conquest of Cool*, 127.

60. Eric Barnouw, *The Sponsor: Notes on a Modern Potentate* (New York: Oxford University Press, 1978), 70.

61. The logic of demographic marketing was irrefutable: the waning of the general interest magazines, such as *Saturday Evening Post, Look, Life, Collier's,* and so on corresponded to the disappearance of general-audience programming on television. See Don R. Pember, "Magazines and the Fragmenting Audience," in *Mass Media in America,* ed. William Vesterman and Robert Atwan (New Brunswick: Science Research Associates, 1974), 334–41.

62. Jerry Dominus, telephone conversation with author, 29 September 1996.

63. Nielsen data quoted in Dick Hobson, "Who Watches What?" *TV Guide,* 27 July 1968, 5–8.

64. Survey results quoted in "What College Students Think of TV," *TV Guide,* 23 January 1971, 8.

65. Aaron Spelling and Jefferson Graham, *Aaron Spelling: A Prime Time Life* (New York: St. Martin's Press, 1996), 66–67.

66. Castleman and Podzarik, *Watching TV,* 208.

67. Advertisement, *Variety,* 3 June 1973, 41.

68. That is, since *Amos 'n' Andy* in 1951—although clearly, *Amos 'n' Andy* represented no "golden age" for blacks. One exception to the fifteen-year drought was *The Sammy Davis Jr. Show,* a short-lived, 1966 variety program featuring the famous "rat pack" entertainer. The show lasted four months before being canceled for poor ratings. For a fuller treatment of the Jim Crow years of network television, see J. Fred Macdonald, *Blacks on White TV: Afro Americans in Television since 1948* (Chicago: Nelson-Hall, 1983).

69. Quoted in Art Peters, "What the Negro Wants from TV," *TV Guide,* 20 January 1968, 7.

70. Klein, interview; Brown, *Television,* 78–79.

71. Malcolm X, "The Ballot or the Bullet," reprinted in *"Takin' It to the Streets": A Sixties Reader,* ed. Alexander Bloom and Wini Breines (New York: Oxford University Press, 1995), 140.

72. Eldridge Cleaver, "Requiem for Nonviolence," reprinted in Bloom and Breines, *"Takin' It to the Streets."*

73. Data for table 2.2 from Tim Brooks and Earle Marsh, *The Complete Di-*

rectory to Prime Time Network TV Shows, 1946—Present (New York: Ballantine Books, 1979), 808.

74. Ed Papazian, *Medium Rare: The Evolution, Workings, and Impact of Commercial Television* (New York: Media Dynamics, 1991), 169. Those few words provide a one-sentence summary of this entire study.

75. Wood quoted in Todd Gitlin, *Inside Prime Time* (New York: Pantheon, 1984), 207. In the telling of Robert Wood's "relevancy" revolution, I drew heavily on Gitlin, *Inside Prime Time*, 203–20, and Brown, *Television*, 98–121, and 262–66. Other useful sources for background include Robert Metz, *CBS: Reflections in a Bloodshot Eye* (Chicago: Playboy Press, 1975), and William S. Paley, *As It Happened* (Garden City: Doubleday, 1979).

76. Wood quoted in Gitlin, *Inside Prime Time*, 207.

77. Andrew Edelstein and Kevin McDonough, *The Seventies: From Hot Pants to Hot Tubs* (New York: Dutton, 1990), 183.

78. Wood quoted in Brown, *Television*, 56. The image is an interesting one, as Todd Gitlin has noted. Television will lead the cultural vanguard but only once the vanguard is established and threatening to march on without television. Wood's image, made at a critical meeting with the single most influential broadcaster in history, captures television's ambivalent attitude toward leading and following.

79. James T. Patterson, *Great Expectations: The United States, 1945–1974* (New York: Oxford University Press, 1996), 753.

80. Wood quoted in Patterson, *Great Expectations*, 209–10.

81. "The Storefront Lawyers—Pilot episode," original broadcast date unknown, LOC shelf no. KSL 3965.

82. Miller, *Boxed In*, 8.

83. Brown, *Television*, 218.

84. Johnson quoted in David Halberstam, *The Powers That Be* (New York: McGraw-Hill, 1979), 436.

85. Agnew quoted in Halford Ross Ryan (ed.), *American Rhetoric from Roosevelt to Reagan*, 2d ed. (Prospect Heights: Waveland Press, 1987), 212–19.

86. For an interesting sympathetic take on Agnew, though one written from a frankly partisan point of view, see John R. Coyne, *The Impudent Snobs: Agnew vs. the Media Establishment* (New Rochelle: Arlington House, 1972). The book is useful as a reference work as well, owing to its comprehensive appendix of transcripts of Agnew's speeches at his demagogic peak. No objective historical work on Agnew currently exists.

87. Gitlin, *The Sixties*, 405.

88. Jonathan Rieder, *Canarsie: The Jews and Italians of Brooklyn Against Liberalism*, quoted in Patterson, *Great Expectations*, 455. Patterson's chapter, "The

Polarized Sixties," is a good starting place for understanding the oppositional nature of the decade. William L. O'Neill's account in *Coming Apart: America in the 1960s* (New York: Free Press, 1969) is even better, although its insights come at times at the expense of the historical objectivity that is Patterson's forte. For a view from the left, see Gitlin, *The Sixties*.

89. For a cogent overview of the ethnic revival within the context of American cultural history, see J. Philip Gleason, "American Identity and Americanization," in *Harvard Encyclopedia of American Ethnic Groups* (Cambridge: Harvard University Press, 1975), 31–58.

90. Crosby, Stills, Nash, and Young, *So Far,* Wea/Atlantic, ASIN: Boooo02JoJ, 1994.

91. Nixon quoted in Peter Carroll, *It Seemed like Nothing Happened: The Tragedy and Promise of America in the 1970s* (New York: Holt, Rinehart and Winston, 1982), 56–61.

3. "The Church of What's Happening Now": The Great Shift, 1970–1972

1. Spiro Agnew, speech delivered in Belleville, Ill., 30 October 1970.

2. James M. Naughton, "Agnew Assails Songs and Films that Promote a 'Drug Culture,'" *New York Times,* 15 September 1970, 17, 91.

3. Naughton, "Agnew Assails Songs," 17, 91.

4. J. Fred Macdonald, *One Nation under Television* (Chicago: Nelson-Hall, 1994), 186.

5. Magruder memo quoted in Gary Edgerton and Cathy Pratt, "The Influence of the Paramount Decision on Network Television in America," *Quarterly Review of Film Studies* 8, no. 3 (summer 1983): 15.

6. Sally Bedell, *Up the Tube: Prime Time in the Silverman Years.* (New York: Viking, 1981), 55.

7. Brooks quoted in *TV Guide,* 19 May 1973, 33.

8. Mary Tyler Moore, Oral History Interview, 23 October 1997, ATAS.

9. Brooks quoted in Paul Kerr, "The Making of MTM," in *MTM: Quality Television,* ed. Jane Feuer (London: BFI, 1984), 75.

10. Moore, Oral History Interview.

11. *Variety,* 1 November 1972, 29.

12. Lear quoted in Donna McGrohan, *Archie and Edith, Mike and Gloria: The Tumultuous History of All in the Family* (New York: Farrar, Straus and Giroux, 1989), 11.

13. Lear quoted in McGrohan, *Archie and Edith,* 23–24.

14. Lear quoted in Todd Gitlin, *Inside Prime Time* (New York: Pantheon, 1984), 212.

15. Wood quoted in Gitlin, *Inside Prime Time,* 212.

16. Tankersly quoted in Richard Adler, *All in the Family: A Critical Appraisal* (Aspen: Praeger, 1979), xxiii.

17. Ella Taylor, *Prime Time Families: Television Culture in Postwar America* (Los Angeles: University of California Press, 1989), 39.

18. McGrohan, *Archie and Edith*, 33.

19. Ed Papazian was one of the first commentators to remark on the show's deep focus; it is his contention that the technique's use in commercials derives from *All in the Family*'s innovation. Ed Papazian, telephone conversation with author, 2 October 1996.

20. Michael J. Arlen, "The Media Dramas of Norman Lear," *New Yorker*, May 1975, 33.

21. McGrohan, *Archie and Edith*, 197.

22. Quoted in Marshall Frady, "It's All in the Family, Too," *Life*, 13 December 1971, 44. CBS executives had expected as much, although they did not believe anyone would ever own up to it. The show tested abominably in previews, but, the report noted, "We believe that many viewers were ashamed to admit, in the test situation, to enjoying certain programs and their characters. We think that when a person's real attitudes conflict with what he believes to be socially proper and desirable, he may express only the latter opinion. Because the main character in Those Were the Days [the pilot's title] expressed views which are not socially desirable, viewers might feel required to criticize him, even if deep down they identify with him" (quoted in Gitlin, *Inside Prime Time*, 36).

23. "Meet the Bunkers," originally broadcast 12 January 1971, LOC shelf no. FBB0102.

24. Petersen quoted in McGrohan, *Archie and Edith*, 33.

25. For the complete texts of both essays, see Adler, *All in the Family*.

26. Neil Vidmar and Milton Rokeach, "Archie Bunker's Bigotry: A Study in Selective Perception and Exposure," *Journal of Communication* (winter 1974). "We found that many persons did not see the program as a satire on bigotry and that these persons were more likely to be viewers who scored high on measures of prejudice. Even more important," the authors went on to say, "is the finding that high prejudiced persons were likely to watch All in the Family more often than low prejudiced persons, to identify more often with Archie Bunker, and to see him winning in the end" (127). Vidmar and Rokeach's study was highly limited and didn't prove anything, but it seemed to fit with the general sense that *All in the Family* did as much harm as good.

27. McGrohan, *Archie and Edith*, 134.

28. Carroll O'Connor, Oral History Interview, 13 August 1999, ATAS.

29. John Leonard, "Ed Sullivan Died for Our Sins," in *Smoke and Mirrors: Violence, Television, and Other American Cultures* (New York: New Press, 1997),

45. Leonard's argument about Sullivan's place in U.S. cultural history more or less mirrors my own, but it is sufficiently obscured by the author's bombast to require a disavowal.

30. Leonard, "Ed Sullivan," 42.

31. The postwar historiographic fashion stressed the essential conservatism of American factions and the extent to which they agreed, rather than disagreed. This was in direct rebuke to the earlier generation of "progressive" historians, who stressed class conflict in their interpretation. Both the name and the most enduring critique of the "consensus" historians are drawn from a seminal essay by John Higham, "The Cult of the 'American Consensus,'" *Commentary,* February 1959, 93–100. See also John Higham, "Beyond Consensus: The Historian as Moral Critic," *American Historical Review,* April 1962, 609–25.

32. From the transcript of Larry Gelbart seminar, Museum of Television and Radio, 5 October 1984, Arts Special Collections, Young Research Library, UCLA.

33. Adler, *All in the Family,* 190. "Archie Bunker for President" was a common graffito of the time. Wags would occasionally respond underneath, "He is."

34. Gitlin, *Inside Prime Time,* 217–18.

35. Quoted in Muriel Cantor, *The Producer's Medium* (New York: Basic Books, 1971), 173–74.

36. Dwight Macdonald, "A Theory of Mass Culture," in *Mass Culture: The Popular Arts in America,* ed. Bernard Rosenberg and David Manning White (New York: Free Press, 1957), 70.

37. J. Fred Macdonald, *Blacks on White TV: Afro Americans in Television since 1948.* (Chicago: Nelson-Hall, 1983), 172. Macdonald's view of Wilson was shared by many blacks at the time. The format of Wilson's show was a forum for various characters the comedian portrayed, each of whom was more or less a stock type: loudmouthed hussy Geraldine Jones, the corrupt Reverend Leroy, pastor of The Church of What's Happening Now, Sonny the Janitor, and others. Just as Julia had been a black Donna Reed, so Wilson was really a kind of reverse image Red Skelton, which made him a delight to audiences but in no way a social advance of the sort represented by the Lear shows.

38. In fact, given the relentless pressure brought on the news divisions by the Nixon administration and its willingness to use the federal government as an instrument of coercion, the entertainment series became more relevant just as the news divisions were becoming more innocuous: an odd reversal, and one that must have contributed to some extent in the former's success.

39. Joseph Morgenstern, "Can Bigotry Be Funny?" *Newsweek,* 29 November 1971, 67.

40. Todd Gitlin, *The Whole World Is Watching: Mass Media in the Making and Unmaking of the New Left* (Berkeley: University of California Press, 1984), 179–

201. See also John Patrick Diggins, *The Rise and Fall of the American Left* (New York: W. W. Norton, 1992); and Alan Matusow, *The Unraveling of America: A History of Liberalism in America in the 1960s* (New York: Harper and Row, 1984). While the latter two books are accomplished scholarly works, care should be exercised in reading them as both have significant ideological biases against the left. Gitlin's book is invaluable, owing not only to his acumen as a student of American media but from his own experience as a former president of Students for a Democratic Society (SDS).

41. Robert Crumb, "Let's Talk Sense about This Here Modern America," *Arcade: The Comics Review,* no. 2 (summer 1975): 8.

42. Nicholas Lemann, "How the Seventies Changed America," *American Heritage,* July/August 1991, 41.

43. James T. Patterson, in *Great Expectations: The United States, 1945–1974* (New York: Oxford University Press, 1996), writes:

> Although highly partisan when it came to his own political survival, [Nixon] did not waste energy trying to stop every liberal idea that came from the Democratic majorities in the Congress. Some of their proposals, such as changes in policy regarding Native Americans, struck him as worthwhile; in any event they did not cost much. Others, such as environmental reforms, enjoyed popularity among the people: it was not worth it, Nixon thought, to oppose them. Still other policies, such as increasing spending for social insurance, had the support of influential lobbies, such as the elderly. Having no strong feelings about issues such as these, Nixon went along with many of them. (741)

44. "The Unemployment Story, Part 1," originally broadcast 10 October 1970, LOC shelf no. VBA 6899.

45. Mark Crispin Miller has described the devolution of the TV dad in a seminal essay ("Deride and Conquer," in *Watching Television,* ed. Todd Gitlin [New York: Pantheon, 1986]) that reads the stripping of paternal authority through the 1960s and early 1970s as a repudiation of the ethic of discipline and restraint that "Dad" represented: "TV . . . wooed the wife and kids . . . with all sorts of bright, delicious images; and yet it contravened its own allurements by giving lots of air time to the Great White Father, who seemed to stand against the universal splurging that TV constantly promoted. Clearly something had to give, and it would soon be Dad, the personification of an outmoded ideology and now an obvious drag on consumption" (200). Miller goes on to point out how this development was nearing its fulfillment as Dad's demotion was "represented as a stroke of liberation. . . . his subversion appeared politically correct," a spurious empower-

ment of Dad's former underlings ("You've Come a Long Way, Baby," as a popular ad of the time said).

46. Speaking of a later hit, Paul Klein told Todd Gitlin how the makers of that show were able to parlay its success into on-air commitments and other network go-aheads: "[the show] goes on the air, and it consistently gets a very big number. Now a bunch of people have leverage. Since CBS has no fucking idea in the world why that is succeeding, and nobody in that company ever watches that show—you've got to take this on faith—they don't know why it works. So everybody connected with that show has leverage . . . because they don't know the reasons for the hit" (quoted in Gitlin, *Inside Prime Time,* 117). Courageous zeitgeist-influenced decisions like Wood's are very much the exception and not the rule.

47. Harry Castleman and Walter Podzarik, *Watching TV: Four Decades of American Television* (New York: McGraw-Hill, 1981), 256.

48. Norman Lear and star Esther Rolle were shocked and hurt by this criticism but understood it as inevitable, given JJ's Fonzie-like popularity. "[JJ] mattered in stories that were very serious . . . and he was wonderful. But we allowed him, for the sake of getting those laughs, those easy laughs, to repeat himself too much" (Norman Lear, Oral History Interview, 26 February 1998, ATAS).

49. Gelbart quoted in Gitlin, *Inside Prime Time,* 216–17.

50. Transcript of Gelbart seminar.

51. "M*A*S*H pilot episode," originally broadcast 25 January 1970, LOC shelf no. FBB 5214.

52. Occasionally, the series would produce an innovative episode, such as a mock documentary, a series of dream sequences, or a whole show shot from the perspective of a bedridden patient, which would garner it unanimous critical praise; but these episodes were carefully crafted exceptions, unrepresentative of the series' bread-and-butter run.

53. John Waters, "Farewell to the *M*A*S*H* Gang," *Newsweek,* 28 February 1983, 87–90.

54. Transcript of Gelbart seminar.

4. "Love Is All Around": Uneasy Footing in the New America, 1972–1974

1. The historiography of American feminism has had an explosive growth in recent years, and emancipatory trends have been found in almost every period, particularly during the war years 1939–1945 and before that in the 1920s. Feminism as a serious political movement began in the nineteenth century, however, and was revived by Friedan as a public-sphere issue only after years of dormancy. For a fuller treatment, see Sara Evans, *Personal Politics: The Roots of the Women's Liberation in the Civil Rights Movement and the New Left* (New York: Random

House, 1980); also see William Chafe, *The Paradox of Change: American Women in the 20th Century* (New York: Oxford University Press, 1992).

2. Interestingly, although the empowered woman was a staple of B movies in the era (owing perhaps to the combination of sex and action it allowed), the major studios produced very few films drawing on the new consciousness. Whereas the comparatively narrow counterculture inspired a slew of films throughout the late 1960s and early 1970s, only a handful dealt with women's problems. A few films of the early 1970s, such as *Klute* (1971) and *Carnal Knowledge* (1971) offered challenging female characters, but they are exceptional, oases of women's parts in a period dominated by he-man directors such as Francis Coppola, Sam Peckinpah, and Irwin Allen. The women's movement's influence on film was limited, ironically, to the drive-in.

3. Helen Reddy, *Helen Reddy's Greatest Hits,* EMI-Capitol Special Products, ASIN: B000002TGF, 1994, CD.

4. Erik Barnouw, *The Sponsor: Notes on a Modern Potentate* (New York: Oxford University Press, 1978), 71.

5. Jack Medelsohn, Executive Story Consultant, to James Lupo, 9 August 1977, Bud Yorkin Papers, Arts Special Collections, Young Research Library, UCLA.

6. Rick Mitz, *The Great TV Sitcom Book* (New York: Richard Marek Publishers, 1980), 291.

7. Christopher Lasch, *The Minimal Self: Psychic Survival in Troubled Times* (New York: W. W. Norton, 1985). *The Minimal Self* was a follow-up to Lasch's better-known study *The Culture of Narcissism* (1978) and provides a gloss on one of that book's pervading notions: that in contemporary society, a strong sense of selfhood was likely to be an encumbrance, one that increasing numbers of Americans were choosing to do without.

8. Michael Arlen, "The Media Dramas of Norman Lear," in *The View from Highway One* (New York: Farrar, Straus and Giroux, 1974), 123.

9. Tom Carson, "The Even Couple," *Village Voice,* 3 May 1983, 58.

10. Jane Feuer, "The MTM Style," in *MTM: Quality Television,* ed. Jane Feuer (London: BFI, 1984), 35.

11. In fairness, it should be noted here that *Maude* offered a level of writing and humor comparable to the best of the MTM shows and only on a structural level seems inferior. Moreover, in grappling directly with social issues such as abortion, racism, alcoholism, and so forth, *Maude* and the Lear programs in general probably did more to transform society than did the MTM shows, which, whatever their artistic merits, tended to stand for a vague middle-class liberalism, if anything. This point is an important one and will get the fuller treatment it deserves further on.

12. For a fuller examination of this theme, see Ella Taylor's *Prime Time Families: Television Culture in Postwar America* (Los Angeles: University of California Press, 1989). Taylor's study covers an overlapping period with this one, and I have drawn on her lucid observations here and elsewhere in describing the evolution of the situation comedy. For Taylor, the signal development in the period is the changing definition of the family from the nuclear unit of *Father Knows Best* and so on to the extended, voluntary groups who make up the casts of such later shows as *The Mary Tyler Moore Show, M*A*S*H, Cheers,* and so on, until the next paradigm shift. The implications of the shift for Taylor are political, and my discussion of them above parallels many of her conclusions.

13. Arlen, "Media Dramas," 64–65.

14. Rick Mitz, *Great TV Sitcom Book,* 265. Mitz's book, a valuable resource for any student of American TV series, has been invaluable throughout the writing of this book. Mitz makes no claim about the significance of Sue Ann Niven's tenure, however, which is my own gloss on a factual point offered by him in passing.

15. Betty White, Oral History Interview, 4 June 1997, ATAS.

16. Taylor, *Prime Time Families,* 116.

17. Taylor, *Prime Time Families,* 41.

18. Arlen, "Media Dramas," 58.

19. The field of inferred sociology, as it were, represents a much larger part of the literature on television than does history. The function of TV in regulating norms has been the theoretical approach most academic work has centered on. The most systematic and comprehensive overview is certainly Robert S. Lichter et al., *Prime Time: How TV Portrays American Culture* (New York: Harper and Row, 1990). Feuer's *MTM* is the best study of the MTM shows and the most insightful; Daniel Hamamoto, *Nervous Laughter: Television Situation Comedy and Liberal Democratic Ideology* (New York: Greenwood, 1995) is not helpful except as a point of departure. David Marc's *Comic Visions* (Malden: Blackwell, 1997) is an insightful and smart, if occasionally facile, take on the sitcom as social barometer; Ben Stein's *The View from Sunset Boulevard* (Garden City: Anchor, 1986) offers a critique of television's liberalism from a conservative point of view. Among the best studies from the era under discussion are Robert Sklar, *Prime Time America* (New York: Oxford University Press, 1980), and the essays of Arlen, particularly *View from Highway One.*

20. Sonny and Cher, *The Wondrous World of Sonny and Cher,* Sundazed Records, ASIN: B0000064Y, 1998, CD.

21. Sonny Bono, *The Beat Goes On* (New York: Harcourt, Brace, Jovanovich, 1990), 160.

22. Silverman quoted in Andrew Edelstein and Kevin McDonough, *The Seventies: From Hot Pants to Hot Tubs* (New York: Dutton, 1990), 197.

23. Bono, *Beat Goes On,* 191.

24. This desire was a constant of karate movies, which saw their first great popularity in this period. Unlike the *mano-a-mano* fisticuffs that were standard in U.S. movies, Chinese films tended to show a prodigal fighter taking on waves of men—but only after being pushed. Bruce Lee became the first Chinese star in American film making such movies, and so successful were they that a number of occidental imitators arose. *Black Belt Jones* was a black Bruce Lee, taking on the mob with a virile swagger; *Billy Jack* was a white hippie Bruce Lee, who lives on an Indian reservation and beats up bigots who insult his friends, such as "Little Bundle of Sunshine from Heaven." *Kung Fu* was originally developed as a vehicle for Lee, but the network thought it would do better with a white star and hired David Carradine to play the part as a Eurasian.

25. Ed Papazian, *Medium Rare: The Evolution, Workings, and Impact of Commercial Television* (New York: Media Dynamics, 1991), 273.

26. Many cultural critics have seen in the basic cop/gangster genre an existential fable—life lived by the will to power in an uncaring, hostile city. The most influential statement of this is Robert Warshow's 1949 essay, "The Gangster as Tragic Hero," in *The Immediate Experience: Movies, Comics, Theater, and Other Aspects of Popular Culture* (Cambridge: Harvard University Press, 2002). The genre came to replace the West as the locus for stark, cosmological battles, and this was not wasted on historians. The cinematic genre of film noir heightened this allegorical reading, and by the time of television's advent, the conventions had hardened into basic elements of violence, pursuit, and capture, all portrayed to a gripping musical score. *Dragnet*'s mundane professionalism was a major innovation, therefore.

27. Tim Brooks and Earle Marsh, *The Complete Directory to Prime Time Network TV Shows, 1946–Present* (New York: Ballantine Books, 1979), 172.

28. David Marc, *Demographic Vistas* (Philadelphia: University of Pennsylvania Press, 1984), 78–79.

29. Webb's greatest moments on the show came when given the opportunity to lecture hippies on the errors of their ways. Friday always had the last word, but in some cases, these lectures grew to homily length, as when Friday was called upon to defend his profession to young cynics; such monologues would be shamelessly punctuated by a fierce orchestral note and a shared nod between Friday and his partner.

30. "The Marcus-Nelson Murders," originally broadcast 8 March 1973, LOC shelf no. FDA 3269–71.

31. *Kojak* was itself inspired to some degree by *Dirty Harry,* the great police zeitgeist movie of 1971. Dirty Harry was an updated version of the Bogart loner— a solitary, cynical figure who did his best to live honorably in a dishonorable

world. That Harry was a policeman (in San Francisco, no less) only made this role more appealing, as the rangy hero swept aside the liberal bureaucracy of the weakened city force and the legal maneuverings of the loathsome villain with equal disdain, solving all problems instead with a massive handgun and a laconic wit. No such taciturn figure Kojak—but he remains Dirty Harry's prototype on the small screen anyway.

5. "Sunday, Monday, Happy Days . . . Tuesday, Wednesday, Happy Days": Return to Normalcy, 1975–1977

1. See, for example, John Robert Greene, *The Limits of Power: The Nixon and Ford Administrations* (Bloomington: Indiana University Press, 1992); James Cannon, *Time and Chance: Gerald Ford's Appointment with History* (Ann Arbor: University of Michigan Press, 1997); and Michael Schudson, *Watergate in American Memory: How We Remember, Forget, and Reconstruct the Past* (New York: Basic Books, 1993).

2. Ford quoted in Peter Carroll, *It Seemed like Nothing Happened: The Tragedy and Promise of America in the 1970s* (New York: Holt, Rinehart and Winston, 1982), 161.

3. Jordan quoted in Carroll, *It Seemed like Nothing Happened,* 261.

4. Philip Slater, *The Pursuit of Loneliness* (Boston: Beacon Press, 1976), 2.

5. Christopher Lasch, *The Culture of Narcissism* (New York: W. W. Norton, 1978), 4–5.

6. Queen, *Jazz,* Pgd/Hollywood, ASIN: B000000OAH, 1998, CD.

7. U.S. Congress, Senate, Committee of Interstate and Foreign Commerce, Subcommittee on Communications, *Hearings on the Issue of Televised Violence and Obscenity,* 94th Cong., 2d sess., 9 July 1976, 270.

8. Robert Sklar, "Does Television Have a Future?" *Emmy,* summer 1979, 58.

9. The phenomenon of 1950s nostalgia has been commented on by a number of critics and historians in recent years. See, for example, Stephanie Coontz, *The Way We Never Were: American Families and the Nostalgia Trap* (New York: Basic Books, 1992); for an incisive discussion of the uses of nostalgia, also see Christopher Lasch, *The True and Only Heaven* (New York: W. W. Norton, 1991), chap. 7.

10. "Love and the Happy Day," originally broadcast 25 February 1972, LOC shelf no. FBB 6115–6117.

11. ABC, for some unknowable corporate reason, decided that the leather jacket had to go—it made Fonzie look too dangerous. But since he rode a motorcycle, Marshall was forced to argue, wouldn't it be unsafe for Fonzie to *not* wear a leather jacket? Fine, ABC replied. But his motorcycle must be clearly shown whenever the character wears the jacket. Thus, for the first season, Fonzie

was shown at all times leaning on or polishing or otherwise fiddling with his bike—a formality that perhaps added to his mystique. See Harry Castleman and Walter Podzarik, *Watching TV: Four Decades of American Television* (New York: McGraw-Hill, 1981), 267.

12. Garry Marshall, letter to author, 13 August 1997.

13. Because soap operas and some other forms of daytime programming are shot in network studios, and because of their large female audience, daytime programming has traditionally been the breadbasket of network profits, since so much of television revolves around power and conspicuous competition.

14. Paul Klein, interview by author, New York City, 1 October 1996. When contacted to confirm this, Marshall replied simply, "we began to look for ways to make Henry Winkler a more integral part of the show" (Marshall, letter to author).

15. Predictably, every show then wanted to have a "Fonzie." A memorandum from the Bud Yorkin series *What's Happening!!* reads, "possibly have a young, streetwise man as the landlord or a tenant in the building who is a sort of black 'Fonzie' type (fatherly to the boys)" ("Points During Meeting with Stu Bloomberg," 6 June 1978, Bud Yorkin Papers, Arts Special Collections, Young Research Library, UCLA).

16. Ed Papazian, *Medium Rare: The Evolution, Workings, and Impact of Commercial Television* (New York: Media Dynamics, 1991), 202.

17. Papazian, *Medium Rare*, 202.

18. Carroll, *It Seemed Like Nothing Happened*, 279.

19. Carroll, *It Seemed Like Nothing Happened*, 280.

20. "Maude's Dilemma," originally broadcast 14 and 21 November 1972, LOC shelf no. FBB 2177.

21. Rick Mitz, *The Great TV Sitcom Book* (New York: Richard Marek Publishers, 1980), 372.

22. The reflexive liberalism of even innocuous TV shows was noted with disdain by many conservatives in the 1970s. As I argue in this study, TV's liberalism existed as an expression of the networks' bottom-line devotion to mainstream norms and consensus, which by the mid-1970s were highly liberalized; but another point of view exists that claims that television's liberalism was the product of the narrow circle of out-of-touch mandarins who produced it. This perspective, though widely held, was given its best and most comprehensive expression by Ben Stein, in *The View from Sunset Boulevard* (Garden City: Anchor, 1986).

23. Klein quoted in Sally Bedell, *Up the Tube: Prime Time in the Silverman Years* (New York: Viking, 1981), 204.

24. Castleman and Podzarik, *Watching TV*, 281.

25. David Marc, *Demographic Vistas* (Philadelphia: University of Pennsylvania Press, 1984), 89.

26. Not that this change represented any great licentiousness—as President Frank Price of Universal Television told *Newsweek* in 1978: "the sexual breakthrough in television has probably taken us to where the movies were in 1935" (*Newsweek,* 20 February 1978, 36).

27. Marshall, letter to author.

6. "It Takes Different Strokes": TV and America, 1978

1. One critic in particular who made this charge was Richard Reeves, in the course of an important document from the period, "The Dangers of Television in the Silverman Era," *Esquire,* 25 April 1978, 45–57. Reeves's essay, although wildly overstated at times, remains the best statement of the case against Silverman and the shows he represented.

2. Quoted in Neil Hickey, "Will The Network System Survive?" *TV Guide,* 6 May 1978, 31–32.

3. "Roots: The Story of an American Family," originally broadcast 23–30 January 1977, LOC shelf no. FBB 5556–59.

4. "ABC, Roots Storm Neilsens for Historic Ratings Victory," *Hollywood Reporter,* 2 February 1977, 2.

5. Neil Hickey, "Changing the Shape of Television," *TV Guide,* 22 April 1978, 5.

6. Nolan Davis, "Is Kunte Kinte the Next Fonzie?" *New West,* 2 February 1977, 38.

7. Hickey, "Changing the Shape," 7.

8. Lear quoted in Hickey, "Changing the Shape," 7.

9. Reeves, "Dangers of Television," 46.

10. Diller quoted in Reeves, "Dangers of Television," 48.

11. The reason for this labored decorum had much to do with the non-WASP origin of all three network founders. Goldenson, Sarnoff, and especially William Paley all made a practice of playing down their Jewishness, even to the point of only hiring Gentiles for elite positions and thus distinguishing themselves from the pushy and vulgar first generation moguls of Hollywood's studio era, such as Mayer, Goldwyn, Cohn, and so on. For a fuller treatment of this subject, see Les Brown, *Television: The Business Behind the Box* (New York: Harcourt, Brace, Jovanovich, 1971), 79–83.

12. Sally Bedell, "The Man with the Golden Gut," *Time,* 5 September 1977, 46.

13. Kevin Phillips, "TV Has Finally Begun to Cover Itself," *TV Guide,* 17 December 1977, A-3.

14. Lewis Lapham, "The Wizard of Oz," *Harper's Magazine,* August 1976, 11.

15. Peter Carroll, *It Seemed like Nothing Happened: The Tragedy and Promise of America in the 1970s* (New York: Holt, Rinehart and Winston, 1982), 211–12.

16. *Statistical Abstract of the United States,* 1980, 587, 589.

17. The film remains the final word on television, satirical or otherwise. Brilliantly walking a thin line between black-humored absurdism (terrorists given cameras to record their bank holdups on *The Mao Tse Tung Hour*) and dead-on industry portraiture (about 75 percent of the dialogue in the film was taken, its author claimed, verbatim from executives), the film centers on the attempt of a last-place network to exploit the anti-TV fury of messianic anchorman Beale. As he subjects the TV audience to repeated jeremiads, the audience gives him his highest ratings ever; later, when his ratings drop, the network has him killed. The scenes in which, apoplectic with rage against television, Beale has an epileptic fit and gets a standing ovation from the studio audiences as the cameras zoom in, remain one of the unforgettable images of omnivorous television. Oblivious to the irony, NBC premiered a TV version of the film, *W.E.B.,* in the 1978 season. "Fittingly," noted Castleman and Podzarik (*Watching TV: Four Decades of American Television* [New York: McGraw-Hill, 1981]), "it was the first show canceled that season" (288). No fatalities were involved, however.

18. Diller quoted in Reeves, "Dangers of Television," 46.

19. In his *Esquire* article ("Dangers of Television"), Reeves quotes a New York radio executive's approval of a young program manager: "He's just brilliant. This kid is analytical and totally research-oriented. Unlike other program managers, he's very objective in his interpretation of research and doesn't let his own tastes or desires interfere with his judgment" (46).

20. *Balkanized* was a term that came into some currency in the late 1970s and was used much as I have used the word *fragmented.* It was introduced by Energy Secretary James Schlesinger, who suggested in 1978 that the energy crisis might bring about the balkanization of America. See Kevin Phillips, "The Balkanization of America," *Harper's Magazine,* May 1978.

21. Aaron Spelling and Jefferson Graham, *Aaron Spelling: A Prime Time Life* (New York: St. Martin's Press, 1996), 123. This anecdote, unconfirmed elsewhere, should probably be taken with some caution. But no student of the networks in this period can reasonably claim that it was improbable.

22. Silverman quoted in Castleman and Podzarik, *Watching TV,* 284.

23. Wood quoted in Todd Gitlin, *Inside Prime Time* (New York: Pantheon, 1984), 219.

24. Probably the definitive study of this genre, and one that I have drawn on in writing on the subject, is Ella Taylor, *Prime Time Families: Television Culture in Postwar America* (Los Angeles: University of California Press, 1989).

25. MTM's Grant Tinker has suggested another theory: "At one time in television Jackie Gleason could sit out there and practically do it all by himself. But

by the 1970s, the attention span of the viewers had shortened. They were spoiled. You had to come at them from all directions to keep their attention. An ensemble could do that" (quoted in Sally Bedell, *Up the Tube: Prime Time in the Silverman Years* [New York: Viking, 1981], 66).

26. Stephen Stark, *Glued to the Set: The 60 Television Shows and Events That Made Us Who We Are Today* (New York: Free Press, 1997), 211.

27. In actuality, this use of the antihero was less of an innovation than a throwback to the sitcoms of early television, before the moralistic suburban freeze set in. The heroes of such shows as *The Honeymooners, The Life of Riley,* and *The Phil Silvers Show* were commonly bumptious oafs who got their comeuppance at the end of each episode.

28. Carroll, *It Seemed like Nothing Happened,* 322.

29. Theodore Roszak, *Person Planet* (Garden City: Pelham, 1978), 289, 271, 291.

30. "Archie Gets the Business," originally broadcast 2 February 1977, LOC shelf no. VBA 7233.

31. Marshall quoted in Horace Newcomb and Robert S. Alley, *The Producer's Medium* (New York: Oxford University Press, 1983), 234.

32. For an interesting inside look at the Silverman/Marshall decision-making process, see Bedell, *Up the Tube,* 124–30.

33. Les Brown, *Television,* 263.

34. Schedule information from *TV Guide,* 12 February 1978, 20–26.

35. See Doug Hill and Jeff Weingrad, *Saturday Night: A Backstage History of Saturday Night Live* (New York: Beachtree Books, 1985), 22–29; also see Tony Hendra, *Going Too Far: The Rise and Demise of Sick, Gross, Black, Sophomoric, Weirdo, Pinko, Anarchist, Underground, Anti-Establishment Humor* (New York: Doubleday, 1987), 433.

36. Michaels quoted in Stark, *Glued to the Set,* 196–97.

37. Quoted in Stark, *Glued to the Set,* 196–97.

38. Michael Arlen, "A Crack in the Greasepaint," *New Yorker,* 24 November 1975.

39. Robert Sklar, *Prime Time America* (New York: Oxford University Press, 1980), 197.

40. David Marc, in *Demographic Vistas* (Philadelphia: University of Pennsylvania Press, 1984), devotes an entire section to an appreciation of this series, which he sees, probably with some justification, as *the new plus ultra* of TV's evolution as a self-reflexive medium. The last quarter of Marc's book is a discussion of self-reflexive television, which he, like Michael Arlen, considered a great advance.

41. Supposedly, it had been the conservatism of these very affiliates that lay behind the networks' reluctance to accept unusual shows. But the combination of

not having to share advertising revenues with the networks, as well as the increasing loosening up of society, combined to sway many affiliates to accept Lear's offer.

42. Jane Feuer, "The MTM Style," in *MTM: Quality Television,* ed. Jane Feuer (London: BFI, 1984), 50.

Epilogue

1. Letterman quoted Harry F. Waters, "David in the Daytime," *Newsweek,* 7 July 1980, 45.

2. Of all Murray's *SNL* characters, none was more famous, or more ironic, than Nick, a lounge singer who spoke (and sang) the purest of all dialects of telethonese. Nick's accompanist in these skits was Paul Shaeffer, whom Letterman would adopt as his own sidekick. In such quiet ways are torches passed.

3. Richard Corliss, "David Letterman Tosses a Late Night Comedy Salad," *Time,* 22 March 1982, 67.

4. Mark Crispin Miller, *Boxed In: The Culture of Television* (Evanston: Northwestern University Press, 1988), 15.

5. Figures supplied by the Barco Library of the National Cable Television Center and Museum, Denver, Colorado.

6. Miller, *Boxed In,* 15.

Selected Bibliography

Adler, Richard. *All in the Family: A Critical Appraisal.* Aspen: Praeger, 1979.

Barnouw, Eric. *The Image Empire: A History of Broadcasting in the United States from 1953.* New York: Oxford University Press, 1970.

———. *The Sponsor: Notes on a Modern Potentate.* New York: Oxford University Press, 1978.

———. *Tube of Plenty: The Evolution of American Television.* New York: Oxford University Press, 1975.

Bedell, Sally. *Up the Tube: Prime Time in the Silverman Years.* New York: Viking, 1981.

Boddy, William. *Fifties Television.* Urbana: University of Illinois Press, 1990.

Bodroghkozy, Aniko. *Groove Tube: Sixties Television and the Youth Rebellion.* Durham: Duke University Press, 2001.

Bono, Sonny. *The Beat Goes On.* New York: Harcourt, Brace, Jovanovich, 1990.

Bradbury, Ray, et al. "A Writers' Symposium." In *Television: The Creative Experience.* New York: Hastings House, 1967.

Brown, Les. *Television: The Business Behind the Box.* New York: Harcourt, Brace, Jovanovich, 1971.

Cantor, Muriel. *The Hollywood TV Producer.* New York: Transaction Publishing, 1970.

Cantor, Paul. *Gilligan Unbound: Pop Culture in an Age of Globalization.* New York: Rowman and Littlefield, 2001.

Carroll, Peter. *It Seemed like Nothing Happened: The Tragedy and Promise of America in the 1970s.* New York: Holt, Rinehart, Winston, 1982.

Castleman, Harry, and Walter Podzarik. *Watching TV: Four Decades of American Television.* New York: McGraw-Hill, 1981.

Chafe, William. *The Paradox of Change: American Women in the 20th Century.* New York: Oxford University Press, 1992.

Coyne, John R. *The Impudent Snobs: Agnew vs. the Media Establishment.* New Rochelle: Arlington House, 1972.

Crosby, Stills, Nash, and Young. *So Far.* Wea/Atlantic ASIN: B000002JoJ, 1994.

Crumb, Robert. "Let's Talk Sense about This Here Modern America." *Arcade: The Comics Review,* no. 2 (summer 1975): 8–13.

Dann, Michael. Oral History Interview, 2 November 1998. Academy of Television Arts and Sciences Archive of American Television, Los Angeles.

Diggins, John Patrick. *The Rise and Fall of the American Left.* New York: W. W. Norton, 1992.

Douglas, Susan J. *Where the Girls Are: Growing Up Female with the Mass Media.* New York: Times Books, 1995.

Edelstein, Andrew. *The Pop Sixties: A Personal and Irreverent Guide.* New York: World Almanac Publications, 1985.

✓ Edelstein, Andrew, and Kevin McDonough. *The Seventies: From Hot Pants to Hot Tubs.* New York: Dutton, 1990.

Edgerton, Gary, and Cathy Pratt. "The Influence of the Paramount Decision on Network Television in America," *Quarterly Review of Film Studies* 8, no. 3 (summer 1983).

Ellison, Harlan. *The Glass Teat.* Los Angeles: The Free Press, 1968.

Evans, Sara. *Personal Politics: The Roots of the Women's Liberation in the Civil Rights Movement and the New Left.* New York: Random House, 1980.

Frank, Tom. *The Conquest of Cool: Business Culture, Counterculture, and the Rise of Hip Consumerism.* Chicago: University of Chicago Press, 1997.

✓ Frum, David. *How We Got Here: American since the Seventies from Better to Worse.* New York: Basic Books, 1999.

Gitlin, Todd. *Inside Prime Time.* New York: Pantheon, 1984.

———. *The Sixties: Years of Hope, Days of Rage.* New York: Bantam Books, 1987.

———. *The Whole World Is Watching: Mass Media in the Making and Unmaking of the New Left.* Berkeley: University of California Press, 1984.

———, ed. *Watching Television.* New York: Pantheon, 1986.

Gleason, Philip. "Americans All: World War II and the Shaping of American Identity." *Review of Politics* 43 (October 1981).

———. *Speaking of Diversity.* New York: Oxford University Press, 1992.

Goldenson, Leonard H., and Marvin J. Wolf. *Beating the Odds: The Untold Story Behind the Rise of ABC: The Stars, Struggles, and Egos That Transformed Network Television.* New York: Scribner's, 1991.

Halberstam, David. *The Fifties.* New York: Villard, 1994.

———. *The Powers That Be.* New York: McGraw-Hill, 1979.

Hamamoto, Daniel. *Nervous Laughter: Television Situation Comedy and Liberal Democratic Ideology.* New York: Greenwood Publishing Group, 1995.

Hendra, Tony. *Going Too Far: The Rise and Demise of Sick, Gross, Black, Sophomoric, Weirdo, Pinko, Anarchist, Underground, Anti-Establishment Humor.* New York: Doubleday, 1987.

Higham, John. "Beyond Consensus: The Historian as Moral Critic." *American Historical Review,* April 1962, 609–25.

———. "The Cult of the 'American Consensus.'" *Commentary,* February 1959, 93–100.

Hill, Doug, and Jeff Weingrad. *Saturday Night: A Backstage History of Saturday Night Live.* New York: Beachtree Books, 1985.

Hobson, Dick. "Help! I'm a Prisoner in a Laff Box!" *TV Guide,* 9 July 1966, 22.

Hoffman, Abbie. *Woodstock Nation.* New York: Vintage Books, 1969.

Hofstatder, Richard. *Anti-Intellectualism in American Life.* New York: Knopf, 1963.

Hurup, Elsebeth, ed. *The Lost Decade: America in the Seventies.* Oakville: Aarhus University Press, 1996.

Jackson, Kenneth. *The Crabgrass Frontier: The Suburbanization of the United States.* New York: Oxford University Press, 1985.

Jones, Landon Y. *Great Expectations: American and the Baby Boom Generation.* New York: Ballantine Books, 1980.

Kearns, Doris *Lyndon Johnson and the American Dream.* New York: Signet, 1976.

Klein, Paul. "Programming." In *Inside the TV Business.* Ed. Steve Morgenstern. New York: Sterling, 1979.

———. "Why You Watch, What You Watch, When You Watch." *TV Guide,* 24 July 1971, 6–10.

Lafferty, Perry. Oral History Interview, 4 December 1997. Academy of Television Arts and Sciences Archive of American Television, Los Angeles.

Lasch, Christopher. *The Culture of Narcissism.* New York: W. W. Norton, 1978.

———. *The Minimal Self: Psychic Survival in Troubled Times.* New York: W. W. Norton, 1985.

Lear, Norman. Oral History Interview, 26 February 1998. Academy of Television Arts and Sciences Archive of American Television, Los Angeles.

Leibman, Nina C. *Living Room Lectures: Fifties Family in Film and Television.* Austin: University of Texas Press, 1995.

Lemann, Nicholas. "How the Seventies Changed America." *American Heritage,* July/August 1991, 41–45.

Leonard, John. *Smoke and Mirrors: Violence, Television, and Other American Cultures.* New York: New Press, 1997.

Leuchetenburg, William. *A Troubled Feast: American Society since 1945.* Boston: Little, Brown, 1973.

Macdonald, Dwight. "A Theory of Mass Culture." In *Mass Culture: The Popular Arts in America,* ed. Bernard Rosenberg and David Manning White. New York: Free Press, 1957.

Macdonald, J. Fred. *Blacks on White TV: Afro Americans in Television since 1948.* Chicago: Nelson-Hall, 1983.

————. *One Nation under Television.* Chicago: Nelson-Hall, 1994.

Marc, David. *Demographic Vistas.* Philadelphia: University of Pennsylvania Press, 1984.

Marc, David, and Robert J. Thompson. *Prime Time Prime Movers: From I Love Lucy to L.A. Law—America's Greatest TV Shows and the People Who Created Them.* Syracuse: Syracuse University Press, 1992.

Matusow, Alan. *The Unraveling of America: A History of Liberalism in America in the 1960s.* New York: Harper and Row, 1984.

McGannon, Donald H. "Is the TV Code a Fraud?." In *Television Today: A Close-Up View,* ed. Barry Cole. New York: Oxford University Press, 1981.

McGrohan, Donna. *Archie and Edith, Mike and Gloria: The Tumultuous History of All in the Family.* New York: Farrar, Straus and Giroux, 1989.

Medelsohn, Jack, Executive Story Consultant, to James Lupo, 9 August 1977, Bud Yorkin Papers, Arts Special Collections, Young Research Library, University of California Los Angeles.

Metz, Robert. *CBS: Reflections in a Bloodshot Eye.* Chicago: Playboy Press, 1975.

Miller, Mark Crispin. *Boxed In: The Culture of Television.* Evanston: Northwestern University Press, 1988.

————. "Deride and Conquer." In *Watching Television,* ed. Todd Gitlin. New York: Pantheon, 1988.

Mitz, Rick. *The Great TV Sitcom Book.* New York: Richard Marek Publishers, 1980.

Moore, Mary Tyler. Oral History Interview, 23 October 1997. Academy of Television Arts and Sciences Archive of American Television, Los Angeles.

Newcomb, Horace, and Robert S. Alley. *The Producer's Medium.* New York: Oxford University Press, 1983.

Nielsen, Arthur C., Jr., and Theodore Berland. "Nielsen Defends His Ratings." In *Television Today: A Close-Up View,* ed. Barry Cole. New York: Oxford University Press, 1981.

O'Connor, Carroll. Oral History Interview, 13 August 1999. Academy of Television Arts and Sciences Archive of American Television, Los Angeles.

O'Connor, John E., ed. *American History/American Television: Interpreting the Video Past.* New York: Frederick Ungar Publishing, 1983.

O'Neill, William L. *American High: The Years of Confidence, 1945–1960.* New York: Free Press, 1986.

————. *Coming Apart: America in the 1960s.* New York: Free Press, 1969.

Paley, William S. *As It Happened.* Garden City: Doubleday, 1979.

Papazian, Ed. *Medium Rare: The Evolution, Workings, and Impact of Commercial Television.* New York: Media Dynamics, 1991.

Patterson, James T. *Great Expectations: The United States, 1945–1974*. New York: Oxford University Press, 1996.

Pember, Don R. "Magazines and the Fragmenting Audience," from *Mass Media in America,* ed. William Vesterman and Robert Atwan. New Brunswick: Science Research Associates, 1974.

Press, Andrea Lee. *Women Watching Television: Gender, Class, and Generation in the American TV Experience*. Philadelphia: University of Philadelphia Press, 1991.

Queen. *Jazz*. Pgd/Hollywood, ASIN: B000000OAH, 1998, CD.

Reddy, Helen. *Helen Reddy's Greatest Hits*. EMI-Capitol Special Products, ASIN: B000002TGF, 1994, CD.

Reich, Charles. *The Greening of America*. New York: Random House, 1970.

Rosenberg, Bernard, and David Manning White, eds. *Mass Culture: The Popular Arts in America*. New York: Free Press, 1957.

———. *Mass Culture Revisited*. New York: Van Nostrand Reinhold, 1971.

Roszak, Theodore. *The Making of a Counter Culture*. Garden City: Doubleday, 1969.

———. *Person Planet*. Garden City: Pelham, 1978.

Schudson, Michael. *Watergate in American Memory: How We Remember, Forget, and Reconstruct the Past*. New York: Basic Books, 1993.

Schulman, Bruce J. *The Seventies: The Great Shift in American Culture, Society, and Politics*. New York: Free Press, 2001.

Schwartz, Sherwood. *Inside Gilligan's Island: From Creation to Syndication*. Jefferson: McFarland, 1988.

Seldes, Gilbert. *The Great Audience*. New York: Viking, 1950.

Sklar, Robert. "Does Television Have a Future?" *Emmy,* summer 1979, 58.

———. *Prime Time America*. New York: Oxford University Press, 1980.

Slater, Philip. *The Pursuit of Loneliness*. Boston: Beacon Press, 1976.

Sonny and Cher. *The Wondrous World of Sonny and Cher*. Sundazed Records, ASIN: B0000064Y, 1998, CD.

Sontag, Susan. *Against Interpretation*. New York: Farrar, Straus and Giroux, 1964.

Spelling, Aaron, and Jefferson Graham, *Aaron Spelling: A Prime Time Life*. New York: St. Martin's Press, 1996.

Spigal, Lynn. *Make Room for TV: Television and the Family Ideal in Postwar America*. New York: Routledge, 1987.

Spigal, Lynn, and Michael Curtain, eds. *The Revolution Wasn't Televised: 60s TV and Social Conflict*. New York: Routledge, 1997.

Stark, Stephen. *Glued to the Set: The 60 Television Shows and Events That Made Us Who We Are Today*. New York: Free Press, 1997.

Statistical Abstract of the United States, 1980.

Stein, Ben. *The View from Sunset Boulevard*. Garden City: Anchor, 1986.

Steinbeck, John. "Have We Gone Soft?" *New Republic,* 15 February 1960, 11–15.

Sturcken, Frank. *Live Television*. Jefferson: McFarland, 1990.

Taylor, Ella. *Prime Time Families: Television Culture in Postwar America*. Los Angeles: University of California Press, 1989.

Tinker, Grant. *Tinker in Television: From General Sarnoff to General Electric*. New York: Simon and Schuster, 1994.

U.S. Congress. Senate. Committee of Interstate and Foreign Commerce. Subcommittee on Communications. *Hearings on the Issue of Televised Violence and Obscenity*. 94th Cong., 2d sess., 9 July 1976, 270.

Van Dyke, Dick. Oral History Interview, 8 January 1998. Academy of Television Arts and Sciences Archive of American Television, Los Angeles.

✓Watson, Mary Ann. *The Expanding Vista*. New York: Oxford University Press, 1990.

White, Betty. Oral History Interview, 4 June 1997. Academy of Television Arts and Sciences Archive of American Television, Los Angeles.

✓Wolfe, Tom. *Mauve Gloves and Madmen, Clutter and Vine*. New York: Farrar, Straus and Giroux, 1976.

Yorkin, Bud. Papers. Arts Special Collections, Young Research Library, University of California, Los Angeles.

Zappa, Frank. *The Real Frank Zappa Book*. New York: Hyperion Press, 1987.

Index

Josh Ozersky has written articles on American cultural history for *Newsday,* the *Washington Post, History: Reviews of New Books,* and other periodicals. He is the author of *Readings for the 21st Century* and is currently at work on a study of American culture in the late 1940s, with special attention to Johnny Mercer, Bob and Ray, and the emergence of "hipster" culture. He lives in New York City.